Rock of Pages

Rock of Pages

The Literary Tradition of 1980s Heavy Metal

Jesse Kavadlo

BLOOMSBURY ACADEMIC
NEW YORK • LONDON • OXFORD • NEW DELHI • SYDNEY

BLOOMSBURY ACADEMIC

Bloomsbury Publishing Inc, 1359 Broadway, New York, NY 10018, USA
Bloomsbury Publishing Plc, 50 Bedford Square, London, WC1B 3DP, UK
Bloomsbury Publishing Ireland, 29 Earlsfort Terrace, Dublin 2, D02 AY28, Ireland

BLOOMSBURY, BLOOMSBURY ACADEMIC and the Diana logo are trademarks of Bloomsbury Publishing Plc

First published in the United States of America 2026

Copyright © Jesse Kavadlo, 2026

For legal purposes the acknowledgments on pp. ix–x constitute an extension of this copyright page.

Cover design by Louise Dugdale
Cover image © Cain Pinto

All rights reserved. No part of this publication may be: i) reproduced or transmitted in any form, electronic or mechanical, including photocopying, recording or by means of any information storage or retrieval system without prior permission in writing from the publishers; or ii) used or reproduced in any way for the training, development or operation of artificial intelligence (AI) technologies, including generative AI technologies. The rights holders expressly reserve this publication from the text and data mining exception as per Article 4(3) of the Digital Single Market Directive (EU) 2019/790.

Bloomsbury Publishing Inc does not have any control over, or responsibility for, any third-party websites referred to or in this book. All internet addresses given in this book were correct at the time of going to press. The author and publisher regret any inconvenience caused if addresses have changed or sites have ceased to exist, but can accept no responsibility for any such changes.

Library of Congress Cataloging-in-Publication Data
Names: Kavadlo, Jesse, 1971- author Title: Rock of pages : the literary tradition of 1980s heavy metal / Jesse Kavadlo. Description: [First edition]. | New York : Bloomsbury Academic, 2026. | Includes bibliographical references and index. | Summary: "In 1985, the Parents Music Resource Center (PMRC), led by "Washington Wives" Tipper Gore and Susan Baker, conducted a moral and legal crusade against the Filthy Fifteen, a list of songs they found to be objectionable from the likes of AC/DC, Judas Priest, Def Leppard, Twisted Sister, and Mötley Crüe. Rock of Pages identifies how the "dangerous" heavy metal of the 1980s can be analyzed through literary criticism, how heavy metal helps us understand what's dangerous about literature, and why this matters" – Provided by publisher.
Identifiers: LCCN 2025025026 | ISBN 9798765140819 hardback | ISBN 9798765140802 paperback | ISBN 9798765140833 PDF | ISBN 9798765140826 ePub Subjects: LCSH: Heavy metal (Music) –History and criticism | Heavy metal (Music)–Moral and ethical aspects | Rock music–1981-1990–History and criticism | Music and literature Classification: LCC ML3534.K385 R63 2026 | DDC 782.42166–dc23/eng/20250604 LC record available at https://lccn.loc.gov/2025025026

ISBN: HB: 9798-7651-4081-9
PB: 9798-7651-4080-2
ePDF: 9798-7651-4083-3
eBook: 979-8765-14082-6

Typeset by Deanta Global Publishing Services, Chennai, India
Printed and bound in the United States of America

For product safety related questions contact productsafety@bloomsbury.com.

To find out more about our authors and books visit www.bloomsbury.com and sign up for our newsletters.

For Pete and Johannes, who would have read this book for opposite reasons.

Contents

Figures	viii
Acknowledgments	ix
Preface: My Double Life	1
Introduction: Won't Somebody Please Think of the Children?	19
1 Nothing. But: A Good Time?: Heavy Metal, the Cold War, and the Long 1980s	35
2 V for Violence	73
3 D/A for Drugs and Alcohol	99
4 X for Sexually Explicit	125
5 O for Occult	159
An Ode to Guitar Solos	201
Conclusion: Let Me Get It Back	205
Notes	219
Selected Bibliography	240
Discography	242
Index	245

Figures

1	Joseph Quinn as Eddie Munson in *Stranger Things*	1
2	The author of this book as Eddie	1
3	Jesse Kavadlo, Professor of English	15
4	Dr. Noize, lead guitarist of Top Gunz	15
5	Krampus (Devil). Greeting card. Postcard by the Viennese Werkstaette	19
6	Hercules liberating Prometheus from an eagle, illustration	35
7	A street in Whitechapel: the last crime of Jack the Ripper, from "Le Petit Parisien," 1891	73
8	Francisco de Goya y Lucientes (1746–1828). Spanish painter	99
9	"Adam and Eve," 1597–1600	125
10	An engraving by the French printmaker Gustave Dore of Satan Smitten by Michael, a scene from John Milton's *Paradise Lost*	159
11	"Angel Musician", *c* 1520	201
12	Orpheus	205

Acknowledgments

This book brings together my vocations and loves: heavy metal and literature. Many people have supported both parts of my life. This book is for them.

My teen dream bands—Checkmate: Pete Cennamo, Drew Fuccillo, Danny Kavadlo, and John O'Reilly; and Sharky: Danny Kavadlo and Anthony Cuccurullo.

My cover band now, Jukebox Heroes: Greg Burrian, John Cochran, Ted Hediger, Kevin Raithel, Erin McRoy, and Rita Srum.

My tribute band that set me (back) on the path of '80s metal that led directly to this book, Top Gunz: Aaron Kist, Kip Kline, Mike Moser, Danny Sheppard, Kelly Bos-Coker, and our fans and friends.

My friends and fellow musicians from the '80s and early '90s New York, Brooklyn, and Staten Island rock scenes at L'Amour, Christopher's, Red Spot, Limelight, Brooklyn College, and more.

My family: my sweet Aura, Jonah, Dorian, and Mars, who listened to a lot of loud music during the writing of this book. If it's too loud, you're too old.

My parents, Rosalie and Carl, and my brothers, Danny and Al.

Bloomsbury editor Rachel Moore, editorial assistant James Eason, and my three peer reviewers. I'm grateful for your advice, efforts, and support.

My students over the years and decades, for keeping me young in mind and heart.

Rebecca Dohrman and John Weiler, for your hospitality and generosity.

Jennifer Yukna and Maryville University's sabbatical committee for giving me the time to single-task for a whole semester, Jason Telford, Maryville's Deans, and the Academic Affairs team.

My English Department: Vaughn Anderson, Jess Bowers, Christi Branson, Dana Levin, John Marino, Germaine Murray, Art Santirojprapai, and Alex Wulff, as well as Theresa Olson, who never got mad about my overdue library books.

My Center for Teaching and Learning team: Chammie Austin, Gifty Blankson, Melissa Childers, and Ashlyn Cunningham.

Laura Ross, Kyra Krakos, Seth Matteson, and Taylor Bell, for always looking out for me.

The editors of *PopMatters*, Karen Zarker and Sarah Zupko, for producing a top-notch magazine and providing my professional foray into writing about music.

Steve Lefridge, who may have helped with the title.

The indefatigable Bob Batchelor, who invited me to speak on his podcast about rock music. The discussion made me realize that I needed to write this book.

Cat Lafuente, who is the closest thing I have to an actual guardian angel.

Chris Schaberg, Kevin Downing, Sam Cohen, Sam Thomas, and Kevin O'Connor, for the help along the way.

Cain Pinto, for this book's original cover painting.

Finally, to my musical idols, the bands that made me who I am today. I cannot imagine what my life would have been like without you, although my hearing would definitely be better.

Preface

My Double Life

Figure 1 Joseph Quinn as Eddie Munson in *Stranger Things*.

Figure 2 The author of this book as Eddie.

> *The double has become an image of terror...*
> —Sigmund Freud, "The Uncanny" (1910)[1]

> *Hello me, meet the real me.*
> —Megadeth, "Sweating Bullets" (1992)[2]

Eddie

After the momentous years of 2020 and 2021—the world shutting down amidst the COVID-19 pandemic, a global economic downturn, mass protests and the famed racial reckonings across the United States, a momentous Presidential election, and an insurrection at the Capitol in its aftermath—by May 2022, Big Cultural Events finally seemed to have slowed down.

Except for one—the release of *Stranger Things*, Season 4, on Netflix.

I kid, but only sort of, at least for me. Yes, of course, it's categorically, exponentially different. But unlike those other world-changing events, this one prompted dozens of people to write to me. Old classmates from elementary school, junior high, high school, college, and grad school. Current friends, acquaintances, and coworkers. The people, especially the kids, who saw my 1980s hard rock tribute band (more on that later), who urgently needed to tell me, seriously, plaintively:

You look like Eddie Munson.

And—twenty-year age difference between me and actor Joseph Quinn aside—I did. Not exactly. But enough for all those people to notice, and to go out of their way to tell me.

It was more than mere appearance. In many ways, I *was* Eddie Munson. *Stranger Things*, together with *Dungeons & Dragons*, will pave the way into this book's subject: heavy metal in the 1980s, and its connections to literature that long predate the '80s. And *Stranger Things* provides an introductory framework for the questions these connections raise: how was heavy metal perceived in its own time? How can we evaluate its cultural context now, during what we retroactively understand to have been the end of the Cold War? And how might we have a different sense of what it means if we think about it as part of a grand, and occasionally not so grand, literary tradition?

Stranger Things, the Netflix series that began in 2016, takes place in the 1980s. The setting allows its adolescent protagonists the Gen X latchkey kid freedom—from parents, cellphones, and social media—to have undocumented, untethered escapades. But *Stranger Things* is a tribute to, not an example of, pop culture of the 1980s itself. It incorporates and alludes to the canon of teen fantasy, adventure, and horror movies: *E.T.* and *The Goonies*, *Carrie* and *Firestarter*, *Aliens* (a Paul Reiser cameo!) and *A Nightmare on Elm Street* (a Robert Englund cameo!), plus many more, even making the theme song from *The NeverEnding Story* a crucial plot point. In that sense, the show is not just set in the '80s, or even about the '80s, but about images of the '80s. It's a pastiche and a bricolage—an homage, sure, but made up of many pieces. It demonstrates how we think of the 1980s in the 2010s and 2020s, with important applications for how we think about 1980s heavy metal now as well.

More than those movies, *Stranger Things* began with, and relied on, *Dungeons & Dragons* to set up its story. *D&D*, as it was usually called, was a role-playing game that rose to prominence among a certain subgroup of adolescents, which included me, during this time. The first episode of *Stranger Things* introduces us to the teen team by showing their gameplay. The monster they face in the game, the Demogorgon, becomes the name they use to identify the real monster they later encounter. I still had my 1980 copy of the *Monster Manual*, and, after dusting it off, I looked it up. There it was.

As Season 4 would later show, many adults and parents saw *Dungeons & Dragons* as dangerous—a gateway into violence, suicide, and satanism. The same people would accuse heavy metal of the same thing. But as someone who played *D&D* at that time, I can tell you what it was really a gateway for. Friendship. Storytelling. And heavy metal. And they were all good.

That's the other point of this book. Everything certain 1980s parents and TV talking heads said was bad turned out to be good. And in retrospect, those parents have a terrible track record of evaluating the fitness of art, music, and literature for young people.

Dungeons & Dragons & Literature

Don't worry. We're working our way towards heavy metal.

To the adults who hated it, *D&D* looked like it revolved around violence and monsters. And it did. Violence and monsters were very much the point. The violence and monsters were awesome. They were also, crucially, imaginary. And because they were not real, *D&D* became a way for at least one 11-year-old—me—to begin understanding fiction, and, maybe, life, by introducing their building blocks in ways that I could understand.

Character: Players would create an entire persona, and then inhabit it. Some of their character's aspects were in their control. What kind of being—human, elf, dwarf, halfling—would they be? What profession: fighter, magic user, cleric, thief? What alignment would govern their behavior—a grid of good, neutral, and evil along with lawful, neutral, and chaotic? Some characteristics were out of the players' control, based on the circumstances they found themselves in and, literally, the roll of the dice. The game, like life, could be arbitrary, capricious. As philosopher Thomas Hobbes famously put it in *Leviathan*, left to ourselves in nature without a society, human life would be "solitary, poor, nasty, brutish, and short." It often was in *D&D*. But, unlike life, the game was safe, a place to explore aspects of identity and morality—and mortality.

Irony: *Dungeons & Dragons* was a role-playing game. Players would naturally experience a distance between their actual selves and their player characters, and learn to inhabit, and switch between, both worlds during gameplay. Something could happen in the game that the players, but not the personas, could understand and appreciate. Personas could act in ways that the players never would in real life: by being brave, or bad; killing monsters, or just killing; defending or taking treasure. Pubescent kids could practice being warriors instead of worriers, all while eating potato chips and sitting around a kitchen table. Some parents thought the game was dangerous. But in an era when television stations would air a public service announcement every night at 10 p.m., asking "Do you know where your children are?" those parents who sanctioned *D&D* always did know. They were home, pretending to cast spells, rolling twenty-sided dice. The most dangerous things, in retrospect, were those potato chips.

Empathy: Players learned to care about their personas, their teammates' personas, and even the fictional non-player characters who populated their imagined world. When a player's character died, it could be devastating. But then, quickly, that player could wipe the tears, stifle the frustration, roll the dice, and create a new character to live again.

Escapism: Along with empathy—that is, feeling things that others feel but one might not feel in one's own life—players got to escape into worlds of weapons and wizards. Escapism and empathy can feel like opposites, but they do not need to be. Escape is sometimes a criticism of games, fiction, and music. I don't think that's the right approach. Players were able to use their minds, emotions, and imaginations as a way to have fantastic experiences, and as a way *not* to have the other feelings left over from real life. In many ways, what could be better than the feeling of escape? As it turns out, not coincidentally, escaping will be an important theme throughout heavy metal.

Storytelling: Character, irony, empathy, and escapism all connect as, and through, storytelling. *Dungeons & Dragons* was an early foray into worldbuilding and lore, ideas that would influence games like *Final Fantasy* and even *Pokémon* later on. More often than not, I was the Dungeon Master. That meant that I would invent the adventure—the plot, the story. What would happen, in what order, and what would it mean? How would it begin, and end? Who would the non-player characters be, and how would they behave? Which monsters would the group face, and for what reasons? I learned that a good story was more than a series of challenges. Unlike history, which is, as the saying goes, just one damned thing after another, an adventure needs coherence, logic, and plenty of surprise and delight. More than anything, *Dungeons & Dragons* raised questions about how fiction works, and its many pleasures, as well as pleasurable pains.

Interpretation: But telling a story is not the end. Experiencing it is. While the Dungeon Master planned the adventure, each player needed to contribute as well. The story didn't exist until it was undertaken by the group, whose collective understanding and decisions would shape its meaning and significance. Some of the fun was in the planning, sure. But most of it came from the human connection, the interaction, the chemistry between friends. At the same time, while *D&D* is meant to be taken literally within the game, it was hard not to understand aspects of it symbolically, metaphorically, as a way of understanding ourselves and the world. This is the part *Stranger Things* takes most seriously: that the self we pretend to be in the game can inspire the self we want to see in the world.

Fun: That's the main reason to play. Anything else is extra. It may have looked like a bunch of kids rolling dice and talking about elves, but make no mistake. The group of players in *D&D* isn't called a "party" for nothing.

A game that ostensibly revolved around mayhem and monsters, that parents decried as paths to suicide and Satan, turned out to teach us about the things that made us most human and most alive.

And, it turns out, all of these elements can help us to understand heavy metal as well, then and now. Heavy metal, like *D&D*, would revolve around personas, ironies, empathy, escapism, story, interpretation, and fun more than anything I'd experience in my life. And it helped me leap from the kitchen table to the stage.

Dungeons & Dragons & Literature & Heavy Metal: "Master of Puppets"

In *Stranger Things* Season 4, enter Eddie Munson, Dungeon Master, but, more importantly, metalhead. His name evoked Eddie Van Halen, king of the electric guitar; Iron Maiden's quasi-undead mascot Eddie; the kid from the '80s heavy metal horror film *Trick or Treat* (1986); and the lycanthropic Eddie Munster from the TV series *The Munsters*, first aired in the 1960s but familiar to '80s kids through nonstop syndication. Eddie, joining the cast after *D&D* provided the initial framework for the series, debuted the Hellfire Club, his group for game play, with custom rock-style three-quarter-sleeve jerseys, naturally. Its demonic-sounding title belied its benign purpose. Like so much else on the show, it was another allusion: to the eighteenth-century gatherings alleged to partake in debauchery, irreligious activity, and worst of all, politics. That it was also a team of villains in the 1980s Marvel comics run of *The Uncanny X-Men* is x-tra.

Eddie was an important addition to the cast, and to the series' overall representation of the 1980s. Unlike the other *D&D*-playing boys—Mike, Dustin, and Lucas—Eddie, gregarious and good-looking (or so I've been told), wasn't a nerd. That word had pejorative meanings in the 1980s, unlike in the 2020s, when everyone gleefully claims to be a nerd over their interest in an esoteric subject. Eddie struggled in school, was not middle-class, and his only family was his uncle. He may not have been a nerd, but he was an outcast. The main reason: he lived and loved heavy metal. He had big, long hair, black clothes, white sneakers, and a wallet chain. He played the guitar—in a nice touch, a B.C. Rich Warlock, popularized at the time by Mötley Crüe's Mick Mars in the "Looks That Kill" video (1984) and yet another allusion, back to spells and magic.

It's hard to explain, let alone understand, how loving music that, in retrospect, was one of the most popular, best-selling genres of the decade could brand someone an outsider. That was certainly how I felt in Brooklyn, New York, where my long hair and denim and leather clothes made me a daily target for street harassment. But even metalheads who didn't have that experience felt like outsiders. It's what we perceived, and what we were perceived as. But being an outsider wasn't a flaw. It was a feature. It was part of the point. It was a version of living as one's own authentic self, regardless of whom it kept out—and also because of who it then invited in.

Eddie wasn't the first metalhead on *Stranger Things*. That was Season 2's Billy Hargrove, Max's step-brother. He wore a mullet—a term, like "hair metal" and "shred," that didn't exist in 1985—an earring, a denim jacket, and a light mustache. His bitchin' Camaro first pulls up to the sound of Scorpions' "Rock You Like A Hurricane." When he appears at the Halloween party, we hear Mötley Crüe's "Shout at the Devil." He lifts weights while listening to Ratt's "Round and Round." That's all cool. But, mainly, unfortunately, Billy was a bully. (One can make the case that he redeems himself at the end of the season. I think he does.)

Not Eddie. Eddie wasn't cool like the cool kids, but that only made him cooler. He was inclusive. He was, mostly, *nice*. But not too nice. And he didn't just listen to music. He played it. Billy came from the dirtbag school of heavy metal, not that there's anything wrong with that. Lots of people adore a dirtbag. The girls on *Stranger Things* kept their eyes on Billy, and Australian actor Dacre Montgomery developed a healthy fan base from his portrayal. But Eddie was a true metalhead: not just the hair, the clothes, and the music, but the fun, the *joy*. Billy didn't look like he was having fun. Even in his final scene, Eddie was having the time of his life.

Time to double back, about Eddie and me. I also played *Dungeons & Dragons* in 1983, when *Stranger Things* Season 1 is set. By 1986, when Season 4 takes place, it was time for me to move on to something that I thought was *very, very different* from *D&D*: heavy metal. My favorite bands were Iron Maiden and Dio. Looking back now, it seems like *maybe* those groups had one foot, or more, in *Dungeons & Dragons*. The cover art for, say, the *D&D* book *The Fiend Folio*, with minor modification, would not be out of place on a Maiden album. Dio's *Sacred Heart* album (1985), featuring a dragon, in a crystal ball, on what appears to be a Latin-inscribed Tarot-style card, wouldn't be out of place on a *D&D* book, either.

There were rock groups from the 1970s with mythic covers and literary lineage. Led Zeppelin had their Icarus (or is it Lucifer, the fallen angel? More in "O for Occult") quasi-mascot, based on a drawing by William Rimmer called "Evening (The Fall of Day)" from 1869–70. Singer Robert Plant also based some Zep songs, like "Ramble On," "Misty Mountain Hop," and "The Battle of Evermore," on J.R.R. Tolkien's *The Lord of the Rings* trilogy. Molly Hatchet had some cool metal-looking album covers, although they turned out to be Southern rock. But the '80s metal covers were a leap forward in their fantasy and ferocity.

Stranger Things Season 4 culminates with Eddie saving his friends, and maybe the world, by staging the epic guitar solo from Metallica's "Master of Puppets" in the Upside Down, a mysterious, nefarious double of our earthly plane. The scene perfectly demonstrates the overlap between *D&D*, fantasy, and heavy metal. Eddie is in full metal gear—bandanna, rings, leather jacket with a cutoff denim vest over it. The vest has a Dio backpatch, naturally. He has his friend Dustin looking on in awe; he has his Warlock guitar and his amplifier. He stands atop a gnarly mountain, as the sky crackles ominous red. Monster bats, foreshadowed by Eddie's own tattoos, blot the sky. The whole thing is a Gothic rock tableau. Eddie uses his strengths—the magic of music and friendship—for battle.

"Master of Puppets"' rapid tempo, odd time signature, and the solo's frenetic arpeggiation and whammy-bar wildness work alongside the lyrics to demonstrate the fight against the show's supernatural monster, Vecna, who will not be the kids' master. The first verse, the only one in the TV cut, demonstrates the monster's threat, if it's read from his point of view, and, equally, the kids' zeal to stop him, if read from theirs: "End of passion play, crumbling away, / I'm your source of self-destruction."[3] It works. Metallica themselves loved it, posting on Instagram that they "were beyond psyched for them to not only include 'Master of Puppets' in the show, but to have such a pivotal scene built around it. We were all stoked to see the final result and when we did we were totally blown away."[4]

As I'll discuss, though, in its own time, "Master of Puppets" can be read as a fight against the real-life monsters of 1986, with its personification of drug addiction and the album's larger theme of manipulation. That the song could conjure disparate meanings, then or now, based on context and the listener's interpretation, is very much the point. Literary study welcomes these kinds of readings. In addition to this book's subtitle of "the literary tradition," I'll be exploring heavy metal and the *literary critical* tradition as well. Heavy metal contains multitudes, as fans have always known.

Metal vs. Literature?

Playing *D&D* led me right to metal. Metal led me right to literature. And literature, now, with this book, leads back to metal.

On the surface, rock & roll, let alone heavy metal, could not seem more different from literature. Literature is, supposedly, highbrow, high culture; written, silent; the result of a single author, for a lone reader. Literature requires uninterrupted time, patience, maturity, and solitude. Drama and poetry began in antiquity. Novels date back to the eighteenth century, all much older than rock & roll. The novel's roots are British and bourgeoisie; its subjects and subtexts, at least during its pre-Victorian ascent, were often marriage, self-improvement, or their intersections. It is the province of the mind.

The rock & roll song is just the opposite: loud, communal, youth-oriented; palpable, physical, uninhibited, and unreserved; its roots are working class and African American. It is tied to the spoken word, the vernacular. Its subjects and subtexts are often sex, self-destruction, or their intersections. It is the province of the body. How does one go from one to the other?

But the better I understood both literature and rock & roll, the less these distinctions held. So much literature is filled with sex and violence—look no further than the center of the Western canon, William Shakespeare himself. His tragedies are revenge bloodbaths; his comedies, sex farces. Shakespeare loved lewd humor. He was writing his words to be performed live on stage, for a diverse and raucous crowd, more like a concert than a classroom. Plus, in most of the pictures we have of him, he has long hair, a beard, and occasionally an earring. Some of the greatest works in the history of literature are devoted to describing hell and damnation. Many more demonstrate a fascination with monsters, with the occult, with death, with life after death and the undead. Literature explores feelings of melancholy, thoughts of suicide, experiences of addiction, fears that one is going mad. We are given the stories, and sometimes perspectives, of killers, victims, heroes, villains, lovers, and those yearning for love. It is celebration. It is condemnation. The language can be beautiful or ugly, realistic or stylized. It's about all unhappy families, people who feel different. Despair and desire, often both. If this sounds familiar, you may be a reader. You're, maybe, also, a heavy metal fan.

The pipeline from *D&D* to metal to literature was, in retrospect, entirely predictable. The book covers for an edition of the *D&D Player's Handbook* and a Manowar album are, to non-fans of either, indistinguishable. (Hint: Manowar features more flags.) Both drew upon the same literary and artistic influences. These include pulps and comics like Conan the Barbarian, who has a literary pedigree going back to the 1930s. Penny Dreadfuls—inexpensive, serialized, sensationalist stories like *Varney the Vampire*—go back further. Artists like Gustave Doré (1832–1883) and poet/watercolorist/visionary William Blake (1757–1827) are even earlier than that. And Doré and Blake both created images to illustrate Dante, from the 1300s, and John Milton, from the 1600s.

Even in 1986, as a 14-year-old, I noticed the overlaps, the parallels. They were right there. I bought Iron Maiden's *Powerslave*, featuring their song "The Rime of the Ancient Mariner," the same semester I read the poem that inspired it, by Samuel Taylor Coleridge. That year, I would also listen to Metallica's "For Whom the Bell Tolls," from *Ride the Lightning*, borrowed from Ernest Hemingway, although in class we read Hemingway's *A Farewell to Arms*, a novel I would not understand for another decade but would then reread and weep every time.

In college, when it was time to choose a major, I chose Political Science. Some of that influence shows up in this book, since heavy metal is, it turns out, implicitly political, except when it's overtly political. Explicit content indeed. But

Poli-Sci wasn't right for me. I needed something in the realm of the imaginary, a pathway to an interior life, apart from the world. Something fantastical. Magical. Real. Ugly. Beautiful. Impractical. Invaluable. Useless. That major was, of course, English.

The major's uselessness is, like heavy metal's feelings of being an outsider, not its flaw but its feature. The same year I ditched *D&D* for music, I formed a band and began writing songs. Within two years, at 16, I was playing rock clubs. This was New York City—if a still ungentrified Brooklyn—so I had opportunities. Throughout high school, and then college, I wrote and performed original music, getting to play the magnificent L'Amour in Brooklyn, home to early-career performances by bands like Metallica (who are everywhere in this book), WASP, Slayer, and many more while they were on the way up, plus the occasional secret show by groups like Iron Maiden and Kiss. It didn't matter what kind of metal it was. I loved it all.

Checkmate, my band, did well. We never got famous, but we wrote, recorded, and performed our own songs, had our fans, and played some great gigs. We opened for bands that never got famous, either, but some of them *almost* did: Dangerous Toys, Enuff Z'Nuff, Tyketto, Danger Danger, White Trash, Child's Play (with requisite backwards *s*), Cycle Sluts from Hell, and Reigndance, featuring Andre Comeau, the rocker from the first season of MTV's *Real World*. Through a lucky connection (thanks, Jennifer), we got to record a demo tape in the middle of the night at Electric Ladyland Studios, used by Kiss, David Bowie, AC/DC, and, of course, Jimi Hendrix.

Meanwhile, soon-to-be-big bands and musicians abounded right in my neighborhood. Checkmate recorded another demo at Sty in the Sky, owned and manned by Josh Silver, who would soon co-found Type O Negative. We rehearsed at Fastlane Studios, where we met the kids in a new band called Life of Agony. Evan Seinfeld, before Biohazard broke, worked at the local late-night pizzeria. The big concerts always rolled through the tri-state area, and I saw Van Halen, Metallica, Scorpions, and Dokken—all on one bill. That was, of course, the Monsters of Rock tour in 1988. It keeps coming back to monsters.

I saw many others at L'Amour—Anthrax, Corrosion of Conformity, Overkill, Stormtroopers of Death, Saigon Kick—plus all my friends in their local bands, every weekend. This was a big deal at the time. I worked evenings and weekends in a record store. OK, it was Sam Goody, the corporate chain, in Kings Plaza, the Brooklyn mall. It was still a record store, or at least a cassette and CD store.

But I got to wear my waist-length hair proudly and listen to new music for my whole shift.

For those eight years, ages 15 to 23, I could only think and dream of music, of being a Famous Rock Star™. It's hard to say how many hours per day or days per week I practiced, because it was never work. Even then, I loved that English used the word *play* for an instrument, because that's what I felt I was doing. *Playing*. It was still, somehow, *D&D*, the band members each taking a different role. It was still a party. Serious play, for hours a day, plus six hours a week of band practice, plus around two gigs each month, plus going to other bands' gigs twice a week. I lived for music. I never wanted to major in music, though, even though I became a proficient guitarist, bassist, singer, and songwriter, plus a decent keyboardist. I learned to be a competent reader of literature in school, but I never learned to read music at all. It never occurred to me to study music in college. Music was special, and I didn't want to ruin it with school. And I *liked* school!

I planned to stay in school until my band and I made it big. Then I graduated from college. We still weren't famous. I started a Master's degree, and I was hired to teach college classes and, separately, high-school equivalency (GED) through the New York City Board of Education. My band still wasn't famous. Then we broke up. I formed a new band, Sharky, and we kept playing, including an opening slot for Dee Snider's post-Twisted Sister group, Widowmaker, in 1994. I finished my M.A., began a Ph.D. program, started teaching full time, and decided, at the age of 23, that I was too old to make it in metal.

By then, my music and scholarly sides had completely separated. I spent the next decade-and-a-half learning to be a writer, teacher, husband, and father. For years, I didn't even have a guitar. No one knew who I used to be, who, in some sense, I really was, my double life. Music was the secret identity I left behind. It was too hard to be everything. Time passed. I couldn't merge my two selves: rocker and reader. I didn't even try. Even though I cut my hair at 27, it stayed long in my dreams for another decade.

In retrospect, retiring from music at 23 was a little hasty.

Paper Beats Rock

I'm not surprised that I couldn't reconcile my double life. School has conflicted with rock since its inception. Rock & roll reveled in rebellion and individuality, of aligning oneself with the marginalized, the underdogs. And for teens, the main source of systemic oppression was school. School rewarded tradition, convention, and conduct, the opposite of what rock stood for. Arguably the very first rock & roll song, "Rock Around the Clock," also became the very first anti-school song, if by accident.[5] The lyrics, setting the precedent for songs like Kiss's "Rock and Roll All Nite," are about rocking, all day *and* all night. So far, so good. But after a disappointing debut, "Rock Around the Clock" was featured in the film *Blackboard Jungle*, in 1955. Like James Dean's *Rebel Without a Cause* from the same year, and Marlon Brando's *The Wild One* from a few years earlier, in 1951, *Blackboard Jungle* depicted the allegedly growing problem of juvenile delinquency, in this case, focused on school.

The film seems to have been intended as a cautionary tale against teen rebellion, with its sympathetic teacher as the protagonist. Instead, teens flocked to *Blackboard Jungle* thanks to its rock & roll soundtrack, the first of its kind, with "Rock Around the Clock" at the forefront. And they didn't see the movie, or the music, as a warning. They thought it looked fun, *cool*. It foregrounded the irony of parental warnings to come, later, in 1985. Kids *wanted* to rock around the clock, just as, thirty years later, Twisted Sister wanted to rock, and Twisted Sister staged the video for "I Wanna Rock" in a school all over again.

Unlike "Rock Around the Clock," Chuck Berry's "School Days" (1957) is explicitly about school. Many bands, including AC/DC, would go on to cover it. Yes, school in "School Days" is awful, but for a particular reason: it suppresses teen spirit, something its opposite, rock & roll, liberates. The song presents the narrative of a single school day, but one that demonstrates emblematic school-day indignities, hence the title's plural, *days*: "Up in the mornin' and out to school, / The teacher is teachin' the Golden Rule," through "Workin' your fingers right down to the bone / And the guy behind you won't leave you alone."[6]

But school is only the first half of the song. "Soon as three o'clock rolls around," the second part tells us, "You finally lay your burden down." How? Through the power of juke joints, dance, and romance. "Hail, hail rock 'n' roll," the final verse beams, "Deliver me from the days of old."[7] Which is dumb old school. The qualities of being good in school—rule-following and sitting in place—become, in the world of rock & roll, liabilities. And the opposite becomes true as well. Unruliness and frenetic movement are the bases of rocking & rolling.

Berry's song is not presented through a racial lens, but it's possible to see one. *Blackboard Jungle*, for example, made the racial dynamics of its white teacher and troubled minority students clear, with the "jungle" of its title, in retrospect, taking a potentially racial cast. "School Days'" reversal represents the archetype of the trickster figure, from Norse mythology's Loki to Native American tales' Coyote. But it is particularly indebted to the African-American folk-tale tradition. Br'er Rabbit famously convinces Fox not to eat him. Instead, Rabbit pleads to be thrown into the thorny briar patch, which he says will be even worse. But it's what Rabbit wanted all along. "Born and raised in the briar patch!" Br'er Rabbit teases, as he easily navigates the thorns to escape, and Fox gets stuck chasing him. The supposedly dangerous juke joints, dens of delinquency, aren't a trap. They're the new home. Rock & roll, supposedly the soundtrack of '50s misbehavior, instead offered teens a respite, even salvation. Hail, hail rock and roll. School, supposedly the source of self-improvement, is the site of social suppression.

This reversal would become the prototype for many more songs. The speaker of Sam Cooke's "Wonderful World" (1960) sings, "[I] Don't know much about history" or any other subject, except love, which is not in the curriculum.[8] Most famously, Alice Cooper's "School's Out" (1972), covered by '80s metal band Krokus (1986), features the excellent puns, "Well, we got no class / And we got no principals."[9] That's meant to be a good thing, in both senses and spellings of the words. The anti-school attitudes would continue with "Rock and Roll High School" by The Ramones (1978) and, in keeping with Chuck Berry, "School Days," by The Runaways (1977). Madam X would celebrate being "High in High School"; the same year, WASP would revise Chuck Berry's title to a punning "School Daze" (1984): "I'm here in a rage, / A juvenile's jail, / And I'm here locked up in their cage."[10] The penitentiary imagery would prove central, as we'll see.

David Lee Roth would imitate the father's voice to ask, "Have you seen Junior's grades?" in Van Halen's "And the Cradle Will Rock . . ." (1980),[11] while "Hot for Teacher" (1984) would make a travesty of the entire educational experience— and include more jail cells in the video. Pink Floyd's "Another Brick in the Wall Part 2" (1979) would get a chorus of children to chant, brilliantly, ironically, ungrammatically in its double negative, "We don't need no education," with their Cockney accents emphasizing class conflict but also class solidarity.[12] Pink Floyd's film *The Wall* (1982) would replace the jails with a more surreal image: students going into a meat grinder. Extreme would drop any pretense for a plaintive, childlike plea: "Mother, [I] don't want to go to school today, / I think I'd rather go outside and play" in 1989.[13]

It's no surprise, then, that I kept my school-self and my metal-self distinct. They weren't just separate, or even just different. They were opposites, contradictions.

But (Metal) Scissors Beats Paper

Then, after years as a college professor at Maryville University, in St. Louis, Missouri, I started playing music again in 2012. I resumed lead guitar and lead singing. My new band was borne of old, playing covers, mostly '80s hard rock, but also some Hendrix, some Pearl Jam, some Green Day. Unlike my romantic, idealistic former self, the one who learned guitar in order to write my own songs, who wrote riffs and lyrics and refused to learn covers, my current self loves playing other people's music. If anything, playing covers is more like what I do as part of my day job—interpreting books, engaging in literary analysis, and guiding others. The joy comes not from sharing my own compositions, but in performing songs that crowds love to hear, when many of the original stars are gone. At first, I couldn't eat before or after each rehearsal, or before any gigs. When we were done playing, I was left wracked with stomach pain. I thought it was the stress of singing after a hiatus, the churn of old pipes, or even nerves. It wasn't. It was a feeling I had forgotten. It was excitement. The kind that only comes from performing. I had to learn to recognize it again.

In 2019, I joined Top Gunz, the biggest '80s hard rock tribute band in the Missouri/Southern Illinois area, as lead guitarist. This meant more—more musical equipment, more gigs and better gigs, getting in shape for regular four-hour performances. It meant creating a persona, and wearing a wig, ripped t-shirts, spandex pants, and stage makeup. It meant playing every weekend, on big stages, with laser lights and smoke machines, to crowds of hundreds and even thousands. They love their '80s heavy metal in the heart of the Midwest. I find myself amazed at where life has taken me. I'm playing more shows, in front of more people, for more money, now, as my midlife crisis side-hustle, than I did when I was young and burning for it.

But school and music were still separate. This was my double life now: Dr. Jesse Kavadlo, Professor of English and Humanities, on weekdays (fig. 3). Dr. NoiZe, lead guitarist for Top GunZ: The '80s Party Rock Tribute Experience, on weekends (fig. 4). Everyone thought Eddie was my double. But I had become my own double.

Figure 3 Jesse Kavadlo, Professor of English. Photo: Maryville University.

Figure 4 Dr. Noize, lead guitarist of Top Gunz. Photo: Gary Donofrio.

Stranger Danger

Stranger Things fans mourned Eddie's sacrifice at the end of his season. I don't like to imagine the futures of fictional characters outside of their stories, but here I'll make an exception. If Eddie had made it (and I'm writing this before Season 5 airs, so who knows what will happen?), I'd like to imagine that his life might have paralleled mine, rather than the other way around. I graduated high school and began college in 1988, and I'd like to hope, his academic struggles to the contrary, that Eddie would have done the same, even in the same year. I don't think he'd have majored in music, either. Colleges weren't doing metal at the time. I think his love of *D&D* would have nudged him into English, too, and, with that as a major, maybe he'd have gone on to teach. In the end, his Hellfire Club was about teaching, after all: having fun, sharing stories, inventing adventures, and making other outsiders feel like they were on the inside. That's also what heavy metal was always about, too. He might need to take some time off from rocking, but he wouldn't stay away for long. I know this for sure.

There is no shortage of doubles in literature, from writers as different as Edgar Allan Poe, Robert Louis Stevenson, Fyodor Dostoyevsky, Philip Roth, and Chuck Palahniuk. And literary doubles tend not to end well, with each half vying for total control. Freud, whose quotation opens this Preface and who will, like the repressed, return throughout these chapters, suggests that doubles are uncanny reminders of death, portents of our own inevitable future corpses.

Rock of Pages: The Literary Tradition of 1980s Heavy Metal is my way to bring the doubles together, what on the surface might seem like two incongruent art forms and two unrelated parts of my life—my study of literature with my passion for heavy metal. As I will discuss, it's more than just that the two have a lot in common. Literature can help us to understand the traditions and cultural conventions that heavy metal builds upon. Literary analysis reveals the songs' and groups' artistry and intelligence, words certainly not ascribed to this genre in the 1980s. Contemporary pop and rap stars have found homes in college classes, with the *HuffPost* obnoxiously proclaiming in 2024 that "poetry and literary analysis are cool for once thanks to Taylor Swift and Kendrick Lamar."[14] Mainstays like Bob Dylan and Bruce Springsteen have been taught and celebrated by academics for decades. But '80s heavy metal, especially what's now called hair metal, is still perceived as being by and for dummies—sometimes even by metal fans themselves.

At the same time, heavy metal can affirm that literature is more rebellious and less stuffy than your teachers have led you to believe. While some of the connections to literature will be plain, I'm as interested in the analytical approach to heavy metal as I am with specific literary correspondences—that is, in providing the close readings and historicist interpretations of the lyrics, music, and artists, with the generosity usually applied to, say, *The Waste Land*, by T.S. Eliot, and not, say "Wasted," by Def Leppard, or even "Wasted Years," by Iron Maiden.

Finally, like *Stranger Things*, this book provides a way of rethinking the 1980s—the Cold War, the youth culture, the backlash against the youth culture, the controversies, the apocalyptic sensibility, and the party-like-it's-the-end-of-the-world debauchery—from the perspective of the twenty-first century, in the way that the study of literature examines cultural contexts and not just cultural productions. In doing so, we'll discuss and analyze a lot of bands and songs, and consider music in conjunction with literary movements, books, and authors. Like Megadeth's "Sweating Bullets" character, I'm chomping at the bit, and I'm sharpening the axe.

But as Dave Mustaine also sang, in that strange song about doubles and "dementia," "Hindsight is always 20–20." It's not always, though, with our prejudices and predispositions. Nostalgia clouds the past and the mind, especially when it comes to the music we came of age to. I'll try to be cautious about nostalgia. As "Sweating Bullets" continues, "But looking back, it's still a bit fuzzy."¹⁵ Indeed. Orpheus, the first metal musician, in that his mythology mingles violence, passion, and the underworld, could not help but look back, despite the consequences.

So let's look back.

Introduction

Won't Somebody Please Think of the Children?

Figure 5 Krampus (Devil). Greeting card. Postcard by the Viennese Werkstätte, Number 542. Color Lithography, 14 : 9 cm. Around 1911. (Photo by Imagno/Getty Images).

Literature is where I go to explore the highest and lowest places in human society and in the human spirit, where I hope to find not absolute truth but the truth of the tale, of the imagination and of the heart.

—Salman Rushdie (1989)[1]

Let me apologize in advance for the profane language and disturbing images that appear throughout this book.
—Tipper Gore, Introduction to *Raising PG Kids in an X-Rated Society* (1987)[2]

What is heavy metal? Leslie West, of the proto-metal band Mountain, may have put it best when he said, "To me, heavy metal is like pornography. I couldn't tell you what it is, but when I see it, I know it."[3] West, whether he knew it or not, was paraphrasing Supreme Court Justice Potter Stewart, who, responding to a 1964 case about exhibiting what was accused of being a pornographic film, said, "I shall not today attempt further to define the kinds of material I understand to be embraced within that shorthand description, and perhaps I could never succeed in intelligibly doing so. But I know it when I see it, and the motion picture involved in this case is not that."[4]

West's analogy provides the context and framing of this book. Heavy metal, however one defines it, along with other art forms in the 1980s, would be accused of being pornography itself, in newspaper editorials all the way to the halls of the United States Congress. In that way, heavy metal is also a part of a darker literary tradition—the many attempts at suppression over decades and centuries. It wouldn't be the first time art would be accused of obscenity by censors who wanted to control and contain it, under the guise of protecting the youth. And, unfortunately, it wouldn't be the last.

Rock Stars throughout the Ages

If one were to look for rock stars—that over-the-top combination of artistry, excess, sex appeal, fame, and scandal—before there were rock stars, or even rock music, one would find writers. Before he was the bane of students' existence, in his own time William Shakespeare was a popular playwright, famous enough that Queen Elizabeth saw him and his troupe perform several of his plays. His most famous poem during his lifetime, "Venus and Adonis," was sexy:

> Touch but my lips with those fair lips of thine,--
> Though mine be not so fair, yet are they red,--
> The kiss shall be thine own as well as mine:
> What seest thou in the ground? hold up thy head:
> > Look in mine eyeballs, there thy beauty lies;
> > Then why not lips on lips, since eyes in eyes?[5]

Shakespeare's plays regularly revolved around murder and crossdressing, not even counting the real-life crossdressing, since men played all the roles. His work consisted of nonstop wordplay, dirty jokes, and appearances by ghosts, witches, and supernatural spirits. That is, in part, because he was writing to entertain people. Students equate Shakespeare with school, but he wrote for the stage, the people, and the world.

In 1812, Lord Byron wrote, "I awoke and found myself famous."[6] His poem, "Childe Harold's Pilgrimage," had made him a rock star. And, like rock stars, Byron was as well-known for his personal and sexual life as he was for his art. His poetry could be sensitive: "She walks in Beauty, like the night / Of cloudless climes and starry skies."[7] Typical male rock star, writing lovely similes to beguile a woman. Meanwhile, Byron slept with anyone and everyone, including his half-sister, creating his own archetype of the Byronic hero—moody, gloomy, perverse, and Gothic, when Gothic was associated with a literary genre more than black eyeliner.

Around the same time, in 1816, Samuel Taylor Coleridge—who also wrote "The Rime of the Ancient Mariner," which Iron Maiden would adapt—published his poem "Kubla Khan." Its concluding lines are intoxicating, powerful, Iron Maiden-esque: "Weave a circle round him thrice, / And close your eyes with holy dread, / For he on honeydew hath fed, / And drunk the milk of Paradise."[8] Rather than drinking metaphorical milk of Paradise, though, Coleridge, like any bona fide rock star, claimed the poem came to him in a dream and was high on opium when he wrote it.

Sex, drugs, and poetry: writers, like rock stars, used their words to enchant and seduce. "The Flea," by John Donne, published posthumously in 1633, begins by observing that the titular insect "sucked me first, and now sucks thee, / And in this flea our two bloods mingled be."[9] That is, the speaker and the woman he's addressing might as well have sex, since their bodily fluids have already mixed anyway in the flea that bit them both. Donne was later ordained as an Anglican priest, which turned out to be another rock star move, if the rock star is Alice

Cooper, Megadeth's Dave Mustaine, or WASP's Blackie Lawless, all of whom became born-again Christians despite decades of profane lyrics.

Another Metaphysical Poet, Andrew Marvell, wrote "To His Coy Mistress," also published posthumously, in 1681. "Had we but World enough, and Time, / This coyness, Lady, were no crime." But since they're mortal, they should have sex now, since "The Grave's a fine and private place, / But none I think do there embrace."[10] It's no "Let's Put the X in Sex" (1988) by Kiss, but, like a good rock song, it manages to be playful, sensual, and morbid at the same time.

Images of sex and death abound. 1980s rock evokes the word *decadence*, hence Mötley Crüe's compilation album *Decade of Decadence*. But 1880s-era poet Charles Baudelaire was part of the original Decadent movement. Earlier, in 1857, six of his poems were banned in France because they "necessarily lead to the excitement of the senses by a crude realism offensive to public decency."[11] Consider these lines from "The Vampire's Metamorphoses" (translated by William Aggeler): "When she had sucked out all the marrow from my bones / And I languidly turned toward her / To give back an amorous kiss, I saw no more / Than a wine-skin with gluey sides, all full of pus!"[12] That's even worse than "looks that kill." The evil woman, the lover as succubus, would strongly influence the Crüe, among many others.

Another member of the Decadent movement, Oscar Wilde, was also as famous for his supposedly indecent work as his supposedly indecent life. He caused a stir with the debauchery implied by the title character in *The Picture of Dorian Gray* (1890), as well as the epigraphs in its Preface, especially the idea that "There is no such thing as a moral or an immoral book. Books are well written, or badly written. That is all."[13] For moralists, then and a century later, that was not all. In 1895, Wilde was sentenced to prison for gross indecency, a euphemism for his homosexual relationships.

Poet Allen Ginsberg, also gay, was the cause of another trial, this time in America, this time closer to the present, in 1957. "Howl" famously opens with these lines:

> I saw the best minds of my generation destroyed by madness, starving hysterical naked,
>
> dragging themselves through the negro streets at dawn looking for an angry fix,
>
> angelheaded hipsters burning for the ancient heavenly connection to the starry dynamo in the machinery of night, [...][14]

In just forty-four words, Ginsberg evokes what would later be the four major objections to metal lyrics: images suggesting violence, drug use, sexuality, and the occult. The case against Ginsberg's publisher, City Lights, was dismissed, even though the poem used the words "cock," "balls," and "asshole." The judge ruled that "Howl" was not without "redeeming social importance" and did not have a "substantial tendency to deprave or corrupt its readers by inciting lascivious thoughts or arousing lustful desires."[15] Rock & roll and heavy metal would not get as generous an interpretation, although in fairness, rock was indeed trying to incite lascivious thoughts and arouse lustful desires.

Payola, McCarthy, and Moral Panic

Around the same time Ginsberg and the literary movement associated with him, the Beats, were emerging, rock & roll finally entered the scene, riled by the same conformist culture that the Beats were howling against. Those conservative forces then began to react against rock & roll in the same way they did to "Howl," in their attempt to contain the new cultural menace. In 1959, Congress held what became known as the Payola hearings. On the surface, the problem seems like straightforward dishonesty. Record companies were paying radio DJs to play their artists' songs without disclosing the payments. The practice sounds shady, even though it was not technically criminal.

What's lesser known, however, is that the songs vying for airplay were mostly a new kind of music called rock & roll—as well as Country—which was being shut out of radio station playlists. The new music's composers were also excluded from membership in ASCAP, the American Society of Composers, Authors and Publishers, and so instead joined BMI, or Broadcast Music, Inc. Payola was, in this reading, less a bribery scam than a way for the old guard to reassert its cultural and economic dominance. And the way to do this was already in place, already handy: the language of the Cold War and McCarthyism. While testifying against Payola, Vance Packard, social critic, journalist, and rock hater, complained that "our airways have been flooded in recent years with whining guitarists, musical riots put to a switchblade beat, obscene lyrics about hugging, squeezing, and rocking all night long."[16] He meant all this is an insult, although Switchblade Beat would be a decent band name. "This," Packard continued, is "the diet served up daily to young Americans whose tastes are still forming."[17] There it was: the unsubstantiated claim of corrupting the youth, a charge that goes all the way back to the 399 BCE trial of Socrates.

The supposed payoffs became known as the "Electronic Curtain," a parallel with the Iron Curtain, and an anti-American conspiracy in keeping with the imagined anti-American conspiracies Senator Joseph McCarthy also intended to expose. Called to testify, Jack Lawrence, a composer and lyricist affiliated with the older ASCAP, claimed that

> to best explain the electronic curtain, I would say that this was a technique perfected by the Communists because they managed to jam the airwaves and keep American words of hope away from the freedom-loving peoples behind the Iron Curtain. Now, the networks have adopted this technique of jamming the airwaves with exactly what they feel should and should not be heard.[18]

As John Brackett writes, "the rhetoric that dominated both" the McCarthy and Payola hearings reflected "ideological debates that were being fought at the height of the Cold War, debates involving the culture of consensus and the image of the 'American Way.'"[19] Like the McCarthy hearings, the Payola hearings sought to stifle a cultural contagion, "enemies from within," under the pretense of probity. It was a moral panic in keeping with the other panics of the 1950s: the "Howl" obscenity trial, the Senate Comic Book Menace hearings of 1954, and *Brown v. Board of Education* from 1952 to 1954. The response to these social threats to the status quo was the same: to contain them.

Containment was famously the response to the threat of creeping Communism abroad, and to the fear of Communism at home. Brackett continues, "When read from the perspective of the nation's dominant strategy for controlling the spread of communism," the Payola hearings "appear less like an inquiry into possible antitrust violations and more like a strategy designed to protect Americans from an imagined threat that seeks to transform the business practices and musical tastes of the nation."[20] This threat came from a new form of music whose roots, practitioners, and audiences were a combination of African American and white working-class. The accusation of payoffs provided cover for the larger fear of a new enemy: rock & roll itself.

The Payola hearings focused on the supposedly corrupting forces of disc jockeys and record companies. They ruined Cleveland DJ Alan Freed's life. But the condemnation included those who played and even listened to the music as well. One senator stood up for the musicians and fans. Senator Albert Gore, Sr., of Tennessee, rejected Packard's "gratuitous insult to thousands of our fellow Tennesseans, both in and out of the field of country music."[21] Senator Gore, Sr., recognized the elitism and grandstanding of the charges.

In an act of historical symmetry and irony, twenty-six years later, in 1985, the son of Senator Albert Gore, Sr., Al Gore, Jr., recognized no such thing. This time, he was the one attempting to stifle the moral contagion of rock & roll. One year earlier, his wife, Tipper Gore, and Susan Baker, wife of Ronald Reagan's Treasury Secretary James Baker, formed the Parents Music Resource Center, or the PMRC. And the PMRC, even more than Lita Ford, Icon, and Pantera, was out for blood.[22]

"Knowing what we know now, the PMRC should have stood for 'Politicians Masked as Reelection Campaigns,'" WASP's Blackie Lawless said, in 2015. "It was Al Gore's 'Joe McCarthy moment.'"[23] Blackie Lawless is exactly right, a statement I relish. The McCarthyite moral panic of the 1950s was revived for the 1980s, with a new attempt to contain the new cultural contagion of heavy metal. Blackie Lawless, the writer of "Animal (F**k Life a Beast)," found himself in the odd historical company of not just Oscar Wilde and Allen Ginsberg, but also fellow literary targets James Joyce (for *Ulysses*), Gustave Flaubert (*Madame Bovary*), D.H. Lawrence (*Lady Chatterley's Lover*), Vladimir Nabokov (*Lolita*), and many others. Leslie West's benign analogy between heavy metal and pornography had come to pass.

"Porn Rock"

Tipper Gore heard songs she didn't like and decided to make a federal case of it.

"A small but immensely successful minority of performers have pioneered the 'porn rock' phenomenon," wrote Gore, in her 1987 book *Raising PG Kids in an X-Rated Society*.[24] "This kind of rock music is only part of an escalating trend toward the use of more explicit sex and graphic violence in entertainment industry offerings, from movies and videos to jeans and perfume ads. Music is the most unexpected medium, and rock music has shown perhaps the least willingness to exercise self-restraint." [25]

Gore was a self-proclaimed rock fan. *Tom Tom Mag* ("Drummers. Music. Feminism.") wrote, later on, in 2019, that "what you may not know [about Tipper Gore] is that through it all, she has maintained a passion for the drums and rock music."[26] It is hard to know what to make of the idea that Gore, rock aficionado, found music to be "the most unexpected medium," or that rock in particular "has shown perhaps the least willingness to exercise self-restraint." It would be *the most expected medium*. Rock music would clearly and obviously be *the least willing* genre to exercise self-restraint. Unwillingness to exercise self-restraint is the defining characteristic of rock music.

In keeping with this book's approach to reading heavy metal as literature, it helps to read *Raising PG Kids in an X-Rated Society* as a work of fiction with an unreliable narrator instead of as a nonfiction diatribe. That is, like novels such as *The Catcher in the Rye*, *Fight Club*, or *Gone Girl*, the narrator seems not to understand the implications of her own language upon herself. If "Tipper Gore"—the perfect parodic name—were a narrator invented by, say, Chuck Palahniuk, *Raising PG Kids in an X-Rated Society* would be a solid satire. Think of the *Simpsons*' Helen Lovejoy endorsing prohibition ("Won't somebody please think of the children!") or *South Park*'s Sheila Broflovski—Kyle's mom—trying to ban a cartoon. Gore's book only makes sense if we imagine that some true behind-the-scenes author has taken on a first-person persona with no self-awareness or knowledge of music or history whatsoever.

How else to make sense of the supposed PMRC origin story and *aha* moment, when Tipper Gore and her 11-year-old daughter listen to Prince's *Purple Rain* album together and mysteriously stumble upon "Darling Nikki," with its slant rhyme of "sex fiend" and "masturbating with a magazine"? "The vulgar lyrics embarrassed both of us," Gore recounts. "I couldn't believe my ears!"[27] *I couldn't believe my ears.* I realize the Internet was still just a gleam in her husband's eye in December of 1984. But one didn't need Google to have heard of Prince. Prince was one of the best-known musicians in the world. By the time the Gores bought it, *Purple Rain* had been the number one album in the country for four months. "Little Red Corvette" was a huge hit in 1983, featuring the lines "Girl, you got an ass like I never seen, ow! / And the ride / I say the ride is so smooth, you must be a limousine."[28] *Purple Rain*, the film, was rated R. That is to say: Prince was hardly an unknown quantity. Gore concludes, "Millions of Americans were buying *Purple Rain* with no idea what to expect."[29] I'm certain that millions of Americans got exactly what they expected, and exactly what they wanted. For an unreliable narrator, the line is fantastic. She's an irony maiden. Unfortunately, Tipper Gore was real.

Tipper Gore writes, of the Senate hearing, "By this time, the United States Congress had begun to take an interest in the issue of labeling records.[30] *Had begun to take an interest in the issue.* As though it happened all by itself. As though it were entirely separate from her marriage to one Senator Albert Gore, Jr. Tipper Gore continues,

Some critics mistakenly assumed that [Al Gore] had asked for the hearing, when, in fact, both he and I had reservations about it. I thought the PMRC would be better off working with artists and the industry on their own terms, instead of dragging everybody before the TV cameras on Capitol Hill. Artists were already screaming about censorship, and this would only give them an excuse to raise the specter of government intervention.[31]

An excuse to raise the specter of government intervention. Excuse. Specter. Was a Senate hearing *not* government intervention? These are the words of an unreliable narrator.

For the hearing, Tipper Gore and Susan Baker compiled what they referred to as the "Filthy Fifteen"—the worst lyrical offenders in rock and pop music, along with their particular category of offense. "Darling Nikki" tops the list, but heavy metal acts comprised nine of the other fourteen: Judas Priest's "Eat Me Alive," Mötley Crüe's "Bastard," AC/DC's "Let Me Put My Love Into You," Twisted Sister's "We're Not Gonna Take It," WASP's "Animal (F**k Like a Beast)," Def Leppard's "High 'n' Dry (Saturday Night)," Mercyful Fate's "Into the Coven," Black Sabbath's "Trashed," and Venom's "Possessed." (The other, non-metal songs were Sheena Easton's "Sugar Walls," Vanity's "Strap On 'Robbie Baby,'" Madonna's "Dress You Up," Mary Jane Girls' "In My House," and Cyndi Lauper's "She Bop.")[32]

Only one musician who had a song on the Filthy Fifteen appeared at the hearing, Twisted Sister's singer Dee Snider. (To their credit, musicians Frank Zappa and John Denver also testified.) It didn't go well—for the Gores. Responding to Tipper Gore's claim that "Under the Blade" encouraged "sadomasochism, bondage, and rape," Snider said,

> The lyrics [Tipper Gore] quoted have absolutely nothing to do with these topics. On the contrary, the words in question are about surgery and the fear that it instills in people... As the creator of 'Under the Blade,' I can say categorically that the only sadomasochism, bondage, and rape in this song is in the mind of Ms. Gore... It was about the fear of operations. I think people imagine being helpless on a table, the bright light in their face, the blade coming down on them, and being totally afraid that they may wake up, who knows, dead, handicapped. There is a certain fear of hospitals. That is what, in my imagination, what I see the hospitals like.[33]

We'll get to Snider's claims and the song itself later on. Images from the day of the testimony show Snider playing the metal card with his sunglasses, irrepressible bleached blond curls, cutoff denim vest, and tee shirt featuring the text of the First Amendment with the word CENSORED covering it. And then there was Al Gore, Jr., Senate nepo baby, thinking that he would easily outsmart Snider. As Snider writes in his memoir, *Shut Up and Pass the Mic*, "I'm sure that looking at my photos and videos, and listening to my music, that they were certain I would be the perfect heavy metal fool to make a very public example of."[34] I don't think anyone watching the interchange can witness anything other than Gore being outmaneuvered and outsmarted at every turn.

Almost anyone. Tipper Gore's account cuts all of it. Of Snider, she writes only this:

> The hearing did not seek to reach any consensus, but on the whole we were pleased to see the facts come out. Twisted Sister's Dee Snider told that committee that he was a Christian who did not smoke, drink, or do drugs, and insisted that he had been unfairly accused. A member of the committee—my husband—asked him the full name of his fan club, SMF Fans of Twisted Sister. Replied Snider, "It stands for Sick Mother Fucking Fans of Twisted Sister."[35]

"My husband," set off by dashes, as though that information is entirely coincidental. Tipper Gore seems to think that getting Snider to say the word "fucking" was some kind of victory, a sign of hypocrisy on his part, as though straight-edge Christians can't say curse words—obscenity is different from blasphemy. As though she doesn't reproduce the word herself in her own text. Instead, the exchange sounds more like the famous response to McCarthy hearings: "Have you no sense of decency?" Not Snider, who is wearing his decency on his sleeve, if he were wearing sleeves. The one lacking decency is the accuser, Al Gore, who, as Blackie Lawless noted, was, in retrospect, using the hearings to establish his own performative moral bona fides in preparation for his Presidential run. (He would lose the nomination to Bill Clinton but then go on to be Clinton's running mate.) As Snider notes, "I took this opportunity to say the F-word, in a federal building, in front of the entire world. Pretty cool when you think about it."[36] Unlike Tipper Gore, Snider chooses not to repeat the F-word in print.

The discussion at the time, for the Gores, concerned explicit language and its potential negative influence on children. For Snider, the recording industry, and musicians, the topic was government censorship—real censorship, not "an excuse to raise the specter of government intervention." The PMRC's point and purpose were to use the might of the federal government to intimidate the recording industry into creating a rating system for albums, which would, in turn, potentially limit where and to whom the albums could be sold. The rating system itself didn't take hold, but the warning stickers did.

Tipper Gore was exactly right. But, in the spirit of unreliable narrators, not in any of the ways she intended. The planned rating system was in keeping with metal's subject matter. But that's because those subjects themselves were perfectly in keeping with the glory and history of literature.

Heavy Metal as Literature

The PMRC wanted albums to contain content warnings, closer to what we see today on video games. These were their intended ratings:

- V for violence
- D/A for drug or alcohol references
- X for sexual explicitness
- O for occult[37]

But such a system would be impossibly unwieldy. Who would listen to and rate every single song? What criteria could they possibly use? Instead, record companies compromised by offering the more generic, but now iconic, "Parental Warning—Explicit Lyrics" label, the black and white sticker that went on to adorn everyone's favorite albums like a badge of honor.

The PMRC was wrong about affixing labels. But it was right about heavy metal's topics. Scholar Robert Walser argues otherwise, saying that his analysis of lyrics "reveals relatively little concern with violence, drug use, or suicide," instead seeing themes of "assertion of or longing for intensity," "lust," "loneliness," "anger, rebellion, madness," and "didactic or critical."[38] He's right, too, but topics and themes are not mutually exclusive. A substantial number of songs include representations of violence, drugs and alcohol, sex, and the occult, but, as Walser also recognizes, they are presented in ways that are more "complex and sophisticated" than critics were willing to acknowledge. Walser wants to defend heavy metal, but a song can describe violence and also act as, say, an "assertion of or longing for intensity." Violence, addiction, and related topics (including madness, in keeping with Walser), sexuality, and the occult are among the best, most favored topics across art, music, and literature.

This book, then, will take two approaches. First, it will examine some of the contexts of 1980s heavy metal, which are easily lost when contemporary listeners pull a playlist or single song from a music streaming service or YouTube. The PMRC and the Cold War provide one kind of context. MTV and videos provide another. The retroactive lens of discussing '80s metal in a twenty-first-century book represents yet another.

At the same time, in Chapters 2, 3, 4, and 5, the book takes the PMRC's own objections and uses them as titles and topics: violence, and, for me, the connected concerns about justice; substance abuse, and the interrelated issues of obsession, madness, suicidal ideation, and mental health; sex, and, concomitantly, representations of women and relationships between men and women; and the occult, along with the problem of the afterlife and morality itself. These categories are just starting points, though. The approach is broad and discursive, with each chapter ending in a Post Script, a retrospective. Beyond even the lens of literature, what can we understand, looking back now with forty years of hindsight?

Chapter 1 will focus on what I'm calling The Long 1980s, which I define as 1978–1991. The period felt like the height of the Cold War, but it turned out to be its end. It was an era of attempted censorship and an extension of Cold War containment culture, but it's now remembered for its freedom of movement and expression—at least for some people. Ronald Reagan promised Morning in America; the possibility of apocalypse foretold The Day After. Meanwhile, MTV took heavy metal from margins to mainstream, and Poison promised nothin' but a good time. But was it?

Chapter 2, "V for Violence," begins with the PMRC's most dramatic objection to heavy metal: that its lyrics and even attendant lifestyle focused on, and promoted, violent behavior among its listeners. The topic lends itself to important questions about how we interpret what we hear, rock star personae, literary perspectives, and how the audience interacts with what it hears. The chapter, however, pivots from violence to its flipside, heavy metal's overt concern for justice, even social justice, during a period not especially known for its sensitivity to those issues.

Chapter 3, "D/A for Drugs and Alcohol," is ostensibly about the supposedly carefree depictions of substances, but it broadens the focus in ways that the PMRC did not consider. On the surface, certainly, some songs had lyrics related to drug and alcohol use, even as, upon closer inspection, they were cautionary tales, not endorsements. But many more songs went into deeper topics that the superficial focus on drugs elided: addiction, as well as connections with suicidal ideation, madness, and mental (or metal) health. Metal bands wailed about their feelings of isolation, like they felt trapped in a sanitarium, a madhouse, or a prison, just as writers and literary theorists were exploring the same ideas.

Chapter 4, "X for Sexually Explicit," examines the intertwined topics of sexuality and love. 1980s metal, especially what came to be known as hair metal, was infatuated with sex and the body, in contradictory ways that, across different artists and songs, evoke archetypes, sexual objectification, the male gaze, and the male gaze's reversal—that is, many of the mainstays of literature and literary theory.

Chapter 5, "O for Occult," discusses the satanic and occult imagery that metal bands were accused of endorsing—another subject of "Stranger Things." Satan was a symbol of rebellion long predating Mötley Crüe's *Shout at the Devil*. Romantic preoccupations with the natural and supernatural paved the way for heavy metal lyricists like Ronnie James Dio. And Dio would lead the effort for metal's answer to USA for Africa, Hear N' Aid, a cause largely ignored by adults at the time and nearly forgotten today. And teens would be hurt, not helped, by adult delusions of satanic influence.

Near the end, where a guitar solo would fall if the book were a metal song, I offer an ode to guitar solos, a nonverbal aspect of the genre that nevertheless deserves inclusion. Finally, I'll conclude the book with the conclusion of 1980's heavy metal itself. What, then, does it mean to look back now?

Certainly, other books have sought to understand heavy metal through an academic lens. *Heavy Metal: The Music and Its Culture*, by Deena Weinstein, from 1991 and revised in 2000, was one of the first and is still one of the best, taking the sociological approach of analyzing the fans and their relationship with the music as a subculture rather than merely an artistic preference. The aforementioned Robert Walser's *Running with the Devil: Power, Gender, and Madness in Heavy Metal Music* (1993) is an astute work of cultural studies and ethnomusicology. Both are required reading. While it's clear from the depth of analysis that Weinstein and Walser are fans, at the time, both seemed cautious and defensive about whether their subjects were worthy of academic study; both made sure to provide the appropriate academic theoretical frameworks and terminology.

In some ways, not much has changed. For all its commercial success, 1980s heavy metal is still outsider art. Weinstein's and Walser's books remain outliers. But other things have changed. More books have been published. Metal Studies emerged as a subset of cultural studies and musicology. The International Society for Metal Music Studies, for one thing, exists, and has its own journal and annual conference. Metal has found its way into college classrooms, including "Reading Rock & Roll," a course (an Honors course!) that I have taught since 2005. Several excellent histories of metal have been published, including *Sound of the Beast: The Complete Headbanging History of Heavy Metal* by Ian Christie (2003) and the more recent and aptly raucous *A History of Heavy Metal* (2018) by Andrew O'Neill. We've come a long way since "School's Out."

And yet, when it comes to history *and*, not history *of*, metal, coupled with the kind of close reading reserved for literature—metal as art, rather than cultural artifact—metal still lags behind other forms of popular music. *Rock of Pages*, then, is an attempt to ask, and answer, these questions: How can literature help us to rethink 1980s heavy metal? How can we analyze the music in the ways we analyze literature? How can heavy metal help us to understand what's important—and maybe even dangerous, in a good way—about literature? What, in retrospect, can this analysis help us to understand about the 1980s, and nostalgia for it today? And why should any of this matter, especially now?

It turns out that 1980s heavy metal, the subject of that potential censorship, provides the perfect way into literature, and vice versa. Many metal bands adapted lyrics from literature: the aforementioned Iron Maiden from Samuel Taylor Coleridge, Metallica from Hemingway, and more. And while the overlap is significant, this book is not primarily about heavy metal's literary adaptations. Instead, I want to analyze metal *as* literature, using the tools and language that we apply to literary studies and analysis. And then, the way in which heavy metal, whether its songwriters were conscious of it or not, continues many literary movements and legacies. When it comes to literature and heavy metal, what are the shared obsessions? How does heavy metal develop literary traditions?

The book's topics take a similarly broad approach: how heavy metal may have gotten its name in part from The Heavy Metal Kid, a character in William Burroughs's avant-garde novel *The Soft Machine*, with "heavy metal" itself borrowing from the uranium-235 used in the atomic bomb. How Van Halen wasn't just a party band, but connected to George Orwell, as well as what it means to be American. Why Bon Jovi can only ever be halfway there. (It's complicated.) How Twisted Sister songs exemplify strategic pronoun use towards self-identification. How Metallica thought they were adapting the film version of Ken Kesey's novel *One Flew Over the Cuckoo's Nest*, but instead were channeling the father of psychoanalysis, Sigmund Freud, whereas Guns

N' Roses were borrowing from Freud's disciple, Carl Jung. How Anthrax amplifies the philosophical pronouncements of Michel Foucault, Iron Maiden's Bruce Dickinson has more in common with poet Emily Dickinson than just a name, what William Shakespeare and Poison's Bret Michaels both think about breakups, and why there might not be heavy metal—and certainly not Ronnie James Dio—without Romantic poet William Blake. Plus, recurring imagery of chains and cages in music videos, why there are so many heavy metal cowboys and rock songs against rock stardom, what Slayer gets right about Dante's *Inferno*, much-needed close readings of WASP lyrics, how heavy metal, just maybe, helped end the Cold War, and what looking back on '80s metal helps its listeners to understand about themselves today. That and much more. Let's rock & roll.

1

Nothing. But: A Good Time?

Heavy Metal, the Cold War, and the Long 1980s

Figure 6 Hercules liberating Prometheus from an eagle. Source: Weltgeschichte 1898 Engraver: H. Leutemanndel.

A world without nuclear weapons may be a dream, but you cannot base a sure defense on dreams.

—Margaret Thatcher (1987)[1]

Giants sleeping, giants winning,
Wars within their dreams.

—"Killer of Giants," Ozzy Osbourne (1986)[2]

Heavy metal was supposedly apolitical, escapist. But was it? Some of it reveled in images of violence and the occult. Other offshoots—glam, the retroactively named "hair metal"—reveled in, well, revelry. It was about partying, nothin' but a good time. Both represent different kinds of adolescent fantasies—but it was anything but apolitical, and there was plenty that was not a good time. In the same way in which literature is bound to its time period, the music under consideration in this book is a distinct product of the 1980s and the Cold War, as close readings of Van Halen, Ozzy Osbourne, and Bon Jovi will attest. And, in the end, even escapism turned out to be political after all.

Breakin' the Chains

In 1985, when I first fell in love with heavy metal, the only time I could hear it on the radio was once a week, at midnight, on a syndicated show called "Metal Shop": "M-m-m-m-m-m-m-m-m-m-m-m-m-m-m-metal shop," for those who know. The only place I could watch the videos was on the UHF[3] station U68 and the occasional clip on the more mainstream, nationally broadcast "Friday Night Videos," network TV's attempt to be MTV, at least for an hour or so. Both were on late at night and became the first reasons for 13-year-old me to stay up late. No one had cable television yet in Brooklyn, New York. I wanted my MTV, but I couldn't have it. This was also, obviously, pre-DVD, pre-DVR, pre-Internet, pre-streaming, pre-all-the-ways-people-watch-and-hear-anything now.

Decades later, in the 2000s, the cable station VH1, what I'd formerly thought of as the adult version of MTV, and not in the good way, started leaning heavily on metal, which I could have taken as a clue that I was now an adult. I didn't. At least I had cable now: "Metal Mania," "That Metal Show," the multi-part documentary "Metal Evolution" by metal anthropologist Sam Dunn, the preponderance of Iron Maiden and Metallica and other documentary metal movies, and Megadeth and Mötley Crüe and more "Behind the Music" episodes.

And then, even more recently, with cable in its last throes, all those specials, and all of those music videos from the 1980s, became available, for instant, easy access, online. This was my chance to go back and re-watch them. And what I found, delightedly rifling through the thousand or so that made it onto MTV's *Headbangers Ball*, surprised me, defying my memory. Metallica sang, "The memory remains," in a different context. But does it?

A huge number of the 1980s metal videos, it turns out, featured futuristic, post-apocalyptic sets reminiscent of *The Road Warrior* and *Escape From New York*.[4] Dust, battle-scarred ground, burned-out cityscapes. Ripped clothes, leather, and boots—on the bands, and on the women who, inevitably, surround them—are somehow right at home in this desolate environment. Sometimes, these wastelands were accompanied by laser guns and robotics. My favorite is Queensrÿche's "Queen of the Reich" video, which even opens with a *Star-Wars*-like crawl, something about a crystal, a queen, a computer, and "five freedom fighters." The video introduces the band members by name as they rock on, even while they fight the queen in a dystopian, or maybe outer-space, future. Her face is covered with a visor like Cyclops from the X-Men. Most of her body is not covered with much of anything.

At other times, they were throwbacks, with faux-Renaissance Faire swords and scepters—where the only remnants of the present-day to survive are guitars, and, fortunately, hairspray. Like the Queensrÿche video, "Screaming in the Night" by Krokus has some kind of fantasy plot, also involving women whose faces are covered, plus an amalgam of pyramids, lightning, dungeons, flags, and singer Marc Storace in a loincloth.

Some videos seemed both in the future and the past, yet somehow neither, like Dio's "Last in Line," another mini-movie starring the kid from the popular-at-the-time TV series "Voyagers," riding a cursed elevator to the underworld. This version is a dystopian combination of ancient Egypt, replete with slaves, along with a scary cyborg and video games that electrocute the losing players.

Kiss, in their big make-up-off reveal video, decided to make "Lick It Up" the one-stop-shopping for dystopia: junked out cars, dirty puddles, women emerging from manholes with amazing '80s curls intact, women *washing* manhole covers for some reason. The street is littered with human skulls as the band, their faces still concealed, strut by in excellent boots given the economic circumstances. The guys sing; the girls jump; fires burn everywhere. Scorpions' "Rock You Like a Hurricane" is similar—more fires, more masks—but with big cats, bigger cages, and better editing.

Welcome (back) to the 1980s. The collective memory and retrospectives have turned the era into a neon-hued, pink party-palooza, bright and bubbly, festooned with tiger stripes and red bandannas. And there is some truth to those images—the effervescent Van Halen, in the early '80s, and the fringe-jacketed, acid-washed denim of Bon Jovi, a little later, both of whom I'll discuss in this chapter. But along with the fun, flying high-wire acts in both the "Panama" and

"Livin' on a Prayer" videos, the endgame of the Cold War created a backdrop for thinking about the end of the world, and *The Day After*. That TV movie, from 1983, was one of many Gen X childhood media traumas, showing kids not just the horror of a nuclear strike—almost everyone will die—but something worse: what happens to those who survive. At the box office, we could choose from *WarGames* (1983), *Red Dawn* (1984), *The Hunt for Red October* (a little later, 1990), *Mad Max* (1979) and its sequel, *The Road Warrior* (1981), and *Escape from New York* (also 1981).

On the news, live every morning and twice in the evening—and to kids, it seemed all adults were watching—a litany of new domestic horrors was entering the cultural lexicon: crack cocaine and the War on Drugs; HIV and AIDS; eating disorders and McDonald's' introduction of Supersizing; the worst decade for American cars and drive-by shootings. As *Stranger Things* chronicles, in its look back on '80s media, American parents become obsessed with missing and kidnapped children after several high-profile incidents. The famous milk carton kids were introduced, and "stranger danger" became integrated into public education.

It's easy to poke fun now, but these early metal videos helped convey Cold War fears, a kind of trickle-down dystopia to match the idea of trickle-down economics taking hold in the Reagan administration. Kids and teens had no control over what they saw on the news, and these videos chronicled the pervasive sense of danger. But it was more than fear.

In *The Interpretation of Dreams* (1899), Sigmund Freud wrote that, in dreams, wishes and fears can be intertwined, related to or even flip sides of each other. And so, along with the fears—of disaster, of the end, of powerlessness—these videos represented wishes as well. REM was singing about the end of the world as we know it at the same time, in 1987, but that was irony, not metal. Let college rock feel fine about the end of the world as we know it. To metal bands and fans, the apocalypse would be awesome. No rules, no clothes, and guitars everywhere.

Crucially, the videos mentioned above, and many more, also featured some kind of bondage: chains for Krokus and the gamers in Dio's underworld; a big cage for Scorpions, although it's hard to tell whether it's keeping them in or the girls out; turning to stone, or something, for Queensrÿche; and other imprisonment scenarios. Sometimes women in strategically ripped clothing are detained as well. Yes, Def Leppard's "Photograph" video director David Mallet said facetiously, "Why did I put the girls in a cage? Girls belong in cages, come on."[5] But more often, it was the band members themselves restrained or incarcerated. The members of Dokken are chained in a fiery dungeon in, not surprisingly, "Breakin' the Chains." Def Leppard's Joe Elliott is quasi-crucified, in chains, on a triangle(?), with more fire, in "Foolin'," not to mention something that looks closer to an actual crucifixion, on a cross, but with chains, in "Bringin' On the Heartbreak." Metallica's imagery featured electric chairs and hospital beds. Quiet Riot's Kevin DuBrow is locked in an iron mask, locked further in a padded cell. Everyone is trapped, confined, restricted, or in somebody else's power.

From a narrative perspective, these scenarios represent the oldest and most reliable story of all time, the master plot of master plots: tension, then release. Conflict, then resolution. In *Beyond the Pleasure Principle* (1920), Freud describes the child's game of throwing an object out of sight—tension—and the joy of its return—release—in an imitation, or even rehearsal, of the mother herself leaving and returning. *Fort* and *Da*, in German—"Gone!" and "There!" In three- to four-minute music videos, viewers get the full narrative ride of rising action, climax, and denouement. Paradise lost, Paradise regained. Gone, there. By the end, usually, the band—or the kid from *Voyagers*—breaks free. (The girls in cages aren't usually so lucky.) Dokken let us know it would work out in their song title. And while Marc Storace doesn't look like he's having much fun, Kiss certainly does. Chains are meant to be broken. Gone, there. Trapped, freed. But first, someone needs to be tied up or tied down.

There were some now-obvious (but at the time, to me, anyway, entirely unrecognized) fetishes at work. At least, they were obvious to the Parents Music Resource Center, who seemed disturbed by the imagery: Tipper Gore objected to what she called "bondage" in Twisted Sister's "Under the Blade" (more on that coming up), even as it seemed to be one of the few videos that *didn't* actually display bondage. But she was not concerned by the underlying problem of powerlessness that the imagery implied, only its surface-level appearance. For me, these emotional metaphors trump the sexual ones. In retrospect, there is the inescapable sense of the inescapable, despite the fact that the bands—and many of the fans, including me—were white, straight, male, irresponsible in the best sense, and at the height of youth, strength, and beauty. Yet in the metal videos, all anyone felt were the metal restraints. All they saw were the bars of their metal cages.

The images can seem kitschy now, and Dokken and many of the artists feel sheepish about them, but at the time, I, and millions of others, identified with the music in a visceral, animal way. Nick Rhodes from Duran Duran said, "I don't think videos have to make sense. They only have to be really cool-looking."[6] They are cool-looking. Many are playful, especially given how grim these descriptions sound in print. But they were much more than cool-looking, and they made Freudian and artistic sense—not literal sense as much as *literary* sense, symbolic sense. These pop apocalypses, and all the chains and cages, make these videos into pop art and historical artifacts of the Cold War, when this supposedly escapist entertainment was busy depicting the opposite of escape: confinement. The prospect of dystopia and detention was pervasive. In their loving parody decades later, in 2014, Steel Panther sum up the ethos most clearly in their song, "Party Like Tomorrow is the End of the World." The videos were ultimately not ridiculous at all—they were impressionistic and surreal artistic renderings of what it felt like to be a certain teen at a certain time. In keeping with the breakin' the chains imagery, the videos were a release, a catharsis, a defiance of power, and a relief from pain and powerlessness. Prometheus unbound—there, then gone, in the mythological imagery and Percy Shelley poem of the same name.

What more can we ask of art?

Like the videos, the term "heavy metal" can be understood here in a Cold War context. After all, the phrase appeared in Beat writer William Burroughs's novel *The Soft Machine* (1961), published the same year as the Bay of Pigs invasion. "Heavy metal" wasn't a musical coinage, not yet. That would come later in Steppenwolf's "Born to Be Wild" and "heavy metal thunder," although it seems to refer to motorcycles, not music. In *The Soft Machine*, the term suggests drugs—not surprising, from the author of *Junky*: "What we call opium or junk is a very much diluted form of heavy metal addiction."[7] But the novel is too strange, too elusive, to take a single line at face value. With Burroughs, "heavy metal" as a drug extrapolates outwardly from the real danger of poisoning by actual heavy metals. But it also seems like more.

One of those heavy metals from the Periodic Table, uranium (or an isotope, specifically uranium-235), also powered the atomic bomb and fueled the entire atomic age. Burroughs uses "Heavy Metal" most frequently in conjunction with the character "Uranian Willy, the Heavy Metal Kid," and the other "blue heavy metal boys." They seem to be aliens whose bodies stand in contrast to Earthlings' softness—hence the book's title, which refers to the human body. "Uranian"—as in, from the planet Uranus, the god of the underworld for which uranium is also named. Heavy metal, literature, and the Cold War were bonded from the beginning.

The Soft Machine is arguably the grandfather of these post-apocalyptic heavy metal videos. (The parents are *Escape from New York* and *The Road Warrior*.) In keeping with videos' frequent camera cuts, the novel was written using the avant-garde cut-up technique, borrowed from the *great*-grandfather of videos, the Dadaist movement. Here, the author or artist isn't writing as much as assembling and reassembling text from other texts that have literally been cut up. The result is a dystopian novel in sensibility, with some recognizable elements of science fiction and pulp fiction, but imagistic and weird, with an uncertain and fragmented narrative—much like those *Road Warrior*-inspired videos. Here, for example, is the paragraph that refers to heavy metal the most frequently. It's easy to see why readers associated the novel with drugs, even aside from actual drug references. It's not about making sense as much as it is about conveying the strangeness of the moment:

> "Citizens of Gravity we are converting all out to Heavy Metal. Carbonic Plague of the Vegetable People threatens our Heavy Metal State. Report to your nearest Plating Station. It's fun to be plated," says this well-known radio and TV personality who is now engraved forever in gags of metal. "Do not believe the calumny that our metal fallout will turn the planet into a slag heap. And in any case, is that worse than a compost heap? Heavy Metal is our program and we are prepared to sink through it . . ."[8]

Despite the novel's fear of a slag-heap planet and the Cuban Missile Crisis just the year after *The Soft Machine* was published, the world didn't end in the 1960s. And despite popular culture and the Cold War seeming to suggest otherwise, the world didn't end in the 1980s either. For metal fans, and maybe William Burroughs, something more surprising happened: it went on. But how did it get to that point? Some metal bands were acutely aware of the Cold War, like the aptly named Nuclear Assault, the equally aptly named Megadeth, and, of course, Metallica, among others. Even Bon Jovi's "Runaway" video opens with an image of a newspaper headline declaring "A Nuclear Accident" before becoming a version of *Firestarter*, the 1981 Stephen King novel released as a film in the same year as the video, in 1984. And yet, the many memoirs, biographies, and oral histories eschew this social context. It's understandable. Social context is for literature. So let's get literary.

Van Halen's Glorious Revolution

In literature, genres are tied to, even synonymous with, their time periods. Medieval literature, from the same period: the anonymously written *Sir Gawain and the Green Knight* and Geoffrey Chaucer's *Canterbury Tales* in England, or Dante Alighieri's *Divine Comedy* in Italy. Victorian literature: the many famous works of Charles Dickens and the Brontë sisters; Bram Stoker's infamous *Dracula*. Even Modern literature—by James Joyce, Virginia Woolf, Marcel Proust, and Franz Kafka—represents the work produced during a period of time, usually around 1910 to 1945, so shortly before World War I to the end of the World War II, as opposed to the way most laypeople use the word "modern" as synonymous with "contemporary."

For some listeners, heavy metal began in the 1970s or late '60s, with Led Zeppelin (even though they have more folky songs than most people credit them for), Deep Purple (metal-ish, but the organ is louder than the guitar half the time), and especially Black Sabbath (yes, they're metal). This certainly makes sense: they have the guitars, the drums, the hair, the hedonism.

But I'm going to suggest two bases for the purposes of this book.

First: *that heavy metal, in keeping with the bars-and-chains videos, is best understood as a cultural product of the late Cold War.* In the same way that, say, new technology and then new wars had an impact on the writers of Modern literature, the World War II period, and the 1970s, but especially the late 1970s and 1980s, are crucial to understanding metal music and musicians. Context is easily lost in the twenty-first century, when we stream songs on Spotify, as opposed to buying an album or hearing a song on the radio, or watch the videos on YouTube, as opposed to watching them in their own time on MTV or *Friday Night Videos*. Heavy metal, as a genre tied to a period, rather than any number of other possible considerations, for me, began in the 1980s.

And second: *that the 1980s did not begin in the 1980s.* They began in 1978.

It's tempting, of course, to think that the 1980s began on January 1, 1980. That's how time and calendars work, for most people, anyway. Fair enough. But literary critics, philosophers, and historians are not most people, and calendars can be capricious cultural measures. Even if the 1980s had begun in the 1980s, I would put the start date as December 8, 1980, in the evening, when John Lennon was murdered in New York City. It was just a month after Ronald Reagan, cowboy California hippie hater, was elected president. The two events are almost too symbolic, too symmetrical: the death of the left-wing, countercultural 1960s with the dawn of the right-wing, consumerist 1980s.

And yet, literary historians will seldom use just the calendar and instead look to events, and to the *zeitgeist*, the spirit of the times. If historians can have their long eighteenth century (the 1688 Glorious Revolution through Napoleon's defeat at Waterloo in 1815) or their long nineteenth century (the French Revolution in 1789 to the First World War in 1914), give me the long 1980s. And so, even more symbolically significant than Lennon or Reagan, I'm going to start with Van Halen.

The 1980s began on February 10, 1978, with the release of Van Halen's self-titled debut album.

Van Halen proclaimed their own Glorious Revolution. They were faster and heavier, yet funnier and lighter, than Styx, the Stones, or Seger, the aging titans of the 1970s, their classic rock calcifying and putting the genre in danger of paralysis. Critics didn't perceive it. Robert Christgau, perhaps the most influential music writer at the time, gave Van Halen's first album a C, saying, "For some reason, Warners wants us to know that this is the biggest bar band in the San Fernando Valley."[9] They were no such thing. They were a pure, uncut arena band, far too bombastic to stay in any bar.

A million words have already been spilled about Eddie Van Halen: his speed, his style, and his customized super-Strat, the Frankenstein guitar, that heralded Eddie as both the scientist and the monster. The famous tension between his musical genius and outsized rock-star maniac and occasional singer David Lee Roth. They took the archetype of brunette axeman vs blond frontman, each vying for the spotlight, chops versus showmanship, substance vs style, started by Led Zeppelin but wiped of its Englishness and rendered American fresh.

Van Halen I, as the album became known, for me simply sounds and looks like the first '80s heavy metal album, even though many fans wouldn't consider it metal at all. It could have come out in any year of the 1980s, and, if it came out today, would blow everyone away as the greatest homage to the '80s. It's still what every Steel Panther album strives to capture, over forty years later.

Today, "Eruption" is arguably both the greatest guitar solo *and* greatest rock instrumental of all time, and it's barely even a song, the one minute and 42 seconds that launched a thousand licks. Like Jimi Hendrix's take on "The Star-Spangled Banner" at Woodstock in 1969, just nine years earlier, Eddie both rewrote the known vernacular of rock playing and pitched it headfirst into the future. Van

Halen took Hendrix's dive bombs—pressing hard on the guitar's tremolo bar for sonic descents—and dived down and bombed bigger. Hendrix added effects pedals for wobbles and whooshes, but Eddie reset Hendrix's phaser from stun to kill. Eddie's left hand fretted faster and his right hand picked quicker.

And then there was the famous finger-tapping. Every guitarist who tapped thereafter, and a few who didn't (George Lynch's solo in Dokken's "In My Dreams") should have been required to cite Eddie in whatever the guitar equivalent of a footnote might be. That ending, with its rapid-fire, modulating arpeggios, concluding with the deep descent courtesy of turning the knob on a delay pedal, sounded like the Heavy Metal Kid's rocket had landed. And it had.

Hendrix's rendition of "The Star-Spangled Banner" was taken as a protest of the Vietnam War, with his guitar's dive bombs added just after the "bombs bursting in air" line, even though, as an instrumental, the words only existed in the listener's mind. The only thing louder than a bomb is a volcanic eruption.[10] But Van Halen's guitar heralded something unnatural, the atomic phase, alluded to in "Atomic Punk," the heavy metal that pays homage to the atomic bomb itself, back to the Uranian Kid in *The Soft Machine*. It takes power and fear and sublimates them into something bigger than even pyrotechnics—it becomes art. "Eruption" is a nuclear war rendered, cut up, and arranged in guitar solo form.

"Eruption" led to one of Van Halen's many better-than-the-original covers, the Kinks' "You Really Got Me," itself sometimes referred to as the first metal song. (It isn't.) As a budding rocker in the 1980s, I heard the original after already knowing Van Halen's version, and there was no way to go back. The Kinks' original sounded tame, despite not really being that old at the time. Then again, it was older than me, making it practically ancient.

Despite Eddie's seemingly effortless virtuosity, the songs were simple, catchy, and populist. Sure, there was excess. Nothing is more thrilling yet hilarious than listening to David Lee Roth's over-the-top shrieks and squeals on "Runnin' with the Devil." I've used the isolated vocal track as a backdrop to exemplify the screams of the damned in a class discussing eternal suffering in Dante's *Inferno*. I made it my ringtone, and it makes everyone jump (more on "Jump" in a minute). But the bass line is just a single, ominous quarter note, and its song structure is simple. The devil of "Runnin'" is metaphorical, idiomatic—the perfect shorthand for the rock & roll life, without even having to get explicit about sex or drugs. The satanic reference is telling and would herald the many metaphorical and literal devils at play in subsequent heavy metal lyrics. Yet the guitar solo is melodic and catchy, repeated twice, almost like a musical bridge.

The devil is a sweet talker. "Ain't Talking 'bout Love," despite the arpeggiated riff, delay, phaser, and—wow—sitar overdub, relies on the elegance of only two chords and Roth's devastating, casual sexuality and equally devastating, casual put-downs. Has there ever been a worse backhanded compliment than "You know you're semi-good lookin'"?[11]

The two best-selling albums of 1978 in the US were both soundtracks: the mainstreamed disco of *Saturday Night Fever*, released in November 1977, and the packaged nostalgia of *Grease*. (It was a great year for John Travolta.) Meanwhile, punk, the grimy flipside of *Saturday Night Fever*'s fashion, seemed to overtake the old rockers with its sneers, attitude, and irony. Van Halen's party music was an alternative to all of it, and, critics like Christgau to the contrary, not an atavistic rock throwback but a multi-hued pop vision of the decade to come.

As punks pouted, *Grease*'s Danny danced, and *Saturday Night Fever*'s Tony posed, Eddie Van Halen smiled and smiled, and when the 1980s finally chronologically rolled around, fans loved him for it. Yet beneath Van Halen's rollicking exterior, mirroring what Reagan would soon call Morning in America, was the same dark animus that fueled both punk and disco.

On the *Saturday Night Fever* soundtrack, The Bee Gees sang, "Life goin' nowhere, somebody help me" on "Stayin' Alive."[12] Early in the film itself, Tony Manero (Travolta) asks for an advance so he can buy a shiny shirt to show off at the disco. When his boss at the paint store implores him to think of the future, Tony scoffs, "Fuck the future."[13] On the other side of the Atlantic, the same year—1977—The Sex Pistols similarly scowled, "No future for you" in "God Save the Queen."[14] In "London Calling," The Clash hoarsely intoned that "The ice age is coming, / The sun's zooming in, / Meltdown expected, / The wheat is growing thin, / A nuclear error, but I have no fear / 'Cause London is drowning and I live by the river!" (1979).[15] No need to worry about dying in a future apocalypse, because the apocalypse is upon us right now.

While "Feel Your Love Tonight" and the cover of "Ice Cream Man," like much of the album, are in good humor, David Lee Roth yowled to the world in "Atomic Punk" that "I am a victim of the science age."[16] It's so close to the Clash's dystopia. In "Runnin' with the Devil," Roth sings, "I live my life like there's no tomorrow." It's almost the Sex Pistols' "no future" nihilism, practically a mirror of the Bee Gees' pleas of "somebody help me." Roth croons, "I got no love, no love you'd call real, / Ain't got nobody waitin' at home."[17] No wonder he ain't talkin' 'bout love. Yet "Runnin' With the Devil" is a rock & roll call to life more than a scoff in wake of possible Cold War death. It's a mirror image, the inverted reflection, of "I live by the river." It's strangely optimistic, a Zen invitation to live in the present moment, another version of breakin' the chains. "And all I've got, I had to steal" in isolation is a lament; coupled with its next line, "Least I don't need to beg or borrow," it becomes a show of strength and pride.

On "DOA," which appeared on *Van Halen II* but was written at the same time as *Van Halen I*, Roth opens with this verse: "We was sittin' ducks for the police man, / They found a dirty faced kid in a garbage can." The chorus laments, "And I'm alone, / I'm on the highway, / Wanted, dead or alive / Dead or alive."[18] Usually, the acronym "DOA" stands for "dead on arrival," but that the group creates the parallel between "dead or alive" and "dead on arrival" is bleak for a supposed party band, suggesting that there's a fragile line between life and death.

A decade later, in 1989, Neil Young would sing a similar line about a kid and a garbage can in "Rockin' in the Free World": "I see a woman in the night / With a baby in her hand, / There's an old street light / Near a garbage can."[19] That song's title helped, but, unlike Van Halen's work, it was immediately understood as political. The song would make Rolling Stone's "500 Greatest Songs of All Time" and eventually end up as 2016 campaign music for both Bernie Sanders *and* Donald Trump.[20] Yet Van Halen understood better than Neil Young or the punks that Cold War apocalypticism, nuclear anxieties, and economic recession weren't reasons to retreat or pout. They were reasons to party. Van Halen initiated what Prince would, in 1984, make explicit, in true 1980s spirit, in "Let's Go Crazy": "We're all excited / But we don't know why, / Maybe it's 'cause / We're all gonna die."[21]

Eddie did die, on October 6, 2020, at 65, youngish for a regular person but ancient in rock star years, which fall somewhere between human and dog years. But what I had not fully considered, really not even fully known until reading the retrospectives, was the full impact of his early life. Eddie and his brother Alex, Van Halen's drummer, were immigrants. And not just immigrants but mixed-race, their father Dutch and their mother Indonesian, having met in Dutch-occupied Indonesia. They and their young family were ostracized when they moved to the Netherlands, so they left for the United States, only to be ostracized again for not knowing the language or culture. Eddie and Alex belonged to two worlds, and neither.

Yet, later in life, Eddie expressed only gratitude. "Coming here with approximately $50 and a piano, not being able to speak the language, going through everything to get to where we are, if that's not the American dream, I don't know what is," he said.²²

Even David Lee Roth, who seems to say and tell everything, also later revealed that he created his stage persona in part as a reaction against being categorized. Everyone who heard Adam Sandler's "Chanukah Song" (2008) knows that "David Lee Roth lights the menorah." But, as writer David Segal summarized, Roth's memoir discussed how "his style and energy came from fury over anti-Semitism and an urge to crush Jewish stereotypes."²³

In retrospect, the 1980s were not exactly known for sensitivity or diversity. Yet it was the tension and teamwork between the immigrant, mixed-race brothers, and the Jew who would not be typecast (and also bassist Michael Anthony, who knew to stay out of the way) that ushered in an era, the sounds and ideas that not just defined but created the '80s. The darkness of their personal and cultural anxieties was sublimated into technicolor dreams.

America made Van Halen possible, and Van Halen made America better.

It's tempting to think that the 1980s ended on December 31, 1989, but the long 1980s ended in 1991, coinciding with Van Halen's *For Unlawful Carnal Knowledge* album, with not-David-Lee-Roth lead singer Sammy Hagar, alongside the more momentous release of Nirvana's *Nevermind*, the death of Queen's Freddie Mercury, and the election of US president Bill Clinton. But every time I listen to *Van Halen I*, I hear the best of the 1980s all over again. Even if it's the 2020s. Even though it was really 1978.

Out of Work and Down: '80s Metal in the UK

Over in England, and in 1980—the '80s proper now—Judas Priest produced *British Steel*, their sixth album. As guitarist KK Downing would later explain, "People were a bit down-spirited in the UK. Nothing was going particularly well."²⁴ So far, so "Anarchy in the UK," "We're the flowers / In the dustbin." But as Downing continues, "It was the kind of album that sent out waves to everybody that said, 'There's good things ahead, and we know how you feel, and we were all feeling the same.'"²⁵ It's the British flipside to Van Halen's American revolution. The title is the perfect pun for the occasion: the English metal band alluding to the nationalized industry. For all of Britain's economic hardship, it was still manufacturing both kinds of metal.

On the one hand, the opening lines of "Breaking the Law" depict the down-spiritedness: "There I was completely wasting, out of work and down, / All inside it's so frustrating as I drift from town to town."[26] Like "Runnin' With the Devil," all they've had, they've had to (British) steal. And yet, the speaker is breaking the law mainly for the thrill of it, to stick it to authority, not overtly for the money. The second verse is almost no-future punk, but with a sincerity that the Sex Pistols would never be caught expressing: "So much for the golden future, I can't even start, / I've had every promise broken, there's anger in my heart."[27] It feels like a universal expression of adolescent anger at life's hypocrisies and disappointments, but it's more culturally specific than that. And yet, the video depicts a comic, Benny Hill-esque bank robbery, almost like the brutal truth of the song alone, with its minor key riff, would be too much to bear. There's danger, but also action and fun.

On the other hand, the album's other big hit, "Living After Midnight," suggests the inverse: action and fun, but also danger. Here's the bridge: "I'm aiming for you, / I'm gonna floor you, / My body's coming / All night long."[28] Like Kiss's "Rock and Roll All Nite" or AC/DC's "You Shook Me All Night Long" and so many others, the song celebrates the revelries of what happens after regular people go to bed. Or, as novelist Djuna Barnes wrote in her Modernist tale *Nightwood* (1937), "Night does something to a person's identity, even when asleep."[29]

The song's imagery implies a combination of possibilities: racing, shooting (a gun? Drugs?), sex. The chorus ends with, "Then I'm gone, I'm gone." The song is upbeat, but is this a lover leaving, or a rocker on the road? Both? Is he high? Is he dead? We don't know, and it doesn't matter. The song fades out. "Living After Midnight" sounds light, especially for heavy metal, with its major-chord melodic chorus, almost pop. But the implications are dark and heavy. It's a party song. But the reason to party isn't for its own sake. It's a way to forget. The speaker lives his life like there's no tomorrow, for better and for worse.

Van Halen Ushers in the Future

In 1949, George Orwell published his novel *1984*, reversing the digits of the year he spent working on it to signify The Future. From that point on, "1984" became the symbol of an ominous, surveillance-driven dystopia, and the term "Orwellian" was born.

Science fiction writers keep picking futuristic-sounding years—say, 1984, or 2001, or 2012—as the settings for their work, but unfortunately—or, really fortunately, given the alternative—the present keeps on catching up. For thirty-five years, 1984 represented the future. For even longer—more than forty years as of this writing—it has represented the past.

Van Halen's own *1984* (or, as the cover refers to it, *MCMLXXXIV*), released on January 9, 1984, was the first album I bought with my own money, missing out on the number one album in the country at the time, Michael Jackson's *Thriller*. Now, as a middle-aged parent, the phrase "with my own money" sounds funny, but it didn't then and presumably still doesn't to today's 13-year-olds. But contemporary baby teens, with their Spotifys and their YouTubes, don't need to make the hard choice that I did: which one album will I plunk down this month's cash for? I chose *1984*, and, in all seriousness, it affected the entire rest of my life. The future lay before me, and unlike Orwell's vision, it would be good.

This was Van Halen. The future would be awesome.

1984 opened with the instrumental "1984," consisting of what can only be called futuristic synthesizers, despite its humble origin as the intro to Michael Anthony's live bass solo. *Blade Runner*, released a little earlier, in 1982, featured similar synths to signify much the same. "1984" wasn't Van Halen's first instrumental. But, unlike "Eruption," there were no smashy drums and certainly not, say, the coolest guitar solo of all time. Like "Intruder," the quasi-intro to their "Pretty Woman" cover from *Diver Down*, and even more like the misleadingly-titled "Sunday Afternoon in the Park" from *Fair Warning*, it was ominous, sinister, maybe even threatening.

"1984" led right into "Jump," suggesting that, having finally arrived, the future would not be Orwellian. It made perfect sense that the movie *Ready Player One* (2018) would open with "Jump" to signify the future, 2045, but at the same time to signal the 1980s, the characters' pop culture preoccupation. With "Jump," the future might be just fine after all. Eddie Van Halen wanted to record a version of "Jump" for years by then, but David Lee Roth and producer Ted Templeman thought it was the wrong sound for a hard rock band famous for its eponymous superstar guitar, with apologies to drummer Alex, who technically shares the name.

They were living in the past. "Jump" was the future. It would hit #1 on the charts.

"Jump" still had that stunning, squealing, syncopated, out-of-nowhere guitar solo, filled with fast runs and finger-taps, as if to remind the listener of the genius behind strings. Eddie, though, was not just a genius guitarist. He was simply a genius. He had already reinvented electric guitar playing, even reinvented the electric guitar itself. Now everyone knew he was the songwriter, the producer, the engineer, and the innovator whose first instrument was in fact the piano.

Yet the "Jump" video—inextricable from the song itself—eschews the futuristic and techie for a lo-fi stage performance, with Eddie playing the guitar for the entire song except for a split screen for the keyboard solo where Eddie, or Eddies, handle(s) both. Another double. The video is notable and memorable for Roth's high kicks and the band's goofy relatability, and he exposed much of America to spandex pants, on a man at least. This future was not Orwell or *Blade Runner*. The future would be fun.

Roth has always been cagy about his lyrics—this is the man who sang "I take a moople at a lookie for a moop meet" (or something; I listened to the line ten times for that elegant transcription) on "Everybody Wants Some." Roth has suggested that "Jump" was about suicide, after seeing a story in the news about a man jumping from a building. Separately, he said it was about a stripper. Both seem entirely plausible, in keeping with the band's semi-concealed darkness, and mostly-unconcealed lightness. "Ah, might as well jump" is equally the hymn of both hope and hopelessness: Søren Kierkegaard's leap of faith, or a deathward plunge.

While "I'll Wait" reuses the synthesizers, it's the opposite feel and message from "Jump"—don't jump. "I wrote a letter and told her these words . . . I never sent it, she wouldn't have heard."[30] It's not very Roth-like in its implication that this affair—with an image of a woman, rather than a real one, similarly to the portrayal in Def Leppard's "Photograph"—can never be realized. For all of its sexualization of women, these songs are closer to the pre-modern notion of courtly love—an exalted passion never to be consummated.[31] It was a love that needn't be debased by lust, even if, in putting women on a pedestal, it became a different form of objectification.

Other songs, like "House of Pain," were based on Van Halen's past unreleased material. It turns out that, in retrospect, much of the rest of *1984* hearkens back to the past, rather than looking into the future, although maybe not as far back as the medieval love of "I'll Wait." "Panama," with another live-action concert video and its revving engines, driving drums, and hot-rod guitar, is in the great rock & roll tradition of comparing fast cars to fast women, or comparing chasing women to a car chase, or something like that, à la "Mustang Sally" or

"Maybellene": "Here she comes, full blast and top down . . . Ain't nothin' like it, her shiny machine . . . You'll lose her in the turn/ I'll get her," and more.³²

"Hot for Teacher" is unambiguous and literal, and its video also looks backward, featuring grainy black and white footage, kid lookalikes of each band member, and a coda parodying the end of the film *American Graffiti* (flash-forwards from the kids to images of their future, e.g., "DAVID LEE ROTH WENT TO HOLLYWOOD AND BECAME AMERICA'S FAVORITE T.V. GAME SHOW HOST," etc.).³³ You'd be forgiven for not remembering anything other than the video's teacher/beauty pageant contestant/stripper, though. Might as well jump. When she first takes off her clothes, the video turns to technicolor like the kids rode the tornado to Oz. But it's not Oz; it's whatever the adolescent male sex fantasy Oz might be. The video for "Hot For Teacher" would be one of only two videos, along with Twisted Sister's "We're Not Gonna Take It," to be shown at the 1985 PMRC congressional hearing. Tipper Gore wrote that it and similar ones "frightened my children; they frightened me!,"³⁴ which may have been the point. But when the video was shown on the congressional floor, it elicited applause and laughter, which was even more the point.

In some ways, *1984* was not the beginning, not the future, but the end, as chronicled in *Runnin' With the Devil*, the memoir by former VH manager Noel Monk. Roth and Van Halen would soon split up. And now, more than forty years later, the album is long in the past. In *1984*, Orwell wrote, "Who controls the past controls the future. Who controls the present controls the past."³⁵ Van Halen controlled their present, and then controlled the past, and not in an Orwellian way. Orwell's Winston, the protagonist of *1984*, would succumb in an unhappy, cautionary ending, but I still think Van Halen is awesome, just as I did when I was thirteen, all sense of maturity or progress be damned. Proust has his madeleine, but for me, music is the best time machine, and *1984* comes pre-time stamped.

As it turns out, even if I had bought *Thriller*, it all would have worked out: Eddie played the solo on "Beat It," too. Yes, Eddie Van Halen would die. But Van Halen would not, and will not. *1984* would be hugely influential to bands and fans alike. The era of hard rock and metal that Van Halen ushered in would peak, then fall, when the '80s ended, but then come back again, as classic rock, for today's 13-year-olds in the era of Spotifys and YouTubes. The 1980s, as I will discuss in the Conclusion, has become a genre, not just an era. And yet despite being titled after a year, and a symbolic year at that, forty years have proven that *1984* transcends time itself. The '80s have come and gone. The Cold War has come and gone. But, in the literary tradition, Van Halen's music is still here. Heavy metals have long half-lives.

Something Other Than a Good Time

By the time we get to the actual 1980s, we can see what Van Halen had wrought: glam metal, and what later became known—first disparagingly, and then embraced—as hair metal. Mötley Crüe, Ratt, and Guns N' Roses, whether they like it or not. The ethos was a decade of decadence, according to Mötley Crüe, or nothin' but a good time, Poison's 1988 anthem. Two different books were published under that name in 2021: Justin Quirk's *Nothin' But A Good Time: The Spectacular Rise and Fall of Hair Metal*, an overview of glam. The other is *Nöthin' But a Good Time: The Uncensored History of the '80s Hard Rock Explosion*, an oral history. It also borrows the Poison song's name but adds an ëxträ ümläüt for ëxträ mëtäl. The overall form resembles the nineteenth-century Sensation Novel, with its multiple unreliable narrators creating ironies and contradictions for the reader to parse. As a technique, it resembles William Burroughs's cut-ups, but guided by purposeful editors instead of chance juxtapositions: reportage as montage. Its chapter titles are direct quotations from the book's huge cast of rock stars, managers, photographers, record executives, and more. From Chapter 1, "The Pussy-Plucking Posse Pocket of Hollywood," through Chapter 20: "We Just Made It a Friggin' Party," to Chapter 49, my favorite: "Saving Whales Doesn't Sell Albums; Leather Pants Do." I'm assuming the elegant semicolon, like the title's umlaut, was added by the book's authors/arrangers, Tom Beaujour and Richard Bienstock.[36]

And yet, interview after interview, we see the possibility that the title is fortified with irony, not metal. There was, very clearly, something other than a good time:

- *Poverty and hunger.* Juan Croucier, bassist in Ratt: "I was a starving musician. So I go, 'How much is the band making?' 'I think we make about fifty bucks a gig.' And I went, 'Fifty bucks? That was groceries for a week.'"[37]
- *Jealousy, infighting, and rejection.* Dokken guitarist George Lynch vs. singer Don Dokken, George Lynch vs. producer Tom Werman, and George Lynch losing the Ozzy audition to Jake E. Lee:

  Ozzy Osbourne: "George Lynch is an excellent guitar player. But Jake was a more tasty guitar player to me."

Jake E. Lee: "If you ask George, he'll say I got the gig because I had better hair."

Sharon Osbourne: "Of course he had better hair! He had better everything."

George Lynch: "I think the big thing with me was that I had cut my hair short. I didn't have that big rock look. But, hey, I could've worn a wig! Ozzy was *bald* at the time!"[38]

- *Drug and alcohol addiction.* Penelope Spheeris, director of the documentary *The Decline of Western Civilization Part II: The Metal Years,* on revisiting the scene of WASP guitarist Chris Holmes smashed in a swimming pool as his mother looks on in shame: "It's not my fault he was that drunk. I didn't want to look at it either . . . The guy was just a total fuckup . . . And then it turns out to be the scene that everyone talks about in the film."[39]
- *Near-death experiences.* Nikki Sixx, bassist/songwriter of Mötley Crüe, on the heroin overdose that had him declared dead, even if reports of his death have been greatly exaggerated: "You take someone who hasn't slept, who's been on the road for almost a year, and whose health is falling apart, and mix that with heroin and pills and cocaine and tons of alcohol, and what happened kind of makes sense. My body just gave out."[40]
- *Actual death experiences.* Vince Neil, singer of Mötley Crüe, on his drunk driving catastrophe that killed Hanoi Rocks' drummer Razzle and severely injured two others: "I definitely deserved to go to prison. But I did thirty days in jail and got laid, and drank beer, because that's the power of cash. That's fucked up."[41] Ratt's Robbin Crosby, who died in 2002 from a heroin overdose and complications from AIDS; Warrant singer Jani Lane, who died from alcohol poisoning in 2011; the pyrotechnics disaster during a 2003 Great White show resulting in a fire that killed one hundred people and injured over 200 more.

It becomes impossible to disentangle the good times from the bad, the upside to the sex, drugs, and rock & roll from the physical and emotional calamities, many of which will be familiar to fans by now. In this way, the separation between art and artist, the easy way in which players in *Dungeons & Dragons* could separate themselves from their characters and personas, became willfully blurred.

The allure of the '80s for people too young to have experienced it comes from an idealization, before the scourges of AIDS or moral crusades, before social media and so-called cancel culture, before people supposedly knew better. It's prelapsarian—before the fall, the 1980s as a kind of Eden before people, young people in particular, had the burdens of knowledge and labor we have today. But this is a misrepresentation. The chart-topping metal of the era (although not all of the metal of the era, as we'll explore later) seemed to extol pleasure, that unholy trinity of sex, drugs, and rock & roll. But a closer look suggests that it was always more complicated. Mötley Crüe's first two albums were filled with danger and cautionary tales. The chorus of "Merry Go Round," from *Too Fast for Love* (1981), repeats "Merry-go-round and round" twenty-two times to put the listener in the position of a depression spiral, playground title to the contrary. *Shout at the Devil*'s "Too Young to Fall in Love" and "Looks That Kill" position love as dangerous, not pleasurable at all. "Your love's a guillotine" is hardly the mantra of a good time.[42]

We know from the collective Crüe memoir *The Dirt* (2001)—and the news reports—that the Crüe was heavily drinking, drugging, and womanizing in real life. But the reader of *The Dirt* can't help but notice that they're suffering. Right at the beginning, we learn that their shared residence, "the Mötley House," "was crawling with vermin."[43] "The whole time we lived there," according the Nikki Sixx's opening chapter, "all we wanted was a record deal. But all we ended up with was booze, drugs, chicks, squalor, and court orders."[44] Nikki elsewhere: "I was broke."[45] Unable to revive Nikki from an overdose, his drug dealer, according to Nikki, "decided to throw me in the Dumpster behind his tenement and leave me for dead."[46] And more:

- Vince, on his ex-girlfriend Lovey: "Just a few months later, I saw her on the news: She had been stabbed sixty times in a drug deal gone wrong, I often wondered what became of her daughter, and hope that she wasn't mine."[47] On the aftermath of his drunk-driving disaster: "It seemed like all my relationships were exploding in my face" and, after his sentence is handed down, "Now people hated me more than they did before."[48]
- Tommy, on Nikki: "I couldn't believe he was shooting up at my fucking wedding" to Heather Locklear; later, describing a day in the life on tour: "Drink. Do drugs. Go on rampage in room, on roof, or in parking lot. Get caught. Get locked in room and handcuffed to bed by road manager. Yell. Scream. Threaten jobs. Shoot up heroin alone . . . Pass out . . . Phone rings. Wake up. Remember nothing, Repeat cycle."[49]
- Mick Mars: "We had sold millions of records and I was still broke."[50]

Yet at the same time, in addition to the partying as well as the suffering, *The Dirt* and *Nöthin' But a Good Time* provide example after example of the incredible hard work and dedication—words not usually associated with a good time—that the musicians and people behind the scenes put in:

- Photographer Don Adkins: "I think one thing I noticed . . . the really good bands that rose to the top . . . were really focused on making it. Absolutely driven."[51]
- Poison singer Bret Michaels: "We were workaholics with a dream."[52]
- Brad Hunt, an executive with Elektra Records: "They [referring to Mötley Crüe but could refer to almost anyone in the book] partied hard, no ifs, ands, or buts about it. But they were really hard workers."[53]
- Tom Whalley, an executive with Capitol Records: "The band [referring to Poison but could refer to almost anyone in the book] was working *incredibly hard*.[54]

A whole chapter of *Nöthin' But a Good Time* —"Flyer Wars"—is dedicated to the countless nights that band after band spent handing out or plastering flyers: "guerrilla marketing," "ten thousand flyers," "every night was promoting night." More exciting than plastering flyers, we get another entire chapter—"It Was a Total Scene Out of *Gunslinger* or Something"—on the dedication to the craft of guitar playing that made the decade a six-string apogee. Guitar god Steve Vai opens the chapter: "We loved playing instruments."[55] Eddie Van Halen's "Eruption" is both the moon launch and the shot heard 'round the world, inspiring a generation of players to be faster, better, louder. If it sounds like sports or athleticism, it was—there was artistry, but there was also physicality, muscle memory that could only come from hours and years of practice. Punks wore their musical amateurism as badges of honor, but metal required proficiency to earn respect. It takes hard work to make it look easy.

The combination of debauchery with overwork—materialism and excess in all forms—is one of the hallmarks of the '80s in America, but it was usually reserved for discussions of the Reagan Revolution, yuppies, and Wall Street—the film and the phenomenon—and not heavy metal. Yet here, with the regular references to drugs, crime, and poverty, the occasional allusion to a world just on the cusp of the AIDS crisis, and the obscene amounts of money the successful bands made, then squandered, metal becomes a microcosm of the Reagan era. Seen in this light, the Hollywood hair band scene is in keeping with *Wall Street*'s Gordon Gekko. Park Avenue leads to skid row, but not for the reason Sebastian

Bach imagined. The bands weren't a form of rebellion against '80s hustle and materialism—they were its flipside and mirror image.

Yet despite the not-quite-behind the scenes *Sturm und Drang*, the near- and actual fatalities, or the work ethic usually associated with a Bruce Springsteen or a Bud Fox, Gekko's *Wall Street* protégé, more than a Faster Pussycat or a White Lion, what the idea of "nothing but a good time" gets absolutely right is that *the music was fun.* Awesome, even. The scene, the bands, the vibe—all fun, all awesome. It's the reason I wanted to read those books and then write this one. I lived it. I loved it. I still do.

After going out of style, '80s metal is enjoying a comeback. Fans who came of age with this music are looking back and seeing it for the good time it was and still is—despite everything. To a newer generation, the 1980s is no longer even a decade, not exactly. For them, the '80s are now, thanks to a decade of iTunes, Spotify, and YouTube, like the '50, '60s, '70s, and '90s, a genre on the Sirius XM Radio station "Hair Nation." The '80s metal scene is more and also less than an actual time period or lived experience—it is an aesthetic.

Which takes us back to that hair.

The Hair in Hair Metal

"Hair bands," the name, was supposed to be derogatory, dismissive. Former *Headbangers Ball* VJ Riki Rachtman hates it. To its detractors, hair represented vanity and frivolity, artifice ahead of authenticity, appearance over music.

But this is wrong. The bands were dedicated to the music, the craftsmanship of songwriting, the mastery of their instruments. They also wanted to amass and entertain fans, foremost, and, yes, they cultivated their image. Yet the hair in so-called hair metal didn't symbolize a lack of substance. It demonstrated their commitment to the cause, to the culture. In the 1980s, long hair on men prevented all kinds of employment and invited all kinds of harassment. It meant choosing the rock identity and life over all others, the badge and uniform that we couldn't change out of or remove. It was a declaration of membership in a tribe, a subcultural invitation to insiders, which also meant that it warded off the outsiders.

Despite the nostalgia, I'm still not convinced that the era was nothin' but a good time. Even the Poison song that became the decade's motto might be another case, like Bruce Springsteen's "Born in the USA" or Neil Young's "Rockin' In the Free World," of a song whose big chorus turns out to be an ironic complement to its verse's lyrics. Between "wooo"s and "yeah"s, Bret Michaels informs us, "Not a dime, I can't pay my rent, / I can barely make it through the week, / Saturday night, I'd like to make my girl, / But right now, I can't make ends meet, no." It's *Saturday Night Fever* all over again. Life goin' nowhere. The work week is not a good time at all, and it doesn't even provide a fair wage. The pre-chorus continues in this vein, about "workin'" and "slavin'," leading into the chorus by saying, "If you could hear me think, this is what I'd say."[56] We *can* hear you think, Bret! You're singing about it right now! And we do hear what he says! It's Poison's version of Loverboy's "Working for the Weekend," but less depressing and sans cowbell, leading into the chorus and title. "Nothin' but a Good Time" eventually builds towards the escapist utopia of its chorus. And then, in the form of the song itself, Poison provides the good time we're hearing about right then in real time, at least for the duration of the song.

The video makes its rock identity politics explicit while even taking a swing at class consciousness and solidarity—less of a surprise than one might think, considering how often Bret extolls his blue-collar Pennsylvania roots. In a conflict redone in a dozen similar videos, a harried, ponytailed dishwasher is threatened and exploited by his boss. But a mystical door opens to a Poison concert, a temporary, fantastical, fun escape before the video concludes back to work in the kitchen. It's another version of the Freudian child's game: Gone, there. But at the end, our rocker's hair is down, and he looms triumphantly over his boss through the magic of metal and the virtue of hard work, '80s style, the other thing the band repeatedly connects to those working-class beginnings. Maybe there's a little Marxist false consciousness—that is, the working class identifies with its oppressors instead of rebelling—in a line like "If wanting a good life is such a crime, / Lord, then, put me away." Maybe it's still not quite "I wanna be anarchy," as the Sex Pistols snarled. It's escapism, sure. But they never lose sight of what they need to escape.

The not-fun parts of the '80s don't go away: AIDS, crime, poverty, drugs, the widening gulf between rich and poor, the apocalyptic threat of Cold War annihilation that was the backdrop of so many of the era's *Mad Max*-style videos. Hair metal, as Poison understood, is the perfect antidote, a genre and movement of what their contemporary Prince expressed openly in "Let's Go Crazy" and even more so in "1999," with lyrics befitting a Megadeth song: "Tryin' to run from the destruction, / You know I didn't even care, / Two-thousand-zero-zero party over / Oops out of time, / So tonight I'm gonna party like it's 1999."⁵⁷ Prince released that song in 1984. It turned out that his timing was perfect. Poison's party is more immediate: tonight we're going to party like it's 1989. And it don't get better than this.

But what if we take Poison's "nothing" in the Existentialist sense, as in philosopher Jean-Paul Sartre's *Being and Nothingness*? *Nothing* is less a negation than a characteristic in and of itself, and a way for us to understand ourselves. Even Sartre, in his play *No Exit*, most famous for its downbeat reveal that "Hell is—other people!," also has a character conclude that "You are—your life, and nothing more."⁵⁸ If Mötley Crüe and Queensrÿche can freely add their umlauts to their names, and if Tom Beaujour and Richard Bienstock can add an umlaut to *Nöthin' But a Good Time*, then in light of the chronicled hardships and dark backdrops, maybe I can add my own punctuation to that song title as well:

The '80s: *Nothing. But, a good time.*

Ozzy Osbourne, Cold War Prophet

No one had a better, and worse, time in the 1980s than Ozzy Osbourne. Van Halen were runnin' with the devil, but John Michael "Ozzy" Osbourne was the Prince of Darkness himself. In 1978, Van Halen, on their way to the top, opened for Black Sabbath, who appeared to be on their way to the bottom. Yet together with Van Halen, no performer set the stage for the decade more than Ozzy did.

By 1980, fighting addictions, his family life falling apart, fired by Black Sabbath, Ozzy was an unlikely candidate for a spectacular solo career. But, surrounded by astonishing musicians, including his answer to Eddie Van Halen, young guitar hero Randy Rhoads, Ozzy released a terrific and impactful series of albums. His infamous antics—biting the head off of a dove, biting the head off of a *bat*, snorting drugs, snorting *ants*, the nonstop alcohol, urinating at the Alamo, the violent episodes—are well documented. Combined with his distinctive and occasionally unintelligible speech, his doughy, tattooed physical mien, his propensity for over-the-top imagery, the rapid turnover and ill will of those great musicians he's played with over the decades, and on and on, it's easy to overlook Ozzy's intelligence, his *brilliance*. It is important to note that the animosity and litigation between Ozzy and his former musicians pose a challenge and complication for analyzing his work. I'm attributing credit to Ozzy here and throughout, even as former bassist Bob Daisley and others dispute that Ozzy wrote much (or any) of the music and, more contentiously, the lyrics. Still, Ozzy has borne the name, the face, the mythos, and the consequences, as well as reaped the rewards.

At least 150 books have been written about Bob Dylan, bard of the 1960s and beyond, who went on to win the 2016 Nobel Prize in Literature—literature! Ozzy has his share of books and music journalism devoted to him, to be sure, and he is a very wealthy man. But, for all his achievements and fame, his fans' love and album sales, unlike Eddie Van Halen, unlike his own guitarists—Rhoads, followed by the fleet-fingered, melodic Jake E. Lee and brutal, squealing Zakk Wylde—Ozzy himself remains underestimated as an artist. And yet he has also used those misjudgments against him, to his advantage. Ozzy is the premier social critic and metal conscience of the 1980s. He remains the unanointed poet laureate of the heavy metal era, self-deprecation to the contrary, and the ironic prophet of the late Cold War. For all those infamous antics, he is, at heart, a sentimentalist, and a sly moralist.

Ozzy seems to have invited the underestimation. He kicked off his first solo album, the playfully titled *Blizzard of Ozz*—cross-referencing L. Frank Baum's famous novel-turned-film, escapism, drugs, and himself all at once—with "I Don't Know." He opens, in true '80s fashion, by referencing the apocalypse: "People look to me and say / Is the end near, when is the final day?" Then, he continues to plead, or maybe feign, ignorance: "What's the future of mankind? / How do I know, I got left behind."[59] No question mark. More fear for the future; more conflict between school, where Ozzy was a disappointment, versus rock & roll, where Ozzy is a deity.

Time and time again, Ozzy engages in Socratic irony—pretending not to understand, and asking questions, so that his listeners, his protegees in metal, can think for themselves. Sure, maybe he really doesn't know. But the effect is the same. Or, if not Socrates, Ozzy is a potbellied metal Buddha, consistently engaging in what Zen practice refers to as "Not-Knowing," the Beginner's Mind. Maybe it's his temperament. Maybe it was the alcoholic blackouts. Or maybe it's neither. It is, ironically, a knowing wink and nod—repeating "I don't know" is a meditative practice and its own kind of wisdom. It's the ability to question received wisdom, a form of clear thinking, not confusion.

He continues: "Fools and prophets from the past, / Life's a stage and we're all in the cast"—an allusion to Shakespeare's *As You Like It*: "All the world's a stage, and all the men and women merely players. They have their exits and their entrances; And one man in his time plays many parts."[60] (Rush liked this line, too, and used it in "Limelight.") Even his use of "fools" is Shakespearean: The Fool in *King Lear*, and the other fools and clowns that go by different names, are able to reveal wisdom and speak truth to power, using clever wordplay, in ways that supposedly wise men know well not to. Ozzy is happy to play the fool, for our amusement, but also, maybe, our benefit.

"I Don't Know" led into what is now Ozzy's signature song, "Crazy Train." Everything about it rocks, and yet, it's quirky, playful: Ozzy bellowing "ALL ABOARD!," followed by the kind of laugh usually reserved only for crazy people in the movies. The menacingly iconic bass intro, Ozzy's weirdly catchy, delayed "Ay (ay-ay-ay-ay-ay-ay)," the eccentric percussion of the vibraslap, and finally, Randy Rhoads's million-dollar, mega-ton riff.

The verse then chugs along, train-like, and Ozzy makes his fears about the future of mankind from "I Don't Know" entirely clear: the whole world, not Ozzy the individual, has gone "Crazy, but that's how it goes, / Millions of people living as foes."[61] Ozzy, the Fool, plainly states the thing that, in 1980, was obvious but politically unsayable. Mutually Assured Destruction, the accepted Cold War peace-keeping doctrine where neither the United States nor the USSR would strike first, knowing that retaliation would destroy them both, is not just MAD; it's crazy. And then, in a line worthy of John Lennon, famous for his Bed-Ins for peace in protesting the Vietnam War, as opposed to Ozzy, famous for his PCP air rifle collection[62]: "Maybe, it's not too late / To learn how to love and forget how to hate."

Ozzy's next verse references fools again: "I've listened to preachers," similar to the prophets of "I Don't Know," "I've listened to fools." But the operative image is not just "crazy," or even the title's "crazy train," the moving deathtrap that everyone in the world of 1980 is unwittingly riding, but the harsher note of "Mental wounds not healing" and, later, "still screaming." And then, he presents a kind of thesis: "Heirs of a cold war, that's what we've become, / Inheriting troubles, I'm mentally numb." It's an image of madness, but, in keeping with the paradoxical craziness expressed in the great Cold War novel *Catch-22*:

> . . . a concern for one's safety in the face of dangers that were real and immediate was the process of a rational mind. Orr was crazy and could be grounded. All he had to do was ask; and as soon as he did, he would no longer be crazy and would have to fly more missions. Orr would be crazy to fly more missions and sane if

he didn't, but if he was sane he had to fly them. If he flew them he was crazy and didn't have to; but if he didn't want to he was sane and had to.[63]

But it is on "Revelation (Mother Earth)" that Ozzy's radical pacifism is its more powerful. The Greek word *apokalypsis*, which we associate with catastrophe, means "revelation." (And the Greek word *catastrophe* means "I overturn.") Yet a revelation is also rooted in revealing, exposing, and that is arguably what the song does. In a combination of humility and chutzpah, in his most mournful voice, Ozzy paraphrases Jesus: "Mother please forgive them / For they know not what they do."[64] Together with Randy Rhoads's neo-classical acoustic-turned-grand-electric guitar playing, along with the chiming of church bells, using a through-composed song structure,[65] Ozzy continues to echo the Bible, while also channeling visionary poet William Blake (whom we'll get to later for Ozzy's replacement in Black Sabbath, Ronnie James Dio): "I had a vision, 1 saw the world burn, / And the seas had turned red ... Mother, please show the children / Before it's too late, / To fight each other, there's no one winning, / We must fight all the hate." It's the same rhyme from "Crazy Train," but now the end of the world threat comes from the twin fronts of nuclear war and environmental degradation. There is, in the end, little difference. Ozzy seems to be channeling poet Robert Frost, who, in one of his shortest yet most powerful poems, "Fire and Ice," writes, "Some say the world will end in fire, / Some say in ice," but both enact equal destruction "And," in the end, "would suffice."[66]

In 1986, on *The Ultimate Sin* album, the intertwining of teleological and technological disaster continues. While the title track is ambiguous about its relationship to nuclear war, the sarcastic "Thank God for the Bomb" is not. However, "Killer of Giants," highlighting the neoclassical skills of guitarist Jake E. Lee after Rhoads's shocking accidental death in 1982, presents the album's most powerful allegory. What are giants if not the world's superpowers of the USA and the USSR? And so, what is the only killer of giants? Nuclear weapons. But, Ozzy warns us, "Killer of giants threatens us all." Throwing off the fool persona, he implores, "Listen to me everyone, / If the button is pushed / There'll be nowhere to run."[67] "Revelation (Mother Earth)" and "Killer of Giants" are not the classic rock radio staples that "I Don't Know" and "Crazy Train" have become, and not only, I think, because they're not as upbeat or catchy. These songs are poignant, and frightening, ill fit for arena chants, headbanging, or car commercials. Yet that's what makes them worth revisiting today.

It will surprise no one that Ozzy was regularly denounced by religious leaders, who saw him as threatening, dangerous, and satanic. Televangelist Jimmy Swaggart, in keeping with Tipper Gore, called rock & roll "the new pornography."[68] And Ozzy *was* threatening—to them. Playing up and joking with his image, Ozzy released *No Rest for the Wicked* in 1989, featuring the song "Miracle Man," which, along with Poison's "Something to Believe In" and Metallica's "Leper Messiah," explicitly calls out the greed and hypocrisy of televangelism. After being attacked as immoral, rockers could be forgiven some *schadenfreude* after the exploits of Jimmy Swaggart and Jim Bakker were revealed. These immensely popular TV preachers were, respectively, caught having sex with prostitutes, and drugging and raping a woman and attempting to cover it up. (If you remember the name "Jessica Hahn" from the 1980s, she was that woman. It's no wonder she aligned herself with the rockers when she went public, appearing in the video for comedian Sam Kinison's 1988 metal cover of "Wild Thing.") Rock stars were many things, but they were not puritanical hypocrites about sex. For all of his joking about the devil, one line from Hosea 9:7 describes Ozzy best: "Because your sins are so many and your hostility so great, the prophet is considered a fool, the inspired man a maniac."[69] Ozzy is not just the ultimate sinner, the maniac, the fool. He is also inspired, and inspirational.

At the end of the 1980s—by which I mean 1991—Ozzy had another hugely successful album, *No More Tears*, featuring the song "I Don't Want to Change the World"; the live version would, two years later, win the Grammy Award for Best Metal Performance. The song's chorus closes the loop begun with "I Don't Know": "I don't wanna change the world, / I don't want the world to change me," and, later, "Tell me I'm a sinner, I've got news for you / I spoke to God this morning and he don't like you."[70] Unlike politicians and preachers, Ozzy has always been honest about who he was. He is a reluctant prophet—aren't they all?—for the nuclear age. But he was also wrong. He changed the world, whether he wanted to or not, for the better, even if the world didn't change him. He was, and still is, Ozzy.

In 2024, Ozzy made news for something other than biting the head off a small animal. He denied permission for rapper/mogul/conspiracy theorist Ye, *née* Kanye West, to sample his music, citing Ye's infamous anti-Semitism. It's not often that a white male Baby Boomer's all-caps social media post about a rapper is the socially conscientious position, but there it was.[71] West's only retort, days later, was to suggest that Ozzy didn't write the post himself, ignoring all of the content and context of the problem. Even today, Ozzy remains underestimated.

Modern Day Cowboys

The video for "The Ultimate Sin," lyrics to the contrary, didn't include imagery of nuclear war or religious revelation. Instead, it featured Ozzy dressed up as a Texas oil tycoon, reminiscent of then-popular TV show "Dallas," cowboy boots and cowboy hat in tow.

In addition to the many videos that used Road Warrior dystopian imagery, there is a second significant, recurring image: the cowboy. The Road Warrior and The Cowboy feel, at first, like opposites: the cowboy recalls the Western movie genre, popular from the 1940s to the 1960s, which itself recalls the expansion of the frontier from 1849 to 1890. It's a throwback to a throwback, nostalgia for nostalgia. The cowboy represents a cinematic idealization of the distant past. *The Road Warrior*'s post-apocalypse is the distant future, representing fear, not nostalgia, the Western's elegiac end of the frontier contrasted with the Road Warrior's apocalyptic end of everything.

Yet the images overlap. They're pulled from movies, and both represent, once again, a kind of fantasy, a wish fulfillment. Their settings are similar: heroes, but also extra-legal justice; open space, but also the possibility of captivity; flashy, utilitarian-yet-performance-oriented clothing: leather, chaps, denim, vests, hats, bandannas, but mired in grit and dust. They're mirrors of the rock & roll fantasy of life on the road. "Road warrior" becomes a pun, the drifter who moves from town to town. Both live outside of convention, outside the law, and make their own morality. They're bound only by their own codes, their own way of living. And they're feared for it by some, but admired, even loved, for it, by others.

Other rock bands before the 1980s saw the analogy: Thin Lizzy's "Cowboy Song," Aerosmith's "Back in the Saddle," The Eagles' "Desperado." Still others would continue the imagery after the '80s ended: Kid Rock in "Cowboy," although he himself is from Michigan and the song is about LA, and Pantera, who were actually from Texas, in "Cowboys from Hell," which is one way to think of Texas.

Tesla's "Modern Day Cowboy" (1986) exists on the exact nexus between Cold War and Cowboy, and Tesla know it. The video incorporates the image of the movie theater and includes clips from three black-and-white movies: first, *High Noon* (1952), a Western; then *Scarface* (the 1932 version), about gangster Al Capone; and finally, the bombers of *Dr. Strangelove* (1964), a Cold War satire that ends in world destruction. (There's also some kind of plot about a spectacled, mustachioed projectionist that is best left alone.) With the film clips, we get the concert-style band footage that's a requirement of the genre.

Unlike other rock & roll cowboys (Ratt and Bon Jovi, coming up), Tesla seems ambivalent about the imagery. From cowboy to gangster to bomber, the video suggests, we see the trajectory of pointless macho violence develop and inflate. Similarly, the lyrics escalate as well: the dissonant pre-chorus of "Bang-bang, shoot 'em up / Bang-bang, blow you away" isn't fun; it's alarming! The "cowboy (cowboy!) of the modern day" who will, if you're still "hangin' 'round" will "blow you away," isn't a figure of admiration as much as fear.[72]

By the final verse, like Ozzy's "Crazy Train" overtly referencing "the Cold War," Tesla is perfectly clear: the showdown is between "The U.S.A. [and] the U.S.S.R. / With their six guns to their sides / I see the message written on the wall / Too much anger deep inside." Unlike, though, say, Bob Dylan's anti-war folk song "Blowin' In the Wind," with its gentle, admonishing conclusion of ". . . how many deaths will it take till he knows / That too many people have died?" Tesla's metal can't help but benefit from the lyrics' high stakes. The final heir to the cowboy-gangster-bomber progression is the metal guitarist. The song's signature is the super-fast scale runs that open it and kick off each chorus, along with the high-wire twin lead for the solo. Metal—planes, bombs—in the Cold War is dangerous. Metal from guitars is, well, dangerous too, but in the good way. Tesla's name comes from inventor Nikola Tesla, who would also inspire a certain car company. They know we should fear nuclear weapons, but they still love electricity.

Along with "Modern Day Cowboy," as Tesla's song suggests, another figure also exists on the exact nexus between Cold War and Cowboy. It's the US president most associated with the 1980s and the end of the Cold War, Ronald Reagan. Reagan, "the Cowboy President," is a modern-day cowboy even more than the guitar slinger is. Reagan wore cowboy hats, boots, and blue jeans when that style was still associated with Westerns, not midwestern suburbs. He bought a ranch, Rancho del Cielo, in 1974, although it was in Santa Barbara, California, not Texas. As an actor, Reagan starred in many cowboy films, including *Santa Fe Trail* (1940), which gave Reagan a life-long nickname and catchphrase, "Just win one for the Gipper." Reagan was also instrumental in escalating the Cold War and vastly increasing defense spending and America's nuclear arsenal. The cowboy comparison cut two ways: an image of protection, but also recklessness. Reagan would escalate but not win the War on Drugs and was, for activists, too late in addressing the burgeoning AIDS crisis. The cowboy represented freedom, sure. But in practice, the Reagan administration was repressive, and it provided the perfect conservative counter against which partakers of sex, drugs, and rock & roll could rebel.

In that sense, Van Halen and "DOA"—dead or alive in the song, but punning on the more familiar acronym, Dead On Arrival—overlap dystopian and Western language. Their "Pretty Woman" video also happened to feature Eddie Van Halen dressed as a cowboy (and Alex as Tarzan, Michael Anthony as a samurai, and David Lee Roth as Napoleon). It also included a woman—or to use the language of the day, someone who turns out to be a female impersonator, which was by itself enough to get the video banned from MTV—who is, as usual, tied up, then released.

Ratt's "Wanted Man" featured a video that looked like it was pulled directly from an old Spaghetti Western. Unlike Tesla, Ratt saw the Western as a playground for the fun side of vice—saloons, guns, and tough-guy acting. The metal band could be like a gang—the "Ratt gang," in the song and video. It's all fun, no danger, a kind of *Westworld* (1973) that ends in 3 minutes and 37 seconds, before anything can go wrong, all the while punning on what being a "wanted man" might mean for a sex-crazed gang of rockers and their equally sex-crazed fans.

No one, though, took the rocker-cowboy comparison more seriously than Jon Bon Jovi. It's easy to make fun of a guy from New Jersey who decided that Western imagery *just speaks to him*. (That other guy from Jersey, one Bruce Springsteen, seems to have gone through a similar cowboy phase, if more recently, with *Western Stars*, in 2019.) Like the rock star and Road Warrior imagery, and, separately, the image of Gypsies[73], the Cowboy is always moving, pushing the boundary of the frontier. At first, Bon Jovi's "Wanted Dead or Alive" feels like an anti-road, anti-rock star song, their "Turn the Page," lamenting, in the opening lines, "It's all the same, only the names will change, / Every day it seems we're wastin' away."[74] The ambivalence is built into the title. Bon Jovi knows he's not really a cowboy, that it's an analogy: "On a steel horse I ride"—the tour bus, or maybe a motorcycle; "a loaded six-string"—the metaphorical weapon of the guitar, as opposed to a loaded six-shooter, a revolver—"on my back."

But even separate from the road-weariness, the idea that the rock star is a wanted man is different from Ratt's more straightforward sexualization. Bon Jovi understands that the rock star is as good to the fans, the public, and the record label dead or alive. When I was working at Sam Goody in 1991, jazz legend Miles Davis died. Immediately, all of his recordings were moved to the front displays. It was, as my manager referred to it, "the Sam Goody death sale." Inevitably, death is an excellent career move, for everyone except the deceased.

Aside from its imagery and overall catchiness, the song is remarkable for two aspects. "Wanted Dead or Alive" opens with, and repeats, a wistful, minor-key acoustic guitar refrain that recurs after each chorus, before slowing down and riding off into the sunset with it at the end. The guitar's repetition matches the final repetition of "And I ride." The song ends, but life on the road will continue indefinitely—or, at least, until the cowboy's divined death. The guitar signifies the cowboy's never-ending travel, moving on to the next town. In spite of its exhaustion, "Wanted Dead or Alive," is, perhaps ironically, in the end, a song about survival—not a small thing, given how many rock stars, and cowboys, died young.

The other remarkable aspect is the song's call-and-response vocal on the chorus: "Wanted"—"Waaa-aanted!"—"dead or alive," provided by loaded six-stringer/backup singer Richie Sambora. The crowd loves it and loves singing it. I'm not Jon Bon Jovi or Richie Sambora by any means, but I've played this song live hundreds of times, sometimes as the lead singer and other times as the backing singer, and even in bars, especially in bars, everyone sings along. Cowboy imagery aside, everyone wants to shout "Wanted!" And everyone wants to *be* wanted, at least sometimes.

Unlike Ratt and their "Ratt gang," Jon Bon Jovi began to see himself as a lone ranger. After the success of "Wanted Dead or Alive," he released a solo album, *Blaze of Glory*, as the soundtrack to the film *Young Guns II*. In keeping, every song was cowboy themed. Around the same time, in 1991, Richie Sambora also released a cowboy-themed solo album, *Stranger in This Town*. At least until they reunited for *Keep the Faith* in 1992, and then after broke up again, this time for good, in 2013, this town ain't big enough for the two of them.

Bon Jovi and the Art of Failure

For all the cowboy cosplay, it is "Livin' On A Prayer" that remains Bon Jovi's smash hit and masterpiece. It is also, in the end, the great anthem of the Reagan '80s, and a harbinger of what would become of the '80s metal generation.

"Livin' on a Prayer" opens with suspenseful, dissonant string-synth keyboards, while, in the video, the silhouettes of the band march forth, *Right*

Stuff-style, portentously, in slow motion, as our speaker solemnly intones, not sings, "Once upon a time, not so long ago." It's a contradiction—"Once upon a time" traditionally evokes, well, a time long ago, as opposed to "not so long ago." But instead of conjuring a fairy tale, of knights and princesses, this will be a folk tale, a story with a lesson about regular human beings, passed on by word of mouth. "Not so long ago" is the opposite of Reagan-era touchstone *Star Wars*' "A long time ago in a galaxy far, far away." This is now, and this is here.

The pentatonic bass riff begins and builds the song further, the big drum fill fires in, and the song's memorable talk-box guitar doubles the bass and leads into a tense verse. As the music comes down, we're introduced to Tommy and Gina, a working-class couple "down on their luck"—union dock work for him, serving in a diner for her. Each section builds upon the last, as a perfect pop song should, from the minor key verse to the escalating pre-chorus, with what are, for me, the most encouraging, inspiring, and true words of poetry to come out of this or any era:

> "We've gotta hold on to what we've got,
> It doesn't make a difference if we make it or not,
> We've got each other and that's a lot for love,
> We'll give it a shot!"[75]

Maybe most importantly, though, the pre-chorus is in quotations. The words are Gina's: "*She says* 'We've gotta hold on . . . ,'" my italics. The voice of perseverance, the reminder that having each other, that love is the most important thing, more important even than success, belongs to her. And thus, with the word "shot," the song explodes into its climactic chorus—in the video, the black and white turns to color with the second chorus, like Bon Jovi finally arrived in Oz.

Every decade gets its own signature nonsense: "Wop bop a loo bop a lop bom bom" for the '50s; "Do Wah Diddy Diddy" for the '60s; "Mah-Nà Mah-Nà" for the '70s (if released earlier). Other songs had a similar chant, but Bon Jovi's "Whooooooa" and "Whoa-oooh"s perfectly embody the 1980s' striving spirit. Add the world's catchiest bassline, the title's "livin' on a prayer," and the classic is cemented.

It is, for me, much more palpable than the equally iconic, similarly dropped -g "Don't Stop Believin.'" That song also has a girl and a boy, but who are they, exactly? They don't have names. What, exactly, should they, and therefore we, believe in? Its openness is part of its massive, cross-generational appeal, to be sure. Everyone loves that song, and its positive ambiguity made it perfect for the finale of HBO's *The Sopranos*, in 2007, where viewers were left unsure of Tony's fate, by design.

But give me the concreteness of the second verse's "Tommy's got his six string in hock, now he's holding in, / When he used to make it talk so tough," and then the talk-box guitar *does* make it talk so tough! Tommy and Gina have, and are, a whole world, where he's not just a dockworker, but a struggling musician, and she has . . . well, Gina has Tommy, so while it's nice that Bon Jovi made her the conscience and voice of the pre-chorus, it's not quite egalitarian. Not bad for the 1980s, though.

It's still better than Journey's "It goes on and on and on and on," because Bon Jovi's chorus suggests just the opposite: it will not go on.[76] It will never go on. Memes and jokes abound about that chorus: *it's been decades—shouldn't Bon Jovi be more than halfway there by now? Shouldn't they be there by now?* It's Zeno's Dichotomy Paradox: "That which is in locomotion must arrive at the half-way stage before it arrives at the goal."[77] That is, using this logic, no one can ever get anywhere, because to get there, you need to get *halfway there* first, and *halfway to halfway*, ad infinitum. If Bon Jovi is always ever halfway there, they can never make it all the way.

Yet it's not a joke. It might be precisely the point.

Like working-class hero film *Rocky* a decade earlier, and like *8 Mile*, sixteen years later, "Livin' On a Prayer" is an ode to failure—or, at least, a particular kind of failure: loss with a silver lining, the small win hidden inside the larger fiasco that, nevertheless, may be even more important than winning itself. Rocky loses his bout to champion Apollo Creed, but he lasted the entire fight. He begins and ends as the underdog, underestimated, but his stature and aura have grown, despite the loss, even with the loss, even *because of* the loss. In *8 Mile*, rapper Rabbit wins his rap battle rematch with Papa Doc, but at the cost of revealing all of his own failures and inadequacies: "I am white, I am a fucking bum, / I do live in a trailer with my mom," and worse.[78] But he has turned his weaknesses into strengths, as his trickster-figure namesake suggests of him. Winning the rap battle does nothing for his workaday life—he's still a fucking bum, still lives in a trailer with his mom, still has to show up the next day at New Detroit Stamping. But he too retains the power of the underdog, his lower class trumping Papa Doc's upper middle-class status for authenticity in the bootstraps-American reversal that being born low and working hard is better than, to paraphrase Ann Richards about George HW Bush, being born on third base and thinking you hit a triple. Tommy and Gina, for example, were statistically unlikely to benefit personally from trickle-down economics.[79]

In "Livin' On a Prayer," it doesn't make a difference if they make it or not, and we'll never know if they do. As far as the song goes, they don't. We do learn, in "It's My Life," fourteen years later, in 2000, that "This is for the ones who stood their ground / It's for Tommy and Gina who never backed down."[80] Good for them! Good to know!

Their love and toughness, their sweat and tears, get them halfway there. The rest is all hope and faith, which will have to be good enough. The final pre-chorus, after the anthemic, chorus-affirming guitar solo, still has Tommy and Gina holding on, but now, like Rocky and Rabbit, "You live for the fight when that's all that you've got." The struggle, not the success, is the thing unto itself; as the Zen koan goes, the obstacle is the path. Or, as Poison would sing in "Cry Tough," "Sometimes the rainbow, baby, is better than the pot of gold."

As if to drive the point of impossibility home even further, the final chorus begins a beat early, staggering dancers everywhere, launching into a key change not the usual half step up—all the worse for the karaoke singers who don't know what they've gotten into—but a whopping *three half-steps up* (from E minor to G minor), pitching the vocals up to the top of the tenor's range, straining all the backing singers, driving the chorus so high it's seemingly just out of reach. It's like the dark joke that the word "free" is purposely out of everyone's range in "The Star-Spangled Banner." And from there, the chorus repeats and fades out, not because the fadeout is a pop convention, but to imply it will go on forever, halfway there and so forever unfulfilled. It's dispiriting, in a way. But at the same time, Tommy and Gina remain forever in place, in love, like the images of the lovers frozen in place and time in John Keats's "Ode on a Grecian Urn" (1819). "Heard melodies are sweet," Keats writes, "but those unheard / Are sweeter."[81] Bon Jovi's melodies are plenty sweet, but Tommy and Gina's unknown future remains sweeter. We wouldn't have it any other way.

"Livin' On a Prayer," a paean to failure, ironically gave Bon Jovi its biggest success. But it was a particular kind of success—popular success in the face of adversity, for those critically maligned underdogs from Sayreville, New Jersey. In the end, the couple's own perseverance and love, rather than, say, a strong social safety net, could win the day in the popular conception of 1980s America. Or maybe it won't. Fade out.

While their original *Slippery When Wet* album cover—a woman in a wet t-shirt, presumably not Gina—was deemed too risqué by record executives to be released in the climate the PMRC had established, Tipper Gore did not target Bon Jovi after all. That was not the case with Twisted Sister, coming up in the next chapter.

Post Script: The Irony Curtain

The 1950s US Cold War policy was clear: preventing the spread of Communism both abroad and domestically. The problem was, Communism at home was not the real problem. McCarthy's own red-baiting and blacklisting were. The Payola hearings, and then, two decades later, PMRC hearings, were extensions of McCarthyism—using the imprimatur of the United States government to contain a perceived threat coming from within the culture. And yet, in the end, the music that the PMRC argued would contaminate the moral purity of America's children helped bring down the Iron Curtain. The very thing Tipper Gore most feared turned out to be the best weapon in the US's anti-Soviet arsenal. Modern day cowboys indeed. It is a great historical irony that heavy metal, not McCarthyism, helped to end Soviet Communism.

This is, admittedly, a tough claim to prove. As my colleagues in the Social Sciences insist, correlation is not causation. So let's analyze the correlation.

The US Festival in 1983 would bring previous touring partners Van Halen and Ozzy together again—along with Judas Priest, Quiet Riot, Mötley Crüe, Triumph, and Scorpions. Organized and sponsored by Steve Wozniak, the co-founder of Apple, the festival title was supposed to be "Us," the pronoun, in contrast with the Baby Boomer's Me Generation. That it was consistently capitalized and so resembled "US," as in "United States," was a coincidence. Or *was* it?

Van Halen would make news—and enter the Guinness Book of World Records—as the highest paid band in the world. It was the perfect convergence of '80s America—a giant music festival, funded by early computer tech dollars, ostensibly to bring people together, that would instead divide the days by genre and lose money yet become the apotheosis of materialism. The Clash, who played the day before Ozzy and Van Halen, complained about the materialist ethos, but they were paid a half a million dollars, too. In the end, David Lee Roth would parade on the stage drunk, forget the words to the songs, and threaten to have sex with a heckler's girlfriend. Van Halen manager Noel Monk said the performance left him "depressed and ashamed."[82] But despite bracing for the bad reviews, "it wasn't nearly as bad as I anticipated." Fans were even more forgiving, generally looking back on it as one of the greatest concerts of all time.

Only six years later, on August 12 and 13, 1989, famous metal manager Doc McGhee would organize another festival. Ozzy Osbourne, Mötley Crüe, and Scorpions would reunite, along with other groups, this time headlined by a band barely formed back in 1983—Bon Jovi. The Moscow Music Peace Festival—symmetrically named with the US Festival, even if "US" never officially stood for "United States"—would be broadcast around the world and expose millions of Eastern Bloc fans to previously prohibited Western music. Three months later, on November 9, 1989, the Berlin Wall would come down. As *Rolling Stone* reported, "The festival gave young Soviet fans a chance to see what life might be like for them—and gave those Americans, Brits and Germans playing a firsthand glimpse of the waning days of the Soviet Union." And as Scorpions' rhythm guitarist Rudolf Schenker said, "It was for us a very big dream, especially coming from Germany, showing the Russians that there is a new generation growing up in Germany who are not coming with tanks and making war, but coming with guitars and playing music and bringing love and peace."[83]

Inspired, Scorpions then wrote their power ballad "Wind of Change" (1990). Wind, not a hurricane this time. A ballad, not about still lovin' you, but about the possibility of lasting peace despite the seeming impossibility of the Cold War—*the Cold War!* Decades in the making!—finally ending. Singer Klaus Meine whistles the opening melody wistfully, in a way that sounds melancholy and hopeful at the same time. The wind of change would be music itself, just as Meine's whistle is both the breeze and the melody.

Then, he begins singing:

> The world is closing in,
> And did you ever think
> That we could be so close like brothers?
> The future's in the air, I can feel it everywhere,
> Blowing with the wind of change.[84]

The song was so effective in spreading the idea of democracy—or, from another perspective, pro-USA propaganda—that a podcast, also called "Wind of Change," would posit the theory that the CIA itself wrote "Wind of Change" to finally topple the Soviet Union.[85] The conclusion: there's not enough evidence to say the CIA did it, but it would have been in keeping with CIA Cold War tactics if it had. Meine denied it, but even if it were true, he would have to deny it.

Finally, Metallica would headline a free concert at Tushino Airfield, in Moscow, on September 28, 1991, as part of the Monsters of Rock Festival, to a crowd of 1.6 million people.[86] Although the Soviet Union wouldn't officially end until three months later, on December 25, 1991, the heavy metal concert—loud, raucous, rebellious, Western, in the final Cowboy linguistic coincidence—might be an even better symbolic representation of the USSR's demise than the eventual removal of the hammer and sickle flag.

The Cold War shaped heavy metal, and heavy metal, just maybe, helped end the Cold War. "Marches of protest / Not stopping the war," Ozzy lamented in "Killer of Giants." But it didn't take marches. The killer of giants turned out to be Metallica, Scorpions, Bon Jovi, and Ozzy himself, heir to the Cold War no more.

2

V for Violence

Figure 7 A street in Whitechapel: the last crime of Jack the Ripper, from "Le Petit Parisien," 1891 (Photo by Stefano Bianchetti/Corbis via Getty Images).

I see thee still,
And on thy blade and dudgeon gouts of blood,
Which was not so before. There's no such thing.
It is the bloody business which informs
Thus to mine eyes.
 —William Shakespeare, *Macbeth* (2.1.45–49; 1606)[1]

A glint of steel, a flash of light
You know you're not going home tonight
Be it jack or switch, doctor's or mind

Nowhere to run, everywhere you'll find
You can't escape from the bed you've made
When your time has come, you'll accept the blade!
—Twisted Sister, "Under the Blade" (1982)[2]

With the Cold War context of the 1980s explored, we can look more closely at the warning labels the PMRC intended to use to label albums. Violence—"V"—is broad, so we'll start with what Tipper Gore thought would be an easy target, Twisted Sister's song "Under the Blade." "Under the Blade," however, proved harder to parse than Gore intended. Representations of violence, it turns out, are pervasive throughout literary history. But the song provides a pathway into understanding how metal lyrics work with and as literature. This chapter will look at a song's use of persona, perspective, and pronoun use to show that, whatever else they were arguing about, Tipper Gore and Dee Snider were also arguing about hermeneutics—that is, the interpretation of literary texts. And, in retrospect, those songs about violence were also about another topic that the PMRC missed entirely, violence's flipside: justice.

Too Much Gore

Twisted Sister frontman Dee Snider sat before the United States Senate. Two of his songs had been targeted. In addition to placing "We're Not Gonna Take It" in the PMRC's Filthy Fifteen, Tipper Gore had written an editorial in *New York Newsday*, Snider's hometown paper, called "The Smut and Sadism of Rock." In it, she declared that "sadomasochism, bondage, incest, and rape are out of the closet and into the lyrics," referring to the Twisted Sister song "Under the Blade" as an example, along with lyrics from Judas Priest and Mötley Crüe.[3]

In response to accusations about "Under the Blade," Snider said that "the lyrics [Tipper Gore] quoted have absolutely nothing to do with these topics. On the contrary the words in question are about surgery and the fear that it instills in people." Then, near the end of his testimony, Snider said, "The beauty of literature, poetry, and music is that they leave room for the audience to put its own imagination, experiences, and dreams into the words. The examples I cited earlier showed clear evidence of Twisted Sister's music being completely misinterpreted and unfairly judged by supposedly well-informed adults."[4]

We'll get to how Gore and Snider interpreted "Under the Blade," and why it matters. But let's start with some ideas about the speaker and the reader in literature and how they might help us with Twisted Sister and the bigger problem that the PMRC raised, which is metal's sometimes violent lyrical content and the possibilities of interpretation.

Although the subject of the hearing was warning labels for albums and, for Snider, the specter of censorship, the rhetoric was that of literary criticism. Tipper Gore and Dee Snider were addressing questions like the ones I've asked thousands of college students since I began teaching in 1994. To paraphrase Raymond Carver's story, *What do we talk about when we talk about literature?* Or, in this case, *What do we talk about when we talk about heavy metal?* How do we talk about it? What is the reader's or listener's role in creating meaning? What does a well-supported reading—that is, a personal, critical interpretation—sound like? How significant is the writer's intention? What should we then do with our interpretations?

To get there, let's start with a question: who is the speaker of "Under the Blade"? We know who the singer is. For literary analysis, the distinction between the perspective of the lyricist/singer and the "I" of the song is crucial, one that might get at the root of Tipper Gore's problem. Or, at least, one of them.

Person and Persona

Here's how Edgar Allan Poe's story "The Tell-Tale Heart" opens: "The old man's hour had come! With a loud yell, I threw open the lantern and leaped into the room. He shrieked once—once only. In an instant I dragged him to the floor, and pulled the heavy bed over him. I then smiled gaily, to find the deed so far done."[5]

No reasonable person should read "The Tell-Tale Heart" and wonder whether the author himself, the real person named Edgar Allan Poe, has actually committed a murder, just as no one should read "Goldilocks and the Three Bears" and wonder when the Brothers Grimm met talking bears.[6] The story is written from the first-person perspective, using the "I" pronoun, but we understand that the conventions of fiction dictate that the speaker is a persona and, in this case, an unreliable narrator who doesn't understand himself or his own actions. The narrator, never named, gets fixated on the appearance of an old man's eye and decides he has to kill him. But the narrator implores, again and again, that he is not mad: "would a madman have been so wise as this?" he tells us of his careful planning. When the police investigate the eventual murder, the narrator almost gets away with it, too, but he hears a noise he takes to be the beating of the dead man's heart. When the police can't hear it, he thinks they're mocking him, and, in the story's last line, admits his crime: "'Villains!' I shrieked, 'dissemble no more! I admit the deed!—tear up the planks!—here, here!—it is the beating of his hideous heart!'" It's a pretty metal story, so much so that Metal Church adapted it for their song "Of Unsound Mind."

The reader is expected to understand what is happening more clearly than the narrator himself—that the heart is the man's own, and its beating signifies his unconscious sense of guilt and anxiety. It could be supernatural—truly the dead man's heart beating beyond the grave—but that interpretation seems less plausible, and less interesting. And the least plausible interpretation would be to think the story advocates murder, even though it's presented through the perspective of the murderer. It is, arguably, a cautionary tale of conscience, but with the thrills of horror. A summary—"A madman kills someone for a bizarre reason but gives himself up because he feels guilty and anxious"—gives us none of what makes the story interesting to read. I read this story when I was 11 years old and got it.

But a song—most songs, at least—is not a story. Is it a poem? Poetic convention refers to the poem's "I" as "the speaker" so as not to conflate the poem's voice with the poet personally. Let's stick with Poe, who was a poet as well as fiction writer. And let's pick a similarly metal poem, the first stanza of "The Raven":

> Once upon a midnight dreary, while I pondered, weak and weary,
> Over many a quaint and curious volume of forgotten lore—
> While I nodded, nearly napping, suddenly there came a tapping,
> As of some one gently rapping, rapping at my chamber door.
> "'Tis some visitor," I muttered, "tapping at my chamber door—
> Only this and nothing more."[7]

Again, it's powerful enough that artists from Alan Parsons Project through Stevie Nicks through Black Rebel Motorcycle Club were inspired to write songs based on it.

On the one hand, the verse is simple enough to be understood straightforwardly, which is why so many middle- and high-school teachers like it: a bird shows up and starts tapping on the speaker's door. Yet there are many ways to think about it: the "once upon a . . ." plays on hopeful fairy-tale expectation, met with the ironic reality of "midnight dreary"; the alliteration ("weak and weary"; "nodded, nearly napping," and more); the rhymes, both at the ends of lines ("lore," "door," "more") and internally ("napping," "rapping," "tapping"). We haven't even gotten to the good stuff—the continued play on "-ore" rhymes, including the alluded "sorrow for the lost Lenore" and the appearance of the Raven itself, speaking: "Quoth the Raven 'Nevermore.'" The poem raises questions: the way it makes the reader feel, the powerful ending, the Goth and metal intertwined themes of love, death, and scary birds, and much more.

But there are wrong questions as well: *Did this really happen? Did Edgar Allan Poe talk to a bird? Will this poem be a bad influence on children?*

Maybe I'm being unfair. And Poe *has* been banned in schools by parents worried "that stories such as Poe's 'The Tell-Tale Heart' . . . , which [has] some violent scenes, may 'plant the seeds' of crime, depression and disobedience in youngsters" even though there's no evidence that such a thing has ever happened or is even possible.[8] In keeping with the PMRC, in the 2020s, book challenges are rising. Maybe I shouldn't be facetious.

Song lyrics can be less clear-cut even than poetry. Even in my Preface, Introduction, and first chapter, when quoting lyrics, sometimes I use "the speaker"; at other times, I'll use the singer's name. But is the person singing the words also "the speaker," like in poetry—again, a persona, from the Latin, for "mask"? Is the singer the "I"? Is the lyricist, if different? Is it a whole band, collectively? Is it possible, especially with figures as famous as David Lee Roth, Ozzy Osbourne, or Dee Snider, that the person and the persona overlap? After all, for fans, the possibility that the person and the persona of their stars are willfully entangled is exciting.

Literary ideas are instructive here. Rock stars are real people, not characters. But they also play and cultivate characters, even if the characters they're playing are versions of themselves.[9] David Bowie, Bob Dylan, and Lady Gaga are prime examples: they use different names and costumes to convey personas, yet, somehow, these personas make them feel more, not less, authentic. Bowie, born David Robert Jones, is a chameleon: Aladdin Sane, Major Tom, Ziggy Stardust, and more. But each act fits the music, and fans don't feel contradictions. The 2007 film *I'm Not There* is inspired by Bob Dylan—born Robert Allen Zimmerman, his chosen name borrowed from poet Dylan Thomas— and features six different actors to convey Dylan's different personas. Lady Gaga—born Stefani Joanne Angelina Germanotta—has so many personas tied to so many looks and videos that she seems most herself acting in the film *A Star Is Born*, where, ironically, she is most straightforwardly playing a role.

Metal stars, outside of Tobias Forge's various Cardinal characters in Ghost, don't usually have Bowie-, Dylan-, or Gaga-esque multiple personas. They are not the roles they play onstage, but they're not quite affectless authors separate from their fictional characters, either. They're something else. As often as I cite the many metal memoirs that have accumulated over the years, I still find it difficult to assess how reliable they are. Like Tipper Gore's book, several memoirs also function like stories with unreliable narrators, like Poe's unnamed "Tell-Tale Heart" narrator, whether it's because of the drug use they recount, the length of time passed, or the fallibility of human memory. Not to mention that many of them are written with ghostwriters, and I don't mean Tobias Forge.

But often, it's more.

David Lee Roth and Mötley Crüe are instructive. Dave is in the business of self-mythologizing. He says what the character of "David Lee Roth" is supposed to say—think "Bop bozadee bozadee bop zitty bop." Mötley Crüe are even trickier. *The Dirt*, arguably the most fun and filthiest of the metal memoirs, is told collectively, switching between narrators, mainly the four band members but also Tom Zutaut, who signed the Crüe to Elektra Records in 1982, manager Doc McGhee, and many more. It's an homage to Wilkie Collins's 1859 novel *The Woman in White*, an early mystery and Sensation novel, which itself was influenced by Collins's friend Charles Dickens and his complex plotting. *The Dirt*—or, for that matter, Collins's *The Woman in White*—does not read like a Modernist novel with multiple narrators, like the works of William Faulkner, to make a statement about the fragmentation of story, memory, or the mind itself, or about order versus chaos. It is an extension of the epistolary novels that preceded it, such as Samuel Richardson's *Pamela* (1740) and *Clarissa* (1749), using letters from different characters as a way to create and develop tension between characters and in the narrative itself.

The result, then, is less a memoir or even a mystery than a kind of modern folk tale. Maybe a rock tale, so much so that *Dirt* co-writer Neil Strauss is the book's true author more than any of its actual narrators, since it is his structure that creates the story. (The same is true of the oral histories *Louder Than Hell* and *Nöthin' But a Good Time*.) Rock stars were the 1980s versions of Paul Bunyan, Davy Crocket, John Henry, and Johnny Appleseed. They lived larger than life, on or even past the cusp of credulity. And they refused to be archetypal heroes. They were closer to those equally American trickster figures like Tricky Fox and Brer Rabbit, getting into trouble of their own making and then miraculously getting out, only for the solution to be the cause of the next round of trouble. Not that their lives were not real. They were real in the way stories are real, to be told and retold, in interviews, memoirs, other people's memoirs, and songs, emblazoned and embellished to each teller's purpose and sensibility, growing larger with each recitation. As Salman Rushdie said, in the quotation that serves as the opening epigraph of the introduction, "Literature is where I go to explore the highest and lowest places in human society and in the human spirit, where I hope to find not absolute truth but the truth of the tale, of the imagination and of the heart."[10] We listen to music for the same reason: to find the truth of the imagination and of the heart.

We already use another literary word for our greatest stars: "legend." Legends are based on true events, but they aren't, by definition, real themselves. They're reality writ large, bigger and better. And, often enough, our best legends, from Gilgamesh to Heracles, from King Arthur to Bloody Mary, are teeming with violence.

Crüel Intentions?

Was Tipper Gore wrong to think that "Under the Blade" depicted "sadomasochism, bondage, incest, and rape"? In short, yes. There is nothing in the lyrics to suggest incest or rape at all. The song does include the line, "Your hands are tied, your legs are strapped, a light shines in your eyes," which Gore quoted out of order in her editorial, as Snider pointed out.[11] Is this "bondage"? Only in the most basic sense of being tied down, but not in the word's traditional denotation of either slavery or as a consensual sexual practice involving restraints, usually associated with a term like "sadomasochism." The line supports Snider's authorial take that it's about surgery.

As a teacher and reader, though, I'm cautious about the word "about." Certainly, songs are *about* topics, but here, and online, often modified under the clickbait headline "*really* about," the word can be reductive, a deliberate conversation ender. This is where Snider is on shakier interpretive ground: "the words in question are *about* surgery and the fear that it instills in people . . . " That's the stated intention. Novelist Michael Chabon distinguishes "two kinds of aboutness . . . One kind is on the plot level: what happens . . . Then there is the other kind of aboutness. There's this question of what is the story About with a capital A. Thematically, that is."[12] When Snider said, "As the creator of 'Under the Blade,' I can say categorically that the only sadomasochism, bondage, and rape in this song is in the mind of Ms. Gore," he certainly brought down the house and ended the conversation, which was his reasonable aim. And the song could imply fear of surgery. But it can be about other things, too, and the author's intention isn't the end of the conversation.

Shouldn't Dee Snider be the ultimate authority on Dee Snider's lyrics? This is what I, as a professor, think of as the *Back to School* problem. In *Back to School* (1986), Rodney Dangerfield plays his usual self-deprecating schlub, but in this version, "Thornton Melon" is a rich businessman schlub who enrolls in college later along with his college-age son. When Melon needs to write an essay on the novels of Kurt Vonnegut, famous for *Slaughterhouse-Five* (1969), *Cat's Cradle* (1963), and many others, Melon hires Vonnegut himself to do the work. Vonnegut's cameo alone is funny, but the punchline is even better: Melon does poorly on the assignment, not just because the professor knows right away that someone else wrote it, but also because "whoever did write [this paper] doesn't know the first thing about Kurt Vonnegut."[13] The joke, I suppose, is on the professor, who, we understand through dramatic irony, only thinks she is an authority on Vonnegut's work. Or worse, she (unknowingly) believes that she knows Vonnegut's novels better than Vonnegut himself.

Literary theory, though, has been working against the idea of the author as final authority for decades. Snider's other point—"The beauty of literature, poetry, and music is that they leave room for the audience to put its own imagination, experiences, and dreams into the words"—alludes to this better way of thinking. The idea that the audience—reader, viewer, listener—creates meaning was cogently argued in 1968 by critic Roland Barthes in "The Death of the Author." It sounds V for Violent, but it's figurative. Barthes wanted readers to break from an "image of literature . . . tyrannically centered on the author, his person, his life."[14] Barthes was working against the assumption that authorial power creates a single, correct interpretation: "The explanation of a work is always sought in the man or woman who produced it, as if it were always in the end, through more or less transparent allegory of the fiction, the voice of a single person, the author 'confiding' in us."[15] Barthes preferred to think of the text as "a tissue of quotations drawn from the innumerable centres of culture."[16] *The Soft Machine*, *The Dirt*, and the oral histories of metal are literally constructed from quotations drawn from if not innumerable then at least polyglot centers of culture.

Some authors really are dead, needless to say. Unlike Vonnegut, who was alive in 1986, Shakespeare can't tell you that your Freudian reading of *Hamlet* wasn't what he intended. How could it be? Freud wasn't around when *Hamlet* was written. But Dee Snider *can* still tell you—and by "you" I mean Tipper Gore—that your reading of "Under the Blade" isn't what he intended. And, unlike in *Back to School*, it would not be a joke. If students worry that they're not entitled to form opinions about Shakespeare because his work is centuries old, endlessly discussed, and firmly canonical, they can feel equally constrained by the living author, because they can still be proven wrong, if the author says so.

Snider's intention may have been an operation allegory, but aside from the reference to a "doctor," in the ambiguous phrase "doctor's or mind"—suggesting that none of it is real?—the other descriptions sound much more like street violence than surgery. Think "You're cornered in the alley way, you know you're all alone." "Under the Blade" could be about a dream-like, horror version of the hospital, but, since it's "under the blade" and not "under the knife," as the phrase goes, a reasonable interpretation could also include that the song narrates the moments before being murdered—or at least attacked—by a Jack the Ripper-style serial killer. Patients simply don't show up for an operation when "You know you're not going home tonight," by which the speaker does not mean inpatient surgery.

You Probably Think This Song Is about You

The lyrics to this tale of ostensible violence raise two important issues related to the study of literature—and, by extension, the study of lyrics, and heavy metal lyrics in particular.

First, as I've been addressing, *who is the speaker?* The song, unlike most literary narrators, never uses the pronoun "I," but the viewpoint of someone witnessing the violence is implied throughout. The ambiguity is part of what makes it literary. What seems like a straightforward song, both musically and lyrically, is open to interpretation. Is it a kind of metaphor, as Snider suggests—the doctor as assailant, cutting into the body? Sure. Is the speaker also the assailant? An observer? The repeated title in the chorus, "Under the Blade," certainly sounds violent, but the whole thing also feels fantastic, imagined. Is this a Gothic-influenced dream expressing fear, but, in reversal, taking the perpetrator's point of view? It's not spelled out. This openness is a good thing—unless you've been called into a Senate hearing.

As we'll see with many other songs, the ambiguity of whether the speaker is describing the violent events or perpetuating them is an important one. It's complicated further by the fact that Dee Snider is singing them, making it appear as though he, personally, is the narrator, as opposed to that Edgar Allan Poe story, when the voice narrating is the one in our heads.

Perhaps the most important word of the song, though, isn't the oft-repeated and obvious use of "blade," or "I," which is only ever implied, but an easily overlooked, although even more repeated word: "you."

"Who are YOU?" the Caterpillar asked Alice in *Alice In Wonderland*. More accurately, if less grammatically, who *is* "you"? That is, in addition to the problem of the song's persona, its "I," and its singer or writer, we have the implicit inclusion of the listener.

"You" has been very busy, at least going by songs. Other genres, even poetry, despite its seeming similarity to lyrics, shy away from using "you." You can count on one hand the number of famous novels written in the second person: *You, Bright Lights, Big City,* Italo Calvino's *If on a Winter's Night a Traveler*, a single chapter of Jennifer Egan's *A Visit From the Goon Squad*, and a handful of others. Instruction manuals and self-help books use "you" aplenty. Nonfiction uses direct address as an occasional rhetorical device ("You can count on one hand . . . ," above), but it doesn't feel like it's for or about the reader in a personal way. That said, many songs are about *you*, or at least it feels that way to us. Carly Simon's "You're So Vain" got it just right.

Here is a brief rundown of some famous rock and metal song titles that include the word *you*:

- "We Will Rock You," Queen
- "You Shook Me All Night Long," AC/DC
- "You Really Got Me," Van Halen/The Kinks
- "Rock You Like a Hurricane" and "Still Loving You," Scorpions
- "You Give Love a Bad Name," Bon Jovi
- "Burnin' For You," Blue Öyster Cult
- "Without You," Mötley Crüe
- "I Hate Myself for Loving You," Joan Jett

- "To Be With You," Mr. Big
- "I Want You to Want Me," Cheap Trick
- "You Could Be Mine," Guns N' Roses
- "You Better Run," Pat Benatar
- "(You Can Still) Rock in America," Night Ranger (parentheses count)
- "You Can't Kill Rock & Roll," Ozzy Osbourne

These represent a fraction of "you"-titled songs. I got these just from my own iTunes library. Pull up your own playlists and see for yourself. And no list can include all the songs that revolve around "you" but don't necessarily place the word itself in the title, since that would encompass thousands of songs. *You* had to be a big shot.

Who is—are—"you," then?

In the songs about rocking itself—"We Will Rock You," "Rock You Like a Hurricane"—the "you" really seems to mean "you"—that is, the listener, the audience. It's a promise from the band to the fans. But even a seemingly straightforward bop like "We Will Rock You" gets complicated fast. Once we get past the opening chorus, the first line—"Buddy, you're a boy, make a big noise"—is not directly addressing the audience at all.[17] I don't have blood in my face, for example, and I certainly hope I'm not a big disgrace. And as the song develops, from the boy, to the young man, to the old man, it feels more and more like a call, couched in the language of the riddle of the Sphynx, for maintaining humility, far less raucous than the anthemic, sing- and stomp-along chorus would suggest. Maybe it's all just an impressionistic tone poem, with the sounds of the words more important than their meanings, but there are still a lot of instances of "you" to contend with.

Sometimes the "you" is adversarial. Lots of Billy Joel songs seem to fall into this category: certainly "Big Shot," but also "Pressure," "You May Be Right," to an extent "You're Only Human," and others. But for metal, the chorus of Ozzy's "You Can't Kill Rock and Roll" sums up the approach: "Leave me alone, don't want your promises no more / 'Cause rock 'n' roll is my religion and my love / Won't ever change, may think it's strange /You can't kill rock 'n' roll, it's here to stay."[18] And yet the verses and pre-chorus opt for a more sinister, almost conspiratorial "they": "How many times can they fill me with lies and I listen again?" to "And they don't really know even what they're talkin' about." Musically, it's one of Ozzy's dreamier songs, like he's in a sad daze.

Kiss's "Crazy Nights"—not one of their dreamier songs but straight-up radio-rock—keeps the scheming "they" and creates a final verse that's practically a case study in the rhetoric of pronoun use in a rock song. I've put each pronoun in bold to show the effectiveness.

> And **they** try to tell **us** that **we** don't belong,
> But that's alright, **we**'re millions strong,
> **You** are **my** people, **you** are **my** crowd,
> This is **our** music, **we** love it loud![19]

This pronoun cycle alone creates a sense of community, from the oppressive outsiders—"they"—versus the more powerful, bigger group of insiders who just need some encouragement courtesy of Paul Stanley's cheerleading, the "we" created by bringing all of "you" together under "our" music. Loudness's "Crazy Nights" is similar and simpler: "Rock and roll crazy night, / You are the heroes tonight."[20]

Judas Priest's "Parental Guidance" also runs the gamut of pronouns but begins with a "you": "You say I waste my life away, / But I live it to the full, / And how would you know anyway? / You're just mister dull," to the chorus: "We don't need no, no, no, no / Parental guidance here."[21] Rob Halford was 35 when the song was released in 1986, so if the "you" is the censor, the "we," including the audience, presumably under 35, becomes the stand-in for the listener.

Stepping away from V for Violence and encroaching on X for Explicit for a moment, the "you" is often a romantic partner. In most of the songs listed above, "you" stands in for "she" and "her." Even in "Rock You Like a Hurricane," one of the big "you" metal choruses, the verse pronouns don't feel like the general audience anymore. They even revert to the third person, representing a woman to have sex with before the speaker (now first person) goes back on the road: "So give her inches and feed her well"; "I've got to leave, it's time for a show."[22] Certainly the "you" of "You Give Love a Bad Name," "Run to You," "Burnin' For You," "I Want You to Want Me," and more are past, current, or prospective romantic partners. But even then, more than a real or single person, the "you" represents a blank character for anyone to project anything onto.

Where does that leave the audience? In short, *involved*. We know we're statistically unlikely to be the "you" of Axl Rose's "You Could Be Mine," but it sounds and feels like he's singing to us. Most of the time, that's a good feeling, even when it's Axl Rose.

But sometimes, for some people, it's not. Before I return to "Under the Blade," let's look at a different controversial song, from 2013, Robin Thicke's "Blurred Lines." It was a huge hit, but also had its detractors, and I believe that much of it came down to this line: *I know you want it*. It's pretty damning out of context, especially the way I used *sinister italics*. Like "Under the Blade," the words are intended to be listened to as part of the song; it's not a work of literature for the eyes on a page, but rather sounds for the ears. And "Blurred Lines" is a catchy, upbeat R&B song: melodic, playful, even a little corny. Not sinister at all.

Stone Temple Pilots' raucous "Sex Type Thing" is much heavier but similar: "You wouldn't want me have to hurt you too, hurt you too," much worse than "I know you want it."[23] And the music to that *is* sinister. The main riff revolves around the flat five interval, the devil in music. (More on that later.) In the song's threats and violence, STP singer Scott Weiland is inhabiting a character, the mind of a rapist, as opposed to *being* that rapist. Taken any other way and he'd be arrested. It's not as clear, though, whether Thicke is using a persona. (The video suggests he's not, unless that's *part of* the persona.) If anything, it's the opposite: we're supposed to feel as though the words are really the singer's, and that the song is supposed to be seductive. Of course, if the *you* in question *doesn't* want it, it's not seductive. It's coercive. Blurred lines indeed.

The use of "you," then, can be inclusive—the listener is involved, in a good way. Or it can feel threatening, unsuspecting. Threatening and unsuspecting are not necessarily bad experiences—think of the joys of roller coasters, or horror films. In fact, the horror film may be the exact analogy.

Rippers, Killers, and Bastards

"Under the Blade" also blurs lines. The "you" is clearly a victim: "You're cornered in the alley way, you know you're all alone, / You know it's gonna end this way, chill goes to the bone."[24] The song itself is fast and galloping, with crunchy minor-key guitars. As much as Dee Snider wants his intention—"the song is about surgery"—to take precedent, the lyrics are certainly open to the interpretation that it's showing an attack: "You've tried to make it to the front, you're pinned against the side, / A monster stands before you now, its mouth is open wide." (Dental surgery?) What Tipper Gore was reacting to, then, is precisely the song's appeal—it's violent imagery.

The thing is this, though: it doesn't matter if the song is about a violent assault, or even bondage, at all. These themes are, in fact, completely in keeping with the literary experience. Its violence is its virtue. Twisted Sister's fans *want that feeling*—of being part of the story, a safe way to channel and control their feelings of helplessness in the world, and the possible real violence around them, in the safe environs of the song's metal fantasy. The "you" may be the victim, but it's using the immersive experience of the music and lyrics to mentally and emotionally transport the listener into a safe place, where the assault is aural and consensual.

Tipper Gore wasn't just taking on "Under the Blade" and Dee Snider. At least twenty-five movies are based on Jack the Ripper, as well as at least another twenty-five novels, not including other forms of media. Dracula may have been partially inspired by Jack the Ripper. Iron Maiden's "Killers" is from the perspective of another knife-wielding maniac. Judas Priest even has a song called "The Ripper," from 1976, featuring lyrics that are reasonably similar to "Under the Blade":

> I'm sly and I'm shameless,
> Nocturnal and nameless,
> Except for "The Ripper,"
> Or if you like, "Jack the Knife."[25]

Presumably, Tipper Gore hadn't heard it, since "Eat Me Alive," the Judas Priest song that did make their Filthy Fifteen list is, in my mind, positively poetic and erudite in comparison: "Wrapped tight around me like a second flesh hot skin, / Cling to my body as the ecstasy begins, / Your wild vibrations got me shooting from the hip, / Crazed and insatiable let rip."[26] They're still thinking about ripping. And where the PMRC read violence, fans felt excitement, pleasure. Literary philosopher Roland Barthes, quoted for his idea about the death of the author, also posited the term and concept of *jouissance*, the pleasure of the text: the bliss a reader experiences that, in its French pun, is analogous to orgasm. Judas Priest simply dispenses with the analogy.

After "Under the Blade" and "Eat Me Alive" (we'll get to "We're Not Gonna Take It" shortly), the other metal song that the PMRC objected to under the auspices of violence was Mötley Crüe's "Bastard." Tipper Gore cited the opening lyrics, which are similar to "Under the Blade" but even more barebones, lazy rhymes in an inconsistent rhyme scheme: "Out go the lights, / In goes my knife, / Pull out his life, / Consider that bastard dead."[27] The PMRC appeared not to comment on the last line of the verse, "You're the king of the sleaze, don't you try to rape me," and, later in the chorus, "We won't get screwed again," lines with no apparent context in the song. Lyricist Nikki Sixx later said, "It was about a manager. So when I write a line like 'don't try to rape me,' I'm saying don't try to screw with me. Don't try to take what we've worked our whole lives for."[28] Nirvana released "Rape Me" in 1991 to make a similar point and to similar controversy, although not a congressional hearing.

Like "Under the Blade," "Sex Type Thing," and "The Ripper," the first-person "my" of "Bastard" is the assailant's perspective; the "you" is the victim's. And as Dee Snider says of "Under the Blade," "Bastard" is also metaphorical. The knives in both songs stand in for something else: for Snider, the surgeon's scalpel and a tomophobic patient; for Sixx, a business-related fantasy-revenge scenario. Not that a song called "Eat Me Alive" aspires to be literary, but, like "Love Gun," "Eat Me Alive" is an extended metaphor of the phallus as weapon, a male power fantasy that Shakespeare wasn't above punning in *Romeo and Juliet* when Sampson unsheathes his sword and declares, with macho gusto, "My naked weapon is out."[29]

These three targeted songs, then, are, at best, dubious examples to highlight violence in rock lyrics. Jack-the-Ripper-inspired music was already so commonplace by 1984, eight years after "The Ripper" and two years after "Under the Blade," that *This Is Spinal Tap* used it as a throwaway joke. Upon retirement, Tap singer/guitarist David St. Hubbins and bassist Derek Smalls would finally have time to get back to working on "a rock musical based on the life of Jack the Ripper, *Saucy Jack*."[30]

But what if a song isn't a metaphor? What if the song is just about killing? The problem for censors is that even if a song has lyrics about killing, it is not itself ever a murder. It has transformed the idea of killing into a work of art. The line, "I'm gonna force you at gun point" from "Eat Me Alive" sounds bad, except that no one did that. The "I" is a persona. The song is imaginary. The supposed violence in lyrics becomes a version of René Magritte's famous painting "The Treachery of Images," an image of a pipe inscribed with the words, "Ceci n'est pas une pipe," French for "This is not a pipe."[31] It's not. It's a painting of a pipe. Jasper Johns would do something similar in his American flag paintings, which were not flags; they were paintings, symbolic representations of something that is already a symbolic representation. No matter how much Tipper Gore wanted "Under the Blade" to be an example of violence, it could only ever be a representation—and therefore, what it represented was open to interpretation.

I suggested that the PMRC's examples were dubious. The problem is that any meaningful example becomes more complex than a single-word, reductive label. And the label was the one thing that was not a metaphor: "Violence," intended to be stickered as "V," the single letter they wanted on the albums, as though they read *The Scarlet Letter*, turned the letter upside down, and, in keeping, took the opposite lesson. Even a brief rundown of possible '80s metal songs that would have been labeled violent demonstrates the problem:

- Slayer, "Angel of Death": borrows its title and images from Nazi torturer Josef Mengele; the descriptions of violence are all based on actual historical occurrences. While the lyrics maintain moral neutrality, the music is heavy and brutal, in keeping with the depictions.
- Metallica, "Creeping Death": based on the biblical plagues in the story of Passover. The chant of "Die!" represents the final plague, the killing of the firstborn.
- Megadeth, "Killing Is My Business. . . and Business Is Good!": a thrash update of AC/DC's "Dirty Deeds Done Dirt Cheap," featuring clever wordplay and based on the Marvel antihero The Punisher.
- Black Sabbath, "Killing Yourself to Live": a quasi-existentialist critique of modernity with more ironic wordplay. Life is suffering, something the PMRC hearings confirmed.
- The Misfits, "Die, Die My Darling"; Mötley Crüe, "You're All I Need"; Guns N' Roses, "Used to Love Her": three different songs about killing loved ones, played for comic horror and cosmic irony. Unreliable narrators are driven to hurt the ones they love most. All three use the same musical/lyrical juxtaposition: the lyrics are about killing, but the pop melodies are relentlessly catchy. Crüe even use a 1950s ballad chord progression, and G N' R go for an acoustic campfire sing-along. It's the opposite of "Angel of Death"—bitter lyrics with sweet sounds. It works either way.
- And, to come full circle back to Edgar Allan Poe, Metal Church, "Of Unsound Mind": once again, based on Poe's story "The Tell-Tale Heart," but worth bringing back because of its shifts between third and first person. "How can he stand to bear the pounding of his heart?" and "It is the eye / That will destroy him" are in the third person. But then, in keeping with the story, "When will it end? What can I do? / Who will believe? Why is this fear

haunting me?"³² Between the shifting perspectives, the lyrics show the effect of the on-the-nose title.

The PMRC simply did not give metal the credit it deserved as art. It's no surprise that at the Senate hearing, Al Gore and others were blindsided by Dee Snider's intelligence, something he counted on and pressed to his advantage. And yet, for me, in retrospect, reviewing the video testimony now as a literature professor and not as a 13-year-old who has just started listening to metal, I can see that Dee Snider's and Tipper Gore's disagreement, once again, boiled down to questions of literary analysis: who is the song's speaker? What is its rhetoric? What are possible interpretations, and how do the music and lyrics together provide the basis for them? What is the role of the writer—and the listener—in creating that meaning? What is the evidence a listener can use to support an interpretation? Great questions for the classroom; bad questions for Congress.

The PMRC's consistent answers to these questions suggest that they thought the artists and songs were too dumb to make use of speakers or personas; the "I" could only be the literal singer of the song, "Twisted Sister" or "Mötley Crüe," gleefully singing about stabbing people. The songs were taken as murders themselves, or at least incitement to murders, never as metaphors, fantasies, escapism, irony, or even art. The audience, they presumed, was also too dumb, not just too young, to know the difference. It is the same moral panic that fueled the backlash against *Dungeons & Dragons*.³³ Whatever they were thinking, the members of the PMRC were not trying to stop violence. There were never any credible claims of violence. They were trying to stop the imagination itself. They were not trying to protect children. They were attacking them. (Metaphorically.) They were undermining kids' intelligence, ability to interpret, and inner lives separate from their parental figures. The lyrics looked like they were violent, but they were doing great service and justice to their young listeners. As strange as it might sound, all those songs about killers and blades didn't make a generation of kids feel victimized, "you" pronouns to the contrary. They made them feel powerful.

What Aren't We Gonna Take, Exactly?

No better song illustrates this idea of power than the other Twisted Sister song that the PMRC went after, "We're Not Gonna Take It." During the hearing, the

PMRC showed the video for that song, rather than just the lyrics themselves, inadvertently revealing that the object was never just to warn parents about lyrical content but was always McCarthyite moralism. With Van Halen's "Hot for Teacher" video and the album covers for Def Leppard's *Pyromania*, Wendy O. Williams's *W.O.W.*, and WASP's "Animal (F**k Like a Beast)," the PMRC needed the visual aid, since, as Dee Snider pointed out, there is nothing remotely "V for Violence" in the lyrics to "We're Not Gonna Take It" themselves.

"We're Not Gonna Take It" is even more than a teen anthem. It's an American anthem. Part melody from "O Come, All Ye Faithful," with chord changes reminiscent of "When the Saints Go Marching In," the song is positively rousing and even sounds vaguely patriotic. It also, once again, relies on its pronoun use, all *we* and *our* against the song's adversarial *you*, *us* vs *them* writ loud and proud (with the pronouns again in bold):

We've got the right to choose, and
There ain't no way **we**'ll lose it,
This is **our** life, this is **our** song.
We'll fight the powers that be, just
Don't pick on **our** destiny, 'cause
You don't know **us**, **you** don't belong.[34]

The *you* is never specified, and it doesn't need to be. In the video, the *you* is the father figure (paging Dr. Freud), played by Mark Metcalf, reenacting his role as an ROTC officer in *Animal House* (1978). That reprisal suggests "you" could be any oppressive authority figure, which is very much the point. Similarly, the referent or antecedent for "it" isn't defined, either. It doesn't matter. The Who had a song of the same title, the last song on *Tommy* (1969), but in context, it completes that concept album's story arc. And even without the rock opera, its lyrics are pointedly political. The brilliance of Twisted Sister's lyrics is their simplicity. They can be applied to anything. And they were.

Dee Snider later approved of the song's use during a 2018 Oklahoma teachers' strike.[35] In 2022, he endorsed Ukrainians' use to protest Russia's invasion. It has appeared in at least twelve movies, from the battle scene of *Ready Player One* (2018) to the ironic battle cry *against* a rock club by the Tipper Gore stand-in (Kathleen Zeta-Jones) in *Rock of Ages* (2012).

Its ambiguity, though, left it open for use as a campaign song by Paul Ryan in 2016. Snider asked him to stop using it. Or for Donald Trump; Snider gave, and then retracted, permission. Or for anti-maskers during the COVID-19 pandemic, which Snider vehemently disliked. Contrasting Ukrainians and anti-maskers, Snider wrote on Twitter, "Well, one use is for a righteous battle against oppression; the other is an infantile feet-stomping against an inconvenience."[36] That same ambiguity left it open to the PMRC's take on the song as well. As Snider said of Tipper Gore in 1985, "The examples I cited earlier showed clear evidence of Twisted Sister's music being completely misinterpreted and unfairly judged by supposedly well-informed adults."[37] You'd think a song called "We're Not Gonna Take It" would be unambiguous. And yet here we are, forty years later, debating who exactly *we* are, and what *it* "we're" not gonna take.

The song is an anthem for the oppressed against subjugation. The problem, then, once again becomes one of audience identification. Tipper Gore and the anti-maskers also thought *they* weren't going to take it anymore. What began, for the PMRC, as straightforward labeling of violence isn't even straightforward for a song called "Under the Blade."

Violence in art is not violence; it's art, as I said. But because it's art, it's also emblematic of more than violence. And what, just beneath the surface, it emblematizes is, often enough, an even bigger problem than violence alone: it also alludes to the problem of justice, and injustice. We're not gonna take it, sure. But, as Faith No More would later ask, "What is it?" And, unanswered in the song but just as important: *why* aren't we gonna take it?

Violent Use Brings Violent Plans: From Violence to Justice

Heavy metal is, as we all know, fascinated with violence. Cartoon violence, like the video for Twisted Sister's "We're Not Gonna Take It," as Snider testified. Horror movie violence, like Twisted Sister's "Under the Blade." Theatrical violence, like Iron Maiden's "Flash of the Blade" and "The Duellists," in the tradition of Shakespeare's frequent use of blades with bloodshed and inspiring the later epic battle songs of bands like Dragonforce. There is no *Romeo and Juliet*, *Macbeth*, *Hamlet*, or *Henry IV* without sword fighting and death. This chapter's opening quotation, from *Macbeth*, and Macbeth's vision of "a dagger which I see before me, / The handle toward my hand? Come, let me clutch thee"—along with that play's many images of blood and bloodshed, especially Lady Macbeth's "out damned spot" soliloquy—connects metal's use of violence as rooted in the literary tradition.[38] But again, just as importantly, it is not just the mere mention of swords or blood in both literature and heavy metal. It is the ways in which both use their art to help us understand them as powerful symbols. *Macbeth*—and *Hamlet*, and *Romeo and Juliet*—enact violence, even entertain us with it. But they are also, as a result, tragedies.

Heavy metal, true to its American working-class roots, has representations of what looks like real-life, not Renaissance, violence. Twisted Sister's lesser-known "Horror Teria: Captain Howdy/Street Justice" (1984), tells a story of a child murderer and his comeuppance. "Horror Teria" is not played for the laughs or drama of their other songs. The flipside of all this violence, then, is an overarching concern with what happens next, after the violence—with justice. Think of it as *after* the blade.

In addition to the influence of *The Road Warrior* and *Escape from New York*, 1980s metal—and comic book characters like The Punisher—was also influenced by the films *Death Wish* (1974) and *Dirty Harry* (1970) from the previous decade. These were violent revenge dramas, a literary form that goes back at least to the 1600s and hit its stride with *Hamlet*. Heavy metal even got its own Goth version of this story in the film *The Crow*, released in 1994 but based on the comics that James O'Barr began in 1981. These films stem from a sense that law and order has broken down, and that the only way to achieve justice is to take it into one's own hands. 1970s and 80s pop culture—and politics—played on not just fears of rising crime, but of the inability, or even corruption, of the institutions that were meant to combat it. Songs like "Under the Blade" and the other riffs on Jack the Ripper reflect and redirect general violent sensibilities, purposing the images of knives and alleyways for visceral but, even in 1984, familiar impact on the listener.

But "Horror Teria: Captain Howdy/Street Justice" is more specific. Inverting "Under the Blade," "Street Justice" features another act of knife-wielding violence: "It happened in the broad daylight, / So unexpected came the knife, / A child's scream sliced through the air, / But no one came or seemed to care, no."[39] And instead of what seems like the perpetrator's perspective, "Street Justice" shows the community's response, issuing a call for communal retribution.

The need for street justice stems from systemic failure: "The man was caught and brought before a judge / . . . His lawyer screamed 'you must set him free,' / And off he went on a technicality, / Since the law don't seem to care, then don't you think it's only fair."[40] Dee Snider was presenting the flipside of the PMRC's own call to action: parents protecting children from a perceived threat. After all, Snider mentioned that he himself was also a parent in his statement.

Twisted Sister, however, did not form or foment a mob. They wrote a song about it. And, like "Under the Blade" and other Jack the Ripper-inspired songs, this one is a fantasy as well, if of a different sort: the crime is clear cut, the court corrupt, the street justice swift and fair. It, once again, in literary and Freudian fashion, represents the fear and the wish: the fear of violence against the innocent, and the wish for uncomplex retribution against the guilty. The PMRC wanted the same, and seemed surprised to discover that life, art, and human beings were more complicated than a song about someone named "Captain Howdy" or called "Under the Blade." This is a good thing—unless you've decided to call for a Senate hearing.

Not every version of justice is street justice, though. Metallica's 1988 album *. . .And Justice for All* followed the death of bassist Cliff Burton in 1986. This was no drug overdose or suicide, no mysterious circumstances, to use the phrase associated with many stars' overdose-or-suicide intrigues. Like Randy Rhoads, Burton was killed in an accident while on tour. He died so senselessly, so young at 24 that he didn't even see 27, the fabled age at which rock stars famously die. After all their imaginary songs about exotic and esoteric deaths, how could the band handle the reality of a true death, from a mundane bus accident?

The answer was to reconsider violence existentially. *. . . And Justice for All* addresses the problem of theodicy, as many philosophers and theologians have done before them. How can evil exist if God is good and omnipotent? In doing so, Metallica developed ideas from previous songs about mere physical violence to loftier themes of social violence. The album doesn't have answers, just explorations. If *Ride the Lightning* demonstrates unfair death and evil in the world, as I will discuss later on, *. . . And Justice for All* raises the question of why that should be. Its answers are wide-ranging but dispiriting: hubris and greed (the title track), authoritarianism ("Eye of the Beholder," practically addressed to the PMRC), McCarthyite witch hunting ("The Shortest Straw" and same), and parental abuse ("Dyers Eve").

Song by song, the album considers the problems of moral violence, and its repercussions, in a more mature way than one might expect from the band that titled their demo *Metal Up Your Ass*. "Blackened" presents a thrashier version of Ozzy's "Revelation (Mother Earth)." If "Fight Fire with Fire," the equivalent opening track on *Ride the Lightning*, was largely descriptive of nuclear war, "Blackened" is poetic and evocative, worrying not just about the end of the human race, but the erasure of human history and all of nature itself, "Throwing all you see / Into Obscurity." What's remarkable, though, is the uneven time signatures throughout the song's verses—it's fast and toe-tapping, but erratic, shifting under one's feet, as disorienting and unsettling as the subject matter.

While "The Frayed Ends of Sanity" continues the perspective of the previous "Welcome Home (Sanitarium)," the breakout song was "One," based on Dalton Trumbo's antiwar novel *Johnny Got His Gun* (1939). Unlike folk music, the genre usually associated with antiwar songs, "One" is not a protest against a current war or to prevent the next war, but as a reminder of a previous war's forgotten consequences, presented through the perspective of a soldier who has been maimed: "Now that the war is through with me, / I'm waking up, I cannot see, / That there's not much left of me."[41] He suffers psychically as much as physically from his erasure of identity. Yet we understand that the song's speaker lost himself figuratively before he lost himself bodily. His loss of agency came from being a soldier in the war itself. Even using the literary convention "speaker" is evocative, since the lyrics make clear that he is no longer capable of speech at all: "Landmine has taken my sight! / Taken my speech!" His "wish for death" feels morally different from that of "Fade to Black," discussed in the next chapter, a question of euthanasia rather than suicide.

By now, though, it's clear that the simplistic, catch-all term "violence" does a great disservice to Metallica's range, but particularly to a song like "One," which is not a mere depiction or glorification of violence—not that there's anything wrong with that. But rather, it challenges the entire philosophical justifications for war by channeling a character through the first person. In its concision and poetry, it is, for me, more effective even than Trumbo's novel.

. . . *And Justice for All*, the song and album, takes the title from the last four words of the Pledge of Allegiance. But the revealing part is not the appropriation itself. It's the use of the ellipsis—the three dots—to alert us to the rest of the Pledge's deliberate omission. The subsequent necessary capitalization of "And," now starting the phrase, places additional emphasis on a word that was supposed to link two words together, but one of them is now gone. The ellipsis erases *liberty*, and as a result, throws *justice* into question. Without liberty, Metallica asks, can there be justice? In isolation, . . . *And Justice for All* becomes an ironic homophone, sounding just like "Injustice for All," as though, maybe, sarcastically, that was the intended meaning all along.

That's a lot for three dots! Considering how Metallica felt about parental warnings, it's no surprise. They included their own sarcastic sticker on *Master of Puppets*, saying, "The only track you probably won't want to play is 'Damage,

Inc.' due to multiple use of the infamous 'F' word. Otherwise, there aren't any 'shits,' 'fucks,' 'pisses,' 'cunts,' 'motherfuckers,' or 'cocksuckers' anywhere on this record."⁴² While unacknowledged, that list comes directly from comedian and free-speech advocate George Carlin's famous monologue, "Seven Words You Can Never Say on Television." Yes, it's a joke, but Metallica understood their cultural history, even if they left off Carlin's seventh word. It must have been an oversight.

Justice in Black and White

It might be surprising to see White Lion, one of the three W bands (with Winger and Warrant) maligned as causing the downfall of '80s metal, singing about violence and justice. Their biggest hit, "Wait," is a pop-metal love song best remembered (by me, anyway) for its excellent guitar solo. While probably unintentional, "The White Lion" was also the name of the very first ship to carry people who would be enslaved from Africa to the colonies, still not yet America, in 1619. Not a great look. That, plus the proliferation of metal bands with the word "white" in their name—Whitesnake, Great White, White Wolf, and, presumably White Lion's main competition, White Tiger—might start to seem like further unintentional racism. (Calling their album *Pride* against a white backdrop, with the "white" of their name above it, suggests more than a mere lion pun, again unintentionally.) On the other hand, there are even more rock, punk, and metal bands with the word "black" in them—Black Sabbath, Black Oak Arkansas, Black Flag, The Black Crows, Black Label Society, and Black Veil Brides. Only the lesser-known band Black Death was playing on the band's actual African-American membership. The rest just know that black is the darkest but coolest color, none more black, as *Spinal Tap* parodied.

And yet, White Lion saw themselves as a political band in ways that their fellow Ws—or, really, any '80s metal bands—did not. "When the Children Cry," from *Pride* (1987), is an acoustic ballad that's not about love, but about being "born into this evil world / Where man is killing man and no one knows just why," with the amazingly depressing chorus, "When the children cry, let them know we tried."⁴³ Their album cover for *Big Game* (1989) features a sad-looking lion hiding in thick brush, with the White House in the distance. "Little Fighter" seems like a take on a spunky love interest—"You were one of a kind, / One who'd never give in"—but darkens: "They took your life but didn't know / That you would never die."⁴⁴ It turns out that the song is taking on the distinctly political and not-fun topic of the Greenpeace boat, The Rainbow Warrior, that was sunk in an act of state terrorism by the French government in 1985.⁴⁵ V for Violence indeed. But this is no fantasy. It was real, and the band is condemning it.

Similarly, "Cry for Freedom" is an anti-apartheid song in support of Nelson Mandela, who was still imprisoned at the time: "Our brother's in prison, / But no crime was ever done, / I call it racism, / Ashamed I face my fellow man."⁴⁶ These stances did not ingratiate White Lion to their record label at the time: Guitarist Vito Bratta was instructed to "tell [singer] Mike Tramp that saving whales doesn't sell albums; leather pants do."⁴⁷ But these songs show the range and complexity of violence as a topic, for a band unfairly branded as superficial because Mike Tramp had amazing cheekbones.

Living Colour managed to get away from band names with either white or black in them. And yet, their status as the only all-African American heavy metal band to break big in the 1980s is not just remarkable on its own. What's even more remarkable is that they wore their identities and politics proudly. Their most popular song, "Cult of Personality" (1988), in addition to its heavy riff and non-stop shred guitar solo, includes samples from Malcolm X, John F. Kennedy, and Winston Churchill. The song is a clear warning against authoritarianism, even when—especially when—it wears an appealing face. But this is not the unnamed, amorphous antiauthoritarianism of "We're Not Gonna Take It." Like the Jack the Ripper songs, "Cult of Personality" is sung from the first-person perspective of the villain, or even the personification of autocracy itself: "I exploit you, still you love me, / I tell you, one and one makes three."⁴⁸ The song's overall infectiousness and title's repetition reinforce precisely the ways in which indoctrination into the cult of personality works.

Finally, as it turns out, in addition to Metallica, a certain other '80s thrash band also liked to include ellipses in its album titles. Megadeth's first three albums all feature them: *Killing Is My Business. . . And Business Is Good* (1985), *Peace Sells. . . But Who's Buying?* (1986), and *So Far, So Good. . . So What!* (1988). Perhaps because founder/singer/guitarist/songwriter Dave Mustaine was so aggrieved at being fired by Metallica, Megadeth has always been preoccupied with the intertwined problems of violence and justice. Unlike his former bandmates, Mustaine tends toward the sarcastic, but he is also more explicitly political.

Most of the lyrics to "Peace Sells" are confrontational, another adversarial "you" vs. another aggrieved "I," with overtones of angry adolescence. But the song builds towards what for me is a sincere question, if snidely delivered: "What do you mean I couldn't be the president / Of the United States of America? Tell me something, / It's still 'we the people,' right?"[49] Like Metallica, Megadeth is throwing our foundational language back at us. The speaker is quoting the preamble to the United States Constitution, but it's another powerful use of pronouns. The United States, for all its flaws and divisions, for a nation that didn't initially allow women to vote and wrote slavery into its Constitution, begins its founding document with the word, the pronoun, "We."[50]

The video for "Peace Sells" is montage as barrage: close-ups of singer Mustaine's angrily enunciating mouth, with rapid, disorienting cuts to the headbanging band, and the headbanging audience, but also street crowds, military operations, and political protests. Then, at the height of intensity, the video shifts and breaks the fourth wall. A father changes the channel on the video that we—and, in the video itself, a teenage metalhead—were just seeing. "What is this garbage you're watching?" the father yells. "I want to watch the news." To which our teen hero replies, "This is the news!" and puts our video back on.[51] The song kicks into double time, and now the images come even faster, overlaying the peace sign, the dollar sign, and various flags with the band and crowd. This is different from the paternal slapstick of "We're Not Gonna Take It," which represents generalized parent/child conflict or, potentially, *any* conflict.

"Peace Sells" is an angry plea for, and from, young people to be taken seriously. MTV must have realized the same, because it used the bass intro for MTV News, and not just because it was an awesome riff. It was a proclamation. The revolution might be televised after all. And, the PMRC's fear of violence to the contrary, it would be peaceful. And not just because peace sells. Because it would consist of visual imagery, music, and language.

Post Script: Vice President Al Gore

By the 1990s, MTV began to embrace politics explicitly. It hired Megadeth's Dave Mustaine as a correspondent to cover the Democratic National Convention. It expanded MTV News for the 1992 presidential election with "Choose or Lose," which looked closely at each of the three candidates. Democratic nominee Bill Clinton would agree to several interviews with MTV, including a town hall of 200 young voters. Independent candidate Ross Perot was also interviewed. In contrast, Republican incumbent George Bush would scoff and disparage MTV before finally acquiescing to an interview 48 hours before the election, when his polling numbers were down. Then he cut the interview short when he didn't like the questions. Bill Clinton won.

At MTV's Inaugural Ball, Bill Clinton announced, "I think everybody here knows that MTV had a lot to do with the Clinton-Gore victory."[52] Thanks to MTV, the platform by which millions of teens got to hear Twisted Sister, Mötley Crüe, Metallica, and Megadeth, Bill Clinton and his running mate, a certain Al Gore, would win the election. Dee Snider, whose videos helped establish MTV as a cultural force in the first place, has since noted, "Metal owes MTV for [its 1980s popularity]. But MTV owes metal."[53] Snider should have gotten a thank-you note from the Gores. He didn't even get an apology.

In 2010, Al and Tipper Gore separated. Dee and Suzette Snider, wed in 1981, are still happily married.

3

D/A for Drugs and Alcohol

Figure 8 Francisco de Goya y Lucientes (1746–1828). Spanish painter. "The Madhouse (Casa de Locos)," 1812–1819. San Fernando Royal Academy of Fine Arts. Madrid, Spain. (Photo by: Prisma/Universal Images Group via Getty Images).

Fame requires every kind of excess. I mean true fame, a devouring neon, not the somber renown of waning statesmen or chinless kings. I mean long journeys across gray space. I mean danger, the edge of every void, the circumstance of one man imparting an erotic terror to the dreams of the republic. Understand the man who must inhabit these extreme regions, monstrous and vulval, damp with memories of violation. Even if half-mad he is absorbed into the public's total madness; even if fully rational, a bureaucrat in hell, a secret genius of survival, he is sure to be destroyed by the public's contempt for survivors. Fame, this special kind, feeds itself on outrage, on what the counselors of lesser men would consider bad publicity—hysteria in limousines, knife

fights in the audience, bizarre litigation, treachery, pandemonium and drugs. Perhaps the only natural law attaching to true fame is that the famous man is compelled, eventually, to commit suicide.
(Is it clear I was a hero of rock 'n' roll?)

Don DeLillo, *Great Jones Street* (1973)[1]

Too much is never enough.

Bon Jovi, "In and Out of Love" (1985)[2]

Since many of metal's supposedly violent lyrics are written from the point of view of a killer, violence as a topic leads more naturally into madness, another of metal's touchstones and an ostensible motivation for the killer's violence, than drugs and alcohol, the next of the PMRC's targets. Madness—or, as we might connect it to today, mental health—is tied to and concomitant with metal's depictions of alcohol and drug use, however, as well as the possibility of suicide, which, separate from the PMRC hearings, was a source of attacks on '80s metal as well. What are metal's connections with the literary themes of addiction, madness, confinement, and suicide? And, if the kids, in retrospect, were never in danger, what if the rock stars themselves were?

This Is Your Brain on Drugs

Putting the band together and the early days of debauchery. The substance-fueled rise to recognition. Fame! And with it, the later stages of depravity. The downturn, attributed in part to drinking and drugs. The band in crisis, also caused by drinking and drugs. The inevitable crash, where the band turns to substances for solace. Finally, the comeback, with the band members clean—or, the end of the band, and sometimes even the true ending of death. The rock & roll *Behind the Music* arc—the rise and the fall—exactly mirrors Aristotle's understanding of how stories work, that faithful high school English parabola of exposition, rising action, climax, falling action, and resolution. Metal's many memoirs and oral histories demonstrate how the cycle of addiction and recovery—the ups and downs, from conflict to resolution, from paradise lost to paradise regained, Freud's child's game of *Fort!* and *Da!*—are the very shape of narrative itself.

It would be easy to fill a chapter—or a book, or several books, once we factor in Mötley Crüe, Ozzy, and Metallica alone—with examples of '80's rock star excesses. Ronald Reagan's other culture war, along with the Cold War, was the War on Drugs. Anyone who came of age in the '80s will remember the famous public service announcement: the frying egg, literal heat instead of metaphorical cold, with the tagline, "This is your brain on drugs." And like the Cold War, America's drug policy was containment—actual incarceration.

The PMRC's targeting of lyrics that refer to drugs and alcohol was of its time, but also harkens back to something more primal, and deeper, than the mere fears of substance abuse alone. The symbolic fears of rock-star drug use were tied into fears about individualism, power, and autonomy—themes we find throughout literature, metal, and adolescence itself. '80s metal artists attempted to represent not just images of drugs, and not just the struggle with mental (and metal) health, but something existential: how does one cope with suffering in life? Despite the chapter title referring to drugs and alcohol, this chapter is, in the end, less about your brain on drugs and more about how metal, like literature, explores yearnings, dread, and the inner workings of the mind itself.

Stranger Things used Metallica's song "Master of Puppets" as the soundtrack for its climactic battle against a mind-invading monster that preyed on teens. It worked. While it's not a proper concept album, many of the songs on *Master of Puppets*, the album, adhere to the title image's theme of relinquishing control—metaphorical puppetry. The title track, discussed in the Preface, features chants of "Master! Master!" On *Stranger Things*, fighting this master meant entering the world of the Upside Down, with its frightening Demobats and its mind-controlling villain, Vecna.

To a hostile 1980s parent, though, Metallica seemed to be the ones in control, the master, metal as its own kind of mind control, a kind of cult. The opening lines of the song do not inspire confidence: "End of passion play, crumbling away, / I'm your source of self-destruction." It's just as Tipper Gore feared.

And, then, worse: "Taste me, you will see / More is all you need, / Dedicated to / How I'm killing you!"[3]

It almost sounds like metal is . . . an addiction.

Except that, once again, the uses of "I" and "you" are a kind of feint. As the song continues, it becomes clear that the "I" is not singer/lyricist James Hetfield, but rather the perspective of *a personification of drugs*. A genuine literary device!

In a heavy metal song! "Master of Puppets" then develops into an extended metaphor, using lines like "Needlework the way," suggesting intravenously injected drugs like heroin, and "Chop your breakfast on a mirror," suggesting cocaine. Drug addiction, not metal, is "Twisting your mind and smashing your dreams." If anything, metal, in the form of this very song, is the cure, or at least the coping mechanism.

Despite the PMRC's concerns that metal was glorifying drug use, many of the most popular songs of the era are solidly anti-drug, even if—or maybe, even because—the bands themselves were using. One of the songs that the Filthy Fifteen labeled for Drug and Alcohol use, Black Sabbath's "Trashed," is straightforwardly against drinking. As singer Ian Gillan—who wrote the lyrics after a drunk-driving mishap—sings during the bridge:

> Ooh Mr. Miracle, you saved me from some pain,
> I thank you Mr. Miracle, I won't get trashed again,
> Ooh can you hear my lies,
> Don't you bother with this fool, just laugh into my eyes.[4]

The song spins a yarn of addiction mixed with self-delusion, ending in what seems like the possibility of the speaker's death at the wheel. Gillan's trademark falsetto shrieks feel scary, and the tempo—which can only be called "driving"— and ominous chorus make the song into what is clearly a cautionary tale. We know that Black Sabbath—and Metallica, and so many more—developed substance abuse problems in real life. It's tempting to say that any representation of drinking and drugs in the songs is, by default, a kind of glorification, even as the lyrics explicitly warn against them. But I think it's more complex, and interesting, than that.

Yes, Hetfield and Gillan were indulging, apparently all the time. But that doesn't negate the lyrical warnings, and it doesn't make them hypocritical. It shows the duality between one's life and one's art, between reality and ambition. The lyrics aspire, even when the lives cannot. In 2004, after driving under the influence again, Gillan would be banned from driving for 16 months. The same year, James Hetfield would enter rehab. He would decide to re-enter in 2019. All I hear or see is laughter, laughing at my cries.

The only other "Drug and alcohol use" song from the PMRC's Filthy Fifteen is Def Leppard's "High 'n' Dry (Saturday Night)." The song is not a cautionary tale, unlike, say, "Me and My Wine," from the same album, where the verse contradicts the apparently denial-filled chorus of "I'm doing fine with just me and my wine: "Now my brain and my body are runnin' on different rails / And I died and just say hi what if all else fails, / Oh I woke up in a subway station, / Lying half dead on the floor, / I don't remember anything that happened the night before."[5]

"High 'n' Dry (Saturday Night)" is not harrowing. It is vaguely celebratory, but small scale. "High 'n' Dry" is a basic male adolescent-perspective song, with the odd reference to alcohol: "I got my whiskey, I got my wine / I got my woman, and this time the lights are goin' out." It feels closer to English working-class pub songs than anything that would particularly inspire teens to emulate it or that could be called "filthy."

The "high" of the title could refer to drugs, but even that is ambiguous, since "dry" suggests the absence of alcohol, and the phrase "high and dry" in any other context means abandonment in a time of need. That might be what the song alludes to. It's hard to tell what it means. In the end, I'm not convinced that the PMRC was as concerned with lyrics about drugs and alcohol as they were about the other categories of violence and sexually explicit language, the subjects of Gore's initial op-ed. These two songs—like many of the metal songs in the PMRC's list—feel obscure, like afterthoughts, compared with, say, Prince's "Darling Nikki." As a classic Baby Boomer, Tipper Gore considered herself a Beatles fan, yet songs like "With A Little Help from My Friends," "Day Tripper," "Doctor Robert," and "Everybody's Got Something to Hide Except Me and My Monkey" are far more pro-drug than the equivocal "Trashed," "High 'n' Dry," or "Master of Puppets."

This could be a very short chapter. But here is where we will reroute and develop the PMRC's simplistic label of "drugs and alcohol." While it's tempting to connect metal musicians to the famous literary drinkers (Ernest Hemingway, F. Scott Fitzgerald, William Faulkner, Dorothy Parker, and too many more to name) and drug users (Charles Baudelaire, Samuel Taylor Coleridge, Elizabeth Wurtzel, and too many more to name again), such a comparison feels superficial, another case of those artists and their addictions. "Trashed" is about drinking and driving. But what drives rock stars to drink? We need to consider metal's drug and alcohol-oriented lyrics on a larger continuum of inner struggle. Drugs and alcohol, it turns out, may be more of a symptom than a problem in and of themselves when it comes to metal songs, although not for the metal artists. I'll return to musicians, drugs, and alcohol for this chapter's conclusion.

Human Diseases

Art-rockers The Talking Heads had a hit with their song "Psycho Killer" in 1977 without managing to launch a Senate hearing, or face any consequences whatsoever, even though it's called "Psycho Killer," it is written from the perspective of the psycho killer, and the Son of Sam murders took place the same year. The worst anyone thought was that it was a distasteful coincidence. That's because the Talking Heads aren't heavy metal and aren't Twisted Sister. "Psycho Killer" has no distorted guitars but does have French in it: "Qu'est-ce que c'est?"[6] (Twister Sister only had Jay Jay French in it.) No one thought singer David Byrne was a psycho killer, or that the Talking Heads' audience would become psycho killers, or that children would be upset by imagined content of "sadomasochism, bondage, and rape." And yet, by including the word "psycho," Byrne helps broaden the scope of what we talk about when we talk about violence in a song. Tipper Gore bemoaned the violence of a song like "Under the Blade," but she was not interested in what it represented. I don't mean Snider's explanation of surgery, or even fantasies of power through the killer's perspective. I mean the prevalence of songs that appear to be about murderous slashers but, looking past the horror façade, are adjacent to the more realistic subject of mental illness. The "psycho" part of "Psycho Killer"—or, to put it in more metal terms, songs about *madness*.

"Got no brain, / I'm insane," Quiet Riot sings in "Metal Health."[7] But why? What is the meaning *behind* the many songs related to compulsion—from drugs to the more complex idea of madness, and how society treats those deemed mad? What literary and philosophical traditions did metal draw upon?

Madness in metal adheres to what Plato wrote in *Phaedrus* as early as 370 BC, attributed to Socrates in dialogue: "There are two kinds of madness, one arising from human diseases, and the other from a divine release from the customary habits."[8] In today's parlance, we might say that the first, "human diseases," would constitute mental illness, which causes suffering, and for which there are medical professionals and medical help today. But the second, "divine release from the customary habits," leads to what we might think of as the connected ways in which being "crazy," or "going crazy," or "losing my mind," to use language that turns up in song after song, may represent a kind of pain. But more importantly, these terms are also associated with positive feelings of desire and release—a crucial metaphor in metal's recurring images of cages and tethers. Think of the many songs that use the word "crazy" not as an informal psychological diagnosis but as a way of demonstrating heightened emotion or awareness.

Socrates further clarifies the different forms of "divine release": "And we made four divisions of the divine madness, ascribing them to four gods, saying that prophecy was inspired by Apollo, the mystic madness by Dionysus, the poetic by the Muses, and the madness of love, inspired by Aphrodite and Eros, we said was the best."[9]

Even if songs and lyrics are not quite in keeping with every aspect of *Phaedrus*, it is an illuminating way of looking at metal's madness as a metaphor—and when, maybe, it is not a metaphor at all.

New Periods of Pain

Take, for example, this stanza from Iron Maiden, with lyrics by singer Bruce Dickinson:

> I felt a Funeral, in my Brain,
> And Mourners to and fro
> Kept treading - treading - till it seemed
> That Sense was breaking through -
> And when they all were seated,
> A Service, like a Drum -
> Kept beating - beating - till I thought
> My mind was going numb –[10]

Wait. That's not Bruce Dickinson. That's *Emily* Dickinson, from around 1861. (Iron Maiden's bassist Steve Harris wrote many of Maiden's signature lyrics anyway.) The first line, which also serves as its title, probably gave it away. Or maybe you know the Clutch song that bears her name.

Anyone familiar with Emily Dickinson knows that many of her poems use proto-metal imagery and feature preoccupations with both the physical and metaphysical mysteries, as well as metaphorical possibilities, of death. As the poem continues,

> And then I heard them lift a Box
> And creak across my Soul
> With those same Boots of Lead, again,
> Then Space - began to toll,

> As all the Heavens were a Bell,
> And Being, but an Ear,
> And I, and Silence, some strange Race
> Wrecked, solitary, here -
> And then a Plank in Reason, broke,
> And I dropped down, and down -
> And hit a World, at every plunge,
> And Finished knowing - then -[11]

Lots of lines would make great metal song titles, and you may have caught "boots of lead," familiar from Black Sabbath's "Iron Man." Like "Iron Man," it's possible to read this poem narratively—that is, like a story—and literally. What would it feel like to retain one's consciousness after death, to be present at one's own funeral? What would happen next? The poem's use of dashes and the equivocal ending raise the problem—"- then -"—but can't resolve it. The experience of such a thing sounds and feels like a terrible form of madness, Socrates' "human disease." But rendered as precisely and exquisitely as Dickinson is capable of, it instead sounds like the poetic inspiration of the Muses, the goddesses of the arts who moved humans to creative heights. This is the madness we associate today, anachronistically, since contemporary diagnoses were not available during their lifetimes, with artists like Vincent Van Gogh, writers like Fyodor Dostoyevsky, and classical composers like Robert Schumann. Dickinson herself probably didn't suffer from any disorders other than being antisocial, which just makes her ahead of her time.

Wanting to know what death feels like is such a pervasive topic in art and literature—to say nothing of philosophy, religion, and medicine—that Iron Maiden's Bruce Dickinson *did* write lyrics that are not far off. "Powerslave," off of the album of the same name, also uses life-after-death imagery, here inspired by Egyptian mythology instead of ontology, and more interested in two of metal's other favorite topics, pride combined with revenge: "A shell of a man God preserved / For a thousand ages, / But open the gates of my hell / I'll strike from the grave."[12]

Yet in 1988's "Can I Play With Madness?" Iron Maiden treats the metaphor of madness differently. The madman here is a prophet who sees the world clearly, a version of Socrates' Apollo-inspired prophecy. "Give me the sense to wonder," Dickinson (Bruce this time) sings, in lyrics replete with images of prophets, crystal balls, and visions.[13] Heavy metal singers, in their ostentatious stage-wear, yowls, and say-anything approach to life, are modern manifestations of the "divine madness" that runs across cultures. Iron Maiden's song is in the tradition of the legend of the Delphic Oracle in Ancient Greek mythology and the Sibyl in Virgil's *Aeneid*.

But for all of Iron Maiden's interest in madness as something to play with, it pales in comparison to the number of songs that associate madness with suffering and death. Of course, many writers of novels, plays, and poems—as well as songs—focus on death, including Dickinson (Emily again), whose poetry seems obsessed with death, as well as anguish:

> I died for beauty, but was scarce
> Adjusted in the tomb,
> When one who died for truth was lain
> In an adjoining room.[14]

And

> Pain has an element of blank;
> It cannot recollect
> When it began, or if there were
> A day when it was not.
> It has no future but itself,
> Its infinite realms contain
> Its past, enlightened to perceive
> New periods of pain.[15]

But Dickinson's poetry doesn't have to be taken straightforwardly as being about death or pain itself. "I Felt A Funeral In My Brain" *could be* taken as a poetic interpretation of the speaker experiencing her own death. It could also represent *feeling like* one is experiencing one's own death. That is, a creeping sense of darkness, of blankness, that is *like* a funeral in one's brain, not the actual funeral. That is to say, once again, a feeling like madness.

Madness exists side by side with the violence and representations of addiction that detractors complained about in heavy metal, and, once again, it finds itself in great company, not just in literature, but as an important idea in literary philosophy. Philosopher, historian, and literary critic Michel Foucault built an important body of work around the ways in which society, power, the powerless, and the idea—even invention—of madness intersect.

It's a Madhouse

Tipper Gore got the idea of bondage right but its meaning entirely, wildly wrong. Anthrax put it succinctly in "Madhouse" (1985): "It's a madhouse / Or so they claim. / It's a madhouse, I'm insane."[16] Armored Saint also had a song called "Mad House" (two words this time) in 1984: "It don't matter what you do—mad house, / Just as long that it's good for you—mad house."[17] With those same video representations of bondage, although not in Tipper Gore's psycho-sexual sense of the word, heavy metal uses the images and language of the madhouse, the insane asylum, bedlam, the mental hospital—in keeping with the ways in which addicts were historically treated as well. Like the tethers and cages, the images reiterate a sense of powerlessness, but this time, the confinement is state-sponsored.

While "Under the Blade" for me evokes images of the slasher more than Snider's professed surgery, in some ways, the idea of compulsory yet unnecessary medical intervention is even scarier. The slasher is a violent individual. Upsetting, yes. But the unwanted operation, or involuntary commitment, represents an entire violent system. Most of the slasher songs are from the perspective of the attacker—upsetting for Tipper Gore, sure, but a fantasy of power for the heavy metal fan, or at least a thrilling ride. The songs about the madhouse are nearly always from the perspective of the imprisoned, the powerless. In that sense, metal's poetics function as Socratic philosophy: they ask uncomfortable questions about power, with potentially distressing answers.

The video for "Madhouse," in keeping, shows the band playing in what appears to be, aptly, a madhouse. You'll notice Anthrax's use of what medical professionals would see as an unfortunate, outdated term. Even "madness" might be considered stigmatizing and unscientific, although it has been used for centuries. But the word has both literary and metal cachet. If "Under the Blade" helps us to understand the importance of using "I" and "you" in the song's persona and relationship to the audience, Anthrax—and many others—use madness as a metaphor for a larger, systemic "Us" and "Them."

"Under the Blade" is important for other reasons as well. Why should people be scared of surgery? Sure, there are the obvious reasons, like the helplessness and the violence of the scalpel. But it's more than that. As Foucault has argued in *Madness and Civilization*, focusing on 1500–1800, hospitals and madhouses had historically been used to coerce and oppress the powerless, even if doctors and the medical establishment have worked hard over the last several decades to try and change that. "Madhouse" opens with the spoken word (and evil laugh, naturally) of "It's time for your medication, Mr. Brown, ha ha ha ha." Then, like "Rock You Like a Hurricane" and the videos I discussed earlier, the images of confinement begin: "White coats to bind me, out of control, / I live alone inside my mind. / World of confusion, air filled with noise, / Who says that my life's such a crime?" It's adolescence as insanity, or insanity as adolescence. The operative image is control—who has it, and who doesn't? And, like the novel that gave rise to the term, *Catch-22*, referenced earlier, it raises a troubling question: what does it mean to feel mad in a world where madness is, ironically, the reasonable response?

The song's central concern, then, title to the contrary, is not the madhouse, not exactly. It's this: "*or so they claim.*" Once again, we face the pronoun problem: who are "they"? Who makes the determination of madness: about who is mad, and how the mad should be treated? In 1983, Suicidal Tendencies similarly sang, in "Institutionalized," "I'm not crazy (Institution), / You're the one that's crazy (Institution)."[18] In its blunt attacks on lyrics supposedly depicting images of drugs and alcohol, the PMRC evokes these exact concerns of abuses of power.

As Foucault explains, the line between the sane and insane is culturally constructed, shifting, and potentially capricious. Without the title and chorus, without the video's straitjackets and padded walls, "Madhouse" sounds almost like everyday teenage anxiety, rather than a committable offense. That there is potentially little distinction is much of the point. Literature and metal arguably romanticize madness, which, for anyone suffering from mental illness, might be upsetting. But madness's very marginalization also provides its metaphorical power. Madmen are so upsetting to the established social order that they must be removed. And, circularly, that removal helps to establish the otherwise arbitrary distinction of who is mad and who is sane.

If the straightjacket and padded cell sound familiar, it's more likely from Quiet Riot than Anthrax. Quiet Riot's *Metal Health* album (1983 and still an excellent pun all these years later), the first mainstream breakthrough LA metal album of the 1980s, laid the groundwork for metal madness. "Metal Health (Bang Your Head)" and its 1984 follow-up, "Mama Weer All Crazee Now" (another Slade cover, with the similarly spelling-challenged "Cum On Feel The Noise") feature lyrics and imagery on the album covers and videos that plainly borrow from the most harrowing version of how people with mental disorders and addictions have been treated historically: ostracized, silenced, tied down, locked up.

The "Metal Health" video shows the straitjacket, the mask, the padded cell—and the escape, to the heavy metal concert. Escape is no small thing. The image of confinement runs deeply throughout metal lyrics and iconography, and the idea of being locked up and silenced—separated—is frightening, especially since the reason for imprisonment is for what the madman *is*, or *might do*, rather than necessarily what he *has done*.

Yet, metal is not just an escape; it represents *escapism* as well. From Poison's "Nothin' But a Good Time" video, with its mystical portal from the kitchen to the concert, to Nelson's "After the Rain" video, with its own magical portal away from an abusive parent to a musical Neverland, to Mötley Crüe pulling their high school protagonist through the bathroom mirror in "Smokin' in the Boys Room," heavy metal routinely relies on images of enchanted escapes from captivity that correspond with the feeling of musical escapism.

The madhouse, then, is not just a metal image of confinement. It creates the conditions for release, in both senses of the word. The metal concert is the other, good version of the madhouse, a way to throw off the shackles, metaphorical this time, and scream, mosh, and bang your head, the corollary to metal health. Metal madness is the flipside to the daily rule-following of institutions—not necessarily an insane asylum, but at least work and school. Goya's painting of the madhouse that opens this chapter would look like a concert if there were a band in the background. It might even look like the cover for Anthrax's single for "Madhouse." This is Socrates' "mystic madness by Dionysus," the Greek god of sex, drugs, and rock & roll. Or close enough—he was the god of wine and wine-making, fertility, parties, theater—and madness.

Diary of a Madman

Once again, all roads lead back to Ozzy Osbourne. Ozzy has an entire album, plus the title track, for "Diary of a Madman." His analysis of madness here is different from his previous album's "Crazy Train." The metaphor of the crazy train and "going off the rails"—insanity, but the dangerous, collective Cold War insanity of "Millions of people living as foes"—intersects with Ozzy's personal feelings of insanity: "Crazy, I just cannot bear." "Crazy Train" combines the struggle, and the madness, of the individual with a larger backdrop of cultural struggle. Ozzy has openly discussed his childhood abuse, learning disabilities, and addictions, as well as his enthrallment to music, and his responses to the ills of the world—all different kinds of "crazy."

In that sense, the cultural madness he describes in "Crazy Train" is different from what he sings of in "Diary of a Madman": "Manic depression befriends me, / Hear his voice, / Sanity now it's beyond me, / There's no choice."[19] Ozzy is embodying every version of Socratic madness: human disease, but also prophecy, poetry, and partying. (Interestingly, there is little of the madness of love in Ozzy's catalogue. Luckily, there is no shortage of other metal bands whose language overlaps with that kind of madness.) On the *Diary of a Madman* album cover, Ozzy looks as mad as a hatter in over-the-top horror makeup amidst a Gothic tableau. A child—who, it turns out, is Ozzy's son, Louis—is visible in the background.

Louis is a coincidence, but it leads directly to Lewis Carroll, inventor of the Mad Hatter, in *Alice's Adventures in Wonderland*: "'We're all mad here,' says the Cheshire Cat to Alice. 'I'm mad. You're mad.' 'How do you know I'm mad?' dear Alice wants to know. 'You must be,' the cat tells her. 'Or you wouldn't have come here.'"[20] *Alice in Wonderland* renders madness circular, self-fulfilling, in a story where, as the PMRC feared, a young person eats and drinks substances that have physical, physiological, and psychological effects. Literature, music, and drugs are all hallucinatory, reality-bending experiences. Rock groups before the 1980s understood Carroll's story as a proto-psychedelic allegory for the entwined madness of drugs and rock & roll, most famously, "White Rabbit" and "I Am the Walrus." It is, as Carroll's title suggests, an adventure.

While Jefferson Airplane and The Beatles make hallucinating sound like a fun trip, Pink Floyd's "Wish You Were Here" and Jimi Hendrix's "Manic Depression" are better antecedents for '80s metal madness, chronicling mental illness as painful and connected to social constraint with musical escape. Ozzy, like Anthrax, fears the power of institutions, in multiple meanings of the word, played for rebellious metaphor. It's powerful enough that the imagery runs throughout the punk and hard rock canon, from The Ramones' "I Wanna Be Sedated," through Green Day's "Basket Case," Cyprus Hill's "Insane in the Membrane," Muse's "Madness," Avenged Sevenfold's "Almost Easy," Slipknot's "Duality," and Korn's "Insane" and "Coming Undone." But one group, once again, understood the spectrum of drugs, madness, institutionalization, and suicide better than any other.

Metallica Masters Madness, Drugs, and Suicide

Metallica's "Welcome Home (Sanitarium)" appears on *Master of Puppets*, another song about being controlled, completing the arc set out by "Madhouse" and "Metal Health." Here, the lyrics are more descriptive and intricate than Anthrax's and Quiet Riot's lyrical blunt instruments, the music off-kilter and disturbing enough that it becomes difficult to tell what to take as a teenage metaphor, hyperbole about isolation, and genuine mental illness. Hetfield's lyrics arguably articulate Foucault's points about institutions more poetically and certainly more succinctly than Foucault himself does:

> Welcome to where time stands still,
> No one leaves and no one will,
> Moon is full, never seems to change,
> Just labelled mentally deranged.[21]

So far, the song uses no "I" or "you" pronouns, just "no one," a pronoun that is almost a negation of identity. The verse seems stripped of agency, with no referents for *who* is "just labelled mentally deranged." The uncertainty seems much the point. Without a specific pronoun antecedent, the "deranged"—"I"? "We"?—have no humanity, and no possibility of progress and therefore freedom. The use of "labelled" is crucial as well: not "is" or "am" "mentally deranged." Derangement is not a state of being. Instead, it is someone else's subjective characterization, through a passive construction—something that *was done*, concealing whoever did the labeling.

Eventually, the characters—the perspective and pronouns—enter: "I see our freedom in my sight," and the chorus, "Sanitarium, / Leave me be, / Sanitarium, / Just leave me alone." No rhyme, not even a consistent rhythm, in keeping with the verse's use of a 10/4 time signature. 10/4 feels almost like a standard rock beat of 4/4 time, but with two extra beats—just enough to throw the listener off balance, in keeping with the metaphorically off-balance lyrics.

Eventually, the song gets heavier, with the bridge: "Fear of living on," rather than fear of death, with "Mutiny in the air," "Kill, it's such a friendly word," and the desperation that killing "Seems the only way, For reaching out again."

Which leads into a frenetic—dare I say crazy?—guitar solo, as opposed to the earlier melodic, sad but sweet solos. The song's lyrics conclude there. We're left only with this image of killing, the only way, and the rest of the song continues, as though musically enacting its violence. The lyrics do not include the title,

"Welcome Home," only the parenthetical "(Sanitarium)." "Welcome home" could be ironic—not welcome; not home—in keeping with the second verse's bitter refrain of "Keep him tied, it makes him well, / He's getting better, can't you tell?" It could be a play on the sanitarium's euphemism as a "home." Or it could refer to the ending's possibility of killing, or death. It's a far cry from Mötley Crüe's sincere "Home Sweet Home," which I'll discuss in the next chapter.

Metallica drummer Lars Ulrich said that "Welcome Home (Sanitarium)" is "a bit like [the film] *One Flew Over the Cuckoo's Nest*. It's from the point of view of a man locked in a sanitarium, but he believes that he is sane, but he's locked up with all these insane people."[22] The film was based on the novel of the same name by Ken Kesey. However, Ulrich's description does not describe the novel or, really, the film at all. It is not from the point of view of the main character, Randle McMurphy, played by Jack Nicholson in the film. It is from the point of view of his observer, Chief "Broom" Bromden, who is locked in the sanitarium but indeed absolutely believes that he is insane. Murphy not only believes that he is sane; he is definitely sane, having lied to be committed rather than go to a prison work farm to serve his criminal sentence.

Like *Catch-22*, *One Flew Over the Cuckoo's Nest* critiques the very definition of insanity. Kesey, who worked as an aide in a mental hospital and became a devotee of LSD and other hallucinogens, suggests that madness is not just a question of an individual's mental state, but rather, in 1960s counterculture fashion, the systemic ways in which a conformist society destroys individuality and autonomy. Chief Broom frequently imagines "the 'Combine,'" "which is a huge organization that aims to adjust the Outside as well as she [Nurse Rached] has the Inside."[23] Readers at first may think that Broom is delusional or hallucinating, but we come to understand that the Combine, for the reader, serves as a metaphor for cultural conformity. Chief Broom, a seemingly unreliable narrator, understands what is happening to the patients, and in the world, better than he, or we, might at first think. He's the opposite of "The Tell-Tale Heart"'s narrator, whose grandiosity prevents him from any insight. His unreliability is a feint. Despite what he, and the institution, tell us, he's a remarkably reliable narrator after all.

One Flew Over the Cuckoo's Nest, both film and novel, do not conclude with the patients' rebellion. Instead, after McMurphy lashes out violently against the novel's antagonist, Nurse Rached, he is forcibly lobotomized. The man who thought the mental hospital would be an easier alternative to prison work has lost all of his freedom, permanently. As Foucault suggests, their functions turn out to be the same. In the end, Chief Broom smothers McMurphy in a mercy killing—very different from Metallica's "got some death to do" bravado—and then escapes, which, it seems, he could have done all along if he were ready. It's an equivocal ending at best. Metallica's sanitarium scenario is, scarily enough, preferable, more palatable, than Kesey's social criticism. "Welcome Home" suggests that working together to overthrow an oppressor might be a path to collective liberation. Kesey suggests that rebellion will always be subsumed by the system, the Combine, which, in the absence of social change, is inescapable, even with Broom's flight. It's rough to realize that, compared with fiction, heavy metal is actually optimistic.

How much should we understand metal madness as social metaphor, as Kesey does? It's hard to say. The PMRC hearings suggest that we should take it literally—not that anyone is mad, but rather that the artists and fans are being treated that way. In metal and Foucault, drug rehab, school, mental institutions, and prisons serve the same symbolic and social function. Detention is a real possibility for teens, especially if one considers school itself a form of detention. (I would like to think it is not, but my experience is not everyone's.) But it is certainly a powerful metaphor for the way metal fans at the time, and maybe now, feel—separate and stigmatized, but also, in the end, different and special, in a good way.

The Problem of Suicide

Detractors of '80s heavy metal seemed to have two complaints. First, that the music is too light: why are there so many songs about partying? See: Poison, Ratt, Warrant. Second, that the music is too dark: why are there so many songs about death, and suicide? See: Metallica, Ozzy, all thrash. The songs about drinking and drugs are, somehow, right in the middle, splitting the difference between the main camps of '80's metal, even as I think those distinctions are long gone. "High n Dry"'s boozing on a Saturday with a girl quickly turns into Black Sabbath's warnings in "Trashed" about how quickly "I drank a bottle of tequila and I feel real good" leads into "death was in my eye." Going crazy, in different senses of the term, and substance abuse, also in different senses, become the twin themes across '80s metal, from Van Halen through Slayer. But they don't just intersect across the different metal genres. Taken together, they lead into another kind of violence, one that the PMRC itself didn't seem concerned about, but that made separate headlines throughout the 1980s: the problem of suicide.

The topic is fraught and delicate, seemingly the province of doctors and psychologists. And yet, again and again, philosophy and literature return to it. Author and philosopher Albert Camus begins his book *The Myth of Sisyphus* with this idea: "There is but one truly serious philosophical problem, and that is suicide."[24] Even for '80s heavy metal, that's a little dark. And yet, what is arguably the most famous, and for many, greatest work of literature, William Shakespeare's *Hamlet*, revolves entirely around murder, madness, and suicide. The most famous soliloquy in all of literature, "To be, or not to be, that is the question," poetically paraphrases (and long predates) Camus's problem of suicide.

Tortured by circumstances and conscience, Hamlet deliberates which might be worse: to die, which is bad, or to be alive, which might be worse. Although the Gravedigger says that Hamlet is 30 years old, I prefer to think of him as younger—maybe even as a metal teen. He's a student. He's unmoored by his father's death and mother's hasty remarriage. He hates his new stepfather and is disgusted by his mother's sexuality. He has girlfriend troubles—and unlike Hamlet, Ophelia goes through with her suicide—as well as girlfriend's father troubles. He's full of angst, volatile. He's famously indecisive, but at other times he's also impulsive.

I've always been sympathetic to Hamlet's supposed tragic flaw of hesitation. A ghost—a ghost!—tells him to kill his uncle, who is also his step-father, who is also the king! I'd be suspicious of anyone who acted too hastily on that intel. Most people would need time and evidence, which are exactly what Hamlet works toward. Given the peculiar circumstances, he's not wrong. For its themes of violence, madness, suicide, sexual situations, and explicit language ("Do you think I meant country matters?" is the sneakiest infiltration of the word "cunt" ever to be read aloud in thousands of schools), *Hamlet* would have gotten all of the PMRC's content labels.

If the greatest work of literature, and much of philosophy, can explore the question of suicide, especially as it pertains to the sufferings and absurdities in the life of a young person, then surely heavy metal as an art form can, and even must, address the question as well. Songs like "Close My Eyes Forever," by Lita Ford and Ozzy Osbourne, and "Don't Close Your Eyes" by Kix use the same operative metaphor of death as sleep that Hamlet develops. Black Sabbath with Ronnie James Dio recorded "Die Young"; Megadeth raised the problem in both "A Tout Le Monde" and "Skin O' My Teeth." Suicidal Tendencies—well, that says it all. And, of course, Ozzy Osbourne's infamous "Suicide Solution" was subject to a lawsuit, all because people again refused to entertain the possibility that Ozzy's lyrics were, of all the unexpected things, *clever*: "Wine is fine, but whiskey's quicker, / Suicide is slow with liquor." The song is not only against suicide; it's also—back to the chapter's *D/A for Drugs and Alcohol* opening conceit—*against drinking*, playing on the double meaning of "solution" as both an answer and a liquid.[25]

Over multiple songs, Metallica develops the drugs-to-madness-to-suicide continuum. The problem of madness as metaphor in "Welcome Home (Sanitarium)" leads directly into the problems of power, control, and drugs in "Master of Puppets," which leads back to the previous album, *Ride the Lightning*, and "Fade to Black." If the concept-but-not-a-concept-album of *Master of Puppets* is being unwittingly manipulated, acted upon by forces outside of one's own control, then the concept-but-not-a-concept-album of *Ride the Lightning* is being unwittingly killed, dying outside of one's control.[26]

Every death is outside of one's control, though, even suicide. Dying is always unwitting. But consider the track list:

- "Fight Fire with Fire": death by nuclear war. "We all shall die."
- "Ride the Lightning": death by capital punishment, via electrocution. "Death in the air, strapped in the electric chair, / This can't be happening to me."
- "For Whom the Bell Tolls": a soldier's death in war. "Take a look to the sky just before you die, / It's the last time you will."
- "Fade to Black": death by suicide; more in a minute.
- "Trapped Under Ice": a metaphor for guilt? "Ice" as a slang term for crystal meth? I . . . don't think there's a metaphor here. "I am dying to live, / Cry out, / I'm trapped under ice." Death by . . . being trapped under ice.
- "Escape": the exception! Not death, but life! "Life is for my own to live my own way." James Hetfield hates it.[27]
- "Creeping Death": the Passover story, death by plague sent by God. "Die by my hand, / I creep across the land, / Killing first born man." It seems closer to the movie *The Ten Commandments* than Exodus, but that's because Kirk Hammett left Exodus.
- "The Call of Ktulu": an instrumental, but the title comes from H.P. Lovecraft's "The Call of Cthulhu," a horror story about an ancient, slumbering squid/god/monster that will drive everyone insane when it awakens. I suppose Metallica wasn't satisfied with a mere instrumental, because *Master of Puppets* would go on to include "The Thing That Should Not Be," a proper Lovecraft adaptation, including a paraphrase from the story itself: "Not dead which eternal lie, / Stranger eons death may die!"[28]

"Fade to Black" is in keeping with the album's death motif, but, as a mediation on suicide, it's different. It sounds different, the closest Metallica had at that point come to a ballad, with its initial slower tempo, clean guitars, and smooth vocal performance. But it is not a ballad. It is not romantic or sentimental. Just the opposite—it is stripped of both romanticism and sentimentalism. The title, never uttered (although eventually sung in "The Memory Remains" in 1997), refers to the gradual decrease in lighting, until there is no lighting left (ride the *lighting*?), first primarily associated with stage plays and then adapted by film as a transition.

As a metaphor, at first glance it feels more appropriate for growing old, the inferior "fade away" half of Neil Young's line "It's better to burn out than fade away" from "Hey Hey, My My."[29] Kurt Cobain would go on to quote that line in his own suicide note, but not with the emphasis on "fade away," since he did not.

And yet, as a metaphor of suicide, the slow "fade" may be more powerful, and more apt, than the quick "burn out," clarified by "Fade to Black"'s opening lines: "Life, it seems, will fade away, / Drifting further, every day."[30] To fade away deconstructs Hamlet's dichotomy of "to be or not to be." One thing, life, *to be*, becomes the other, death, *not to be*, painfully, slowly, as the lights dim gradually on the stage. A fade to black does not represent death. Worse, it represents life. As Camus continues in *The Myth of Sisyphus*, "Living, naturally, is never easy. You continue making the gestures commanded by existence, for many reasons, the first of which is habit. Dying voluntarily implies that you have recognized, even instinctively, the ridiculous character of that habit, the absence of any profound reason for living, the insane character of that daily agitation, and the uselessness of suffering."[31]

"Fade to Black"'s first verse continues:

I have lost the will to live,
Simply nothing more to give,
There is nothing more for me,
Need the end to set me free.

The pretense of poetry drops. All that is left is plaintive statement, which, in many ways, is more powerful than the artifice of poesy. It is easy, and tempting, to see what some adults in the 1980s were concerned about.

And yet, one small, easily overlooked phrase, an aside between commas on the page but rushed breathlessly together, like one word, in Hetfield's vocal delivery, is "it seems," in that opening line, "Life, it seems, will fade away." Not

"Life will fade away." As I said about slasher songs and in keeping with Magritte's famous pipe painting, a song is not a murder; it is representational. "Fade to Black" is not a suicide. Even if the lyrics dispense with metaphor, the song *itself* is a metaphor, a representation, a substitution. The song itself replaces the suicide. Poet Wallace Stevens wrote, "Let be be finale of seem. / The only emperor is the emperor of ice-cream" in "The Emperor of Ice-Cream."[32] "Be" and "seem" are both linking verbs, but their significance is crucially different. "Be"—reality— is the ultimate form of *what might be*—"seem." Like Metallica, Stevens is also talking about death, and alluding to Hamlet's line to Claudius about everyone's eventual fate as food for worms. But Stevens also wants us to enjoy life, to eat the ice cream, even though, like ice cream, life can be cold, and easily melts away. Black Sabbath's "Paranoid" ends in the same way: "I tell you to enjoy life, / I wish I could, but it's too late."[33] That the line was misheard as "end your life" is as alarming as it is ironic.

While one could see suicide as taking control of one's life and death, I see it in keeping with the other tracks of *Ride the Lightning*, another example of death that is outside of one's own control, like war or capital punishment. And Hetfield did not attempt suicide in any case. He wrote a song. In addition to revisiting the idea on "The Memory Remains," the opening verse's "Nothing matters" would resurface in "Nothing Else Matters," with the opposite sentiment. Here, Hetfield is practically channeling Jean Paul Sartre:

> I never opened myself this way,
> Life is ours, we live it our way,
> All these words, I don't just say,
> And nothing else matters.[34]

"Nothing matters" could be nihilistic, a prelude to suicidal ideation. But it can equally become the basis for Existentialism's radical freedom, the idea that, if nothing matters, then we can do whatever we want, live it our way. And, in keeping, we are responsible for whatever we do. Adding "else" suggests, in fact, that something is powerfully important after all.

Even Camus didn't end *The Myth of Sisyphus* with suicide. His final lines are even more famous than his opening: "The struggle itself toward the heights is enough to fill a man's heart. One must imagine Sisyphus happy."[35] It's a punchline for today's philosophy memes, but for Camus, it was deadly serious. For all the death—imagined in the songs, and sadly real for Cliff Burton—one must imagine Metallica happy as well. Their distorted, discordant, often dissonant music about violence, war, madness, drug addiction, and suicide has brought tremendous joy to the world.

Post Script: Rock Stars, Wanted Dead or Alive; or, the Limits of the Literary

The PMRC targeted songs for depicting drug and alcohol use, and, separately, Ozzy Osbourne and Judas Priest were subject to lawsuits alleging that their songs encouraged suicide. The supposed victims were teens, thought of as children. And perhaps they were victims, but not of heavy metal. And no one at the time was looking out for the rock stars themselves, who, in retrospect, *were* victims, not perpetrators.

In Don DeLillo's black comic 1985 novel *White Noise*, college lecturer Murray J. Siskind is attempting to stake out an academic niche in Elvis Studies. "Elvis," he says, "fulfilled the terms of the contract." "Excess, deterioration, self-destructiveness, grotesque behavior, a physical bloating and a series of insults to the brain, self-delivered. His place in legend is secure. He bought off the skeptics by dying early, horribly, unnecessarily. No one could deny him now."[36] At the time, Elvis Studies read as academic satire. In an age of Metal Studies, I'm glad it doesn't anymore.

What is less parodic and more ambiguous is "the terms of the contract": an anodyne, clinical phrase that DeLillo turns malignant. How satirically or seriously should we take this passage? If satirically, who is it satirizing? If seriously, can it be that audiences see rock star excess, leading to horrible, unnecessary death, as a cultural contract? Or worse, that we want it that way?

DeLillo used a similar phrase—"It's one of the terms in the standard contract"—in his earlier novel, *Great Jones Street*.[37] *Great Jones Street* revolves around a fictitious rock star, Bucky Wunderlick, who tries to escape the burdens of fame and what the market and his fans expect of him. The fantastic, mic-drop opening quotation to this chapter, about the nature of excess, whether it's excess of sound, style, sex, or substances, also opens *Great Jones Street*. In keeping with the passage from *White Noise*, it is difficult to tell how seriously or satirically to take it, especially given that it was published in 1974, well before the further excessive scope of the bands in this book. But in 1974, the deaths of Jim Morrison, Janis Joplin, Jimi Hendrix, and Brian Jones were still fresh in the public mind. DeLillo, perhaps thinking of Bob Dylan's at-the-time recent retreat from public life, already understood the fantastical narrative of *rock star* even before it had become everyday and cliché. As Wunderlick explains to his girlfriend Opal, "Suicide was nearer to me than my own big toe. It was the natural ending. I mean it was right there. No one would have been surprised or shocked. I really think it was expected of me."[38] But Bucky doesn't attempt suicide. Instead, he inadvertently becomes enmeshed in a conspiracy of drugs—but not the kind you'd think—corporate malfeasance, and violence at the hands of his supposed admirers.

As though building on DeLillo, music journalist Ian Winwood published one of the few books to address the cultural violence inflicted upon rock stars, as opposed to the PMRC's imagined violence that rock music supposedly causes. *Bodies: Life and Death in Music* (2022), is a memoir and, by turns manifesto. For real-life people, as opposed to the fantasy of song lyrics, addiction, excess, and madness are not metaphors at all. As Winwood explains,

> Over the course of my career I've spoken with many scores of musicians whose behavior might reasonably be described as deranged… I've written about people who, like me, have seen the insides of psychiatric care facilities. I've transcribed with words of performers who have since taken their own lives. Drink and drugs are everywhere. Like a magnet, the music business attracts people hardwired for self-destruction; as well as this, it provides an unsafe environment for those who might not otherwise give it a go. A perfect monster, it is both the chicken and the egg.[39]

For fans, lyrics about violence, drugs and alcohol, death, suicide, and madness can be sources of solace, means of expression, and fantasies of power and escape. Thinking about them from the point of view of the songwriter, however, one begins to consider that a list of rock lyrics about death is simply a list of rock lyrics. From the Who: "I hope I die before I get old." From Metallica: "I have lost the will to live." From Nirvana: "I Hate Myself and Want to Die," although, in fairness, this song title's words are never uttered. Led Zeppelin's "In My Time of Dying," not as a mediation on a biblical passage but as personal. Even pop's Cutting Crew, in "(I Just) Died in Your Arms," suggests that the metaphor of the broken heart might be fatal. REM's "Try Not to Breathe" is poetry to listeners, but is it just that? Megadeth's "In My Darkest Hour" (1988) becomes confessional: "Feels so cold, very cold, / No one cares for me."[40]

This kind of reading is risky. It opens up the possibility of Tipper Gore's own misreadings: overly intrusive, overly literal. But the point is not what this kind of reading says about the listener. The point is to consider, in its overwhelming aggregate, what the preponderance of this language says about its composers. Roland Barthes's death of the author is no longer a metaphor when the authors of some of these lyrics keep unceremoniously dying.

By the same token, a list of rock stars who died unnatural, premature deaths is simply a list of rock stars. For every David Bowie, who died of liver cancer in 2016 at 69—too soon but not tragic—there is a Wendy O. Williams, a Chris Cornell, a Chester Bennington, a Per "Dead" Ohlin of Mayhem, a Kurt Cobain, all of whom, and more, died by suicide. For every Chuck Berry, who died at ninety, there is a Jim Morrison, a Jimi Hendrix, a Janis Joplin, a Billy Holiday, a Whitney Houston, a Prince, an Andrew Wood (Mother Love Bone), all of whom suffered from drug-related or -suspected early deaths. If this rate of, say, elementary school teachers, or product managers, instead of musicians, died by suicide and substance abuse, how long would it take to become a national emergency?[41] But then again, as DeLillo understood, this is how we want our rock stars. These are the terms of the contract.

In Baz Luhrmann's biopic *Elvis* (2022), Presley's longtime manager, Colonel Tom Parker (played by Tom Hanks), rejects the idea that Elvis died at the age of forty-two ("Old Elvis"!) from a drug overdose or drug-induced heart attack. He instead suggests that Elvis died for his fans, from his need for their attention, their adoration, their love. Even if this is Hollywood malarkey, or, more generously, the deathbed drama of Parker as an unreliable narrator, then why didn't anyone take Elvis seriously when he sang, plaintively, believably, night after night, "I'll be so lonely I could die"?[42] But more: why did Parker and everyone around Elvis stoke his insecurities and fuel his drug dependences? Was it just for the money, as the film suggests, or the control? Or was it DeLillo's terms of the contract—what we have come to expect and demand of our rock stars?

Alice In Chains released *Dirt* in 1992, and the album's songs were a litany of heroin addiction and death: "Rain When I Die," "Sickman," "Junkhead," "Godsmack," "Down in a Hole." Recalling his 1993 interview, Ian Winwood writes, singer Layne Staley "was the first obviously damaged person I'd ever met."[43] Staley and bassist Mike Starr would both subsequently die of overdose. We want songs to be poetry, metaphors, and hyperbole. And they are. But what if they are also more? What if they're (also) cries for help? What if they're (also) suicide notes? We want our stars to be personas, ironically distanced and detached from their lyrics' affectations and afflictions, as I have suggested. And they are. But what if the characters they are playing are the saddest versions of who they are? Or who they don't want to become?

What if rock & roll's morbidity is a systemic problem rather than one of individual aberration and accountability? What if rock-star death is a social problem rather than social expectation—the terms of the contract—or, worse, a gruesome, salacious form of entertainment? What if Jim Morrison, Janis Joplin, Layne Staley, Elvis Presley, and the rest are not Byronic heroes, in dreamy thrall to Eros and Thanatos, worshippers of Dionysius and the Muses? Reading rock & roll as Platonic madness, divine release, as I mostly have, suits the listener far better than the artist. Rock star mortality and morbidity might be enough to convert one's literary mindset to a literal one. As much as we would like it to be true, our rock stars are not necessarily truth-tellers, saviors, or demigods, sacrificing themselves for art, for us. Or at least not only that. Their appetites for destruction captivate us, but at a cost. Thinking of them as "bodies" reminds us of the connection between our stars' fleshly objectification and their subsequent corpses.

Our idols are addicts, potential addicts, and real people struggling with mental health. Rather than protect them, every aspect of the music and fame machines enables their worst impulses, throwing gasoline—or alcohol—on their fires, because their continued performance is more important than their health and their lives. Dirt sells tickets, *Dirt* sold for Alice In Chains, and "The Dirt" sold books for Mötley Crüe. When James Hetfield of Metallica, in the documentary *Some Kind of Monster* (2004), takes a leave of absence from recording their next album to treat his alcoholism, everyone involved worries about the life of the band, not the life of the bandmate. "A number of the band's supporters," Winwood writes, were disappointed that Hetfield "was no longer the person he used to be. 'How much that hurt me is so amazing,' [Hetfield] says."[44]

Of course, rock stars are excessive—*that's what being a rock star means*. The very obviousness, the cliché, the way we instantly understand what DeLillo meant in 1985 about Elvis's decline and demise, means that we, like Elvis, have accepted the terms of the contract. Or worse: we have offered them.

After reviewing decades of his interviews, and speaking again to members of Foo Fighters, Smashing Pumpkins, Green Day, and many more; after chronicling his addictions, his near-death experiences, and his father's death, finally, three-quarters of the way through *Bodies*, Winwood feels ready to deliver a thesis:

> In the past, if I considered the matter at all, I guess I used to think that the bloodstains on the otherwise exquisitely woven tapestry of music were mere spillages. But the closer I looked, the more I saw them as being part of the fabric. In this new light, even the unlikeliest people can be a VH1 Behind the Music special waiting to happen. Pick a band, any band.[45]

The reference to *Behind the Music* presses Winwood's point even further. Not only do we accept unnecessary deaths as par for the star course, as DeLillo suggests, but we celebrate them. They entertain us. As I began this chapter suggesting, in the overlap between the band narrative, addiction/recovery narrative, and the actual accepted shape of a narrative, we look forward to death as the most satisfying conclusion to the rock & roll story. Sure, a recovery, a comeback—the most typical *Behind the Music* ending—is fine. But the second most typical conclusion—not coming back, dying, the narrative of the film *Elvis* and Elvis himself—is even better. The maxim is that growing old is bad but it beats the alternative. True, unless you're a rock star. Paul McCartney's continued performances will never be as cool as John Lennon's unlived potential. Bill Wyman's quiet old age can't compete with Brian Jones's exquisite corpse. Bon Scott's infamy ironically outlives Brian Johnson's longevity.

How bad is the problem? Only four months after Winwood's *Bodies* was published, in April 2022, two more of his interviewees, Taylor Hawkins, the drummer of Foo Fighters, age fifty, and Mark Lanegan, singer of the Screaming Trees, age 57—appearing only a page apart—died. In each case, Winwood was making a point about how Hawkins and Lanegan had, previously, only *almost* died but defied the odds and managed to recover. In a macabre reversal of Mark Twain's apocryphal quotation, the reports of their survival were greatly exaggerated.

Winwood's conclusion, his "Bonus Track," reminds readers of the joy that music and musicians offer. But that hope also comes earlier and stronger, from Simon Neil, the Scottish singer, guitarist, and songwriter of Biffy Clyro:

> Music saved my life. When I'm writing songs, when I'm not worrying about anyone else, that's when I'm at my happiest... I'm in a moment of pure unadulterated happiness and I don't give a fuck what anyone else says. It's me saying that I'm proud of who I am, And I'm proud of what we've done.
>
> This is who we are.[46]

Music, or at least the music business, has wrought sorrow and carnage for its practitioners. But at the same time, all those songs, those lyrics, even those about addiction and death, even especially those about addiction and death, have improved millions of people's lives. Elvis's life, not death, brought joy to millions of fans. In the movie theater where I saw *Elvis*, the average attendee's age was at least seventy, and the film's ending, even preordained, brought them to tears.

I remain convinced that "Fade to Black" has prevented suicides, not caused them. James Hetfield, as of this writing, has not burned out or faded away. Some contracts were made to be broken. But imagine, in 1985, that Tipper Gore, or anyone in power, had thought about the rock stars, wanted dead or alive, who actually needed help, and not the kids, who did not.

4

X for Sexually Explicit

Figure 9 Adam and Eve, 1597–1600. Found in the Collection of Rubenshuis. Artist Rubens, Pieter Paul (1577–1640). (Photo by Fine Art Images/Heritage Images via Getty Images).

> *Woke up to the sound of pouring rain,*
> *Washed away a dream of you.*
> *But nothing else could ever take you away,*
> *'Cause you'll always be my dream come true,*
> *Oh my darling, I love you!*
>
> Skid Row, "I Remember You" (1989)[1]

> *We fucked a flame into being.*
>
> D.H. Lawrence, *Lady Chatterley's Lover* (1928)[2]

When asked what he'd do if he weren't in a band, fictional Spinal Tap drummer Mick Shrimpton says, during end credits of *This Is Spinal Tap* (1984), "As long as there's, you know, sex and drugs, I can do without the rock and roll."[3] It's a joke, but a revealing one. Having discussed drugs, we can move on to sex—and, because the songs insist on it, love, as well as what we might call metal's ontology of women. Perhaps the worst offender on their Filthy Fifteen, the PMRC's (literal) poster child for sex intertwined with violence, WASP's "Animal (F**K Like A Beast)" gets the close reading, and maybe redemption, it deserves. Then, we'll consider the ways in which literature and literary theory can help us understand the contradictory and sometimes fantastical ways in which women have been depicted—as devils, angels, and monsters—in some of metal's most popular songs. If violence fosters fantasies of power and justice, and drugs and alcohol set the conditions for fantasies of escape, images of sexuality are the most overt fantasies of all, even as they conceal male fears of sexuality and the feminine.

WASP and Other Animals

For all of the supposed sexism of metal lyrics, only three of the metal songs on the PMRC's Filthy Fifteen were flagged for sexual lyrics: Judas Priest's "Eat Me Alive," AC/DC's "Let Me Put My Love Into You," and WASP's "Animal (F**k Like A Beast)."

AC/DC's song is a curious addition. Its meaning is unambiguous, but the inclusion feels arbitrary. Any number of AC/DC songs could have made the list, including several from the same album, *Back in Black* (1980), in which "Let Me Put My Love Into You" (no metaphors; a single entendre) appears.

Why not "Shoot to Thrill"? (A pun!) "Givin' the Dog a Bone"? (A metaphor? Technically.) "What Do You Do for Money Honey"? (A rhetorical question.) The mega-hit "You Shook Me All Night Long"? (Another single entendre. Two single entendres in series do not make a double entendre.) *Back in Black* was already an enormous hit, and not even AC/DC's most recent album at the time. AC/DC was too big to fail, a phrase that did not yet exist. It's easy to forget that AC/DC was even targeted, and almost no retrospectives about *Back in Black* mention it. Which is almost a shame, because the final line of the chorus—"Let me cut your cake with my knife"—is my second-favorite '80s sexual metaphor, just after Kiss, "I wanna put my log in your fireplace," from "Burn Bitch Burn."[4]

WASP was not too big to fail. Their debut album was still unreleased when the PMRC drew up its list. The song's lyrics were flagged for three separate offences—"Sex/language/violence." (No occult? No drugs? It could have worked.) WASP were old-fashioned shock rockers, taking Alice Cooper's '70s stage show into the '80s. The fake blood and raw meat they used onstage and in pictures have a long theatrical tradition, going back further than, say, the play *Sweeney Todd* (1979) or the bloody Hammer horror films of the 1960s. The Grand Guignol, the theater in Paris from 1897 to 1962, specialized in horror and violence. French writer Antonin Artaud developed the idea of the Theatre of Cruelty, which was intended to help people throw off the shackles of repression that civilization has imposed on us: "We are not free," Artaud wrote. "And the theater has been created to teach us that first of all. I call for actors burning at the stakes, laughing at the flames."[5] Mötley Crüe's Nikki Sixx even said he was reading Antonin Artaud while working on his similarly-named *Theatre of Pain*.[6]

And yet, especially in retrospect, the most offensive part of "Animal" is the simple inclusion of the word "fuck," which was a surprise in, say, *The Catcher In the Rye*, in 1951, or Kurt Vonnegut's *Slaughterhouse-Five*, as late as 1969, and got both of those books banned. By 1984, the year of "Animal"'s release as a UK single, "I fuck like a beast" or the chorus's refrain of "I come 'round, 'round I come feel your love (like an animal)" was already domesticated. "Feel your love" had already been one of Van Halen's more pop-sounding songs, and it sounds almost romantic. The song itself has a catchy chorus and would have made a great opening track to WASP's debut album, as intended, although "I Want to Be Somebody," a plaintive paean to fame and fortune, unlike the anti-fame songs this chapter will discuss later, turned out fine. "Animal" even had the courtesy of putting its profanity in parentheses and bowdlerizing it with asterisks.

Tipper Gore may have felt as though she didn't have as much to work with as she'd hoped. While the PMRC's campaign was against obscene lyrics, Gore and Susan Baker also must have understood that lyrics outside of the band's imagery might not make enough of an impression. To bolster the case, Paula Hawkins, Republican Senator from Florida, brandished "Animal"'s 12" single cover, a close-up of singer/bassist/bandleader Blackie Lawless's crotch outfitted with a circular saw codpiece. Blackie Lawless, the stage name for Steven Edward Duren, reads as pure cartoon villainy in the tradition of Dick Dastardly, which I'm surprised no rocker ever used, or Cruella de Vil, which Poison's C.C. would indeed appropriate. It is a persona, and clearly so. A work of art in its overt Freudianism, the circular saw takes the place of the phallus as a weapon designed to eviscerate a woman's body, but it also reads as a phallic replacement, and the only blood on that cover is on Blackie Lawless himself. It signifies hyperbolic anti-sex Puritan propaganda as much as rock & roll hedonism. The image is too over the top, too surreal, to be understood literally or as anything other than pure horror and stagecraft.

Tipper Gore, continuing her stint as our unreliable narrator, understood no such thing. And yet, the opening lyrics to "Animal," like the exaggerated cover, suggest that the extreme imagery is a feint, a ruse:

> I got pictures of naked ladies lying on their beds.
> I whiff that smell and sweet convulsion
> Starts a-swelling inside my head.
> I'm making artificial lovers for free, I start to howl I'm in heat.
> I moan and growl and the hunt drives me crazy,
> I fuck like a beast![7]

Wait a minute. Is Blackie Lawless suggesting that the song is a *fantasy*? Or at least, *about* fantasy? Sexual fantasy? Masturbation? If the naked ladies (jeepers, what a quaint phrase) are magazine pictures (equally quaint, in the internet age), the smell he whiffs is his own. Not that that masturbation would be much better for the PMRC, which flagged Prince's "Darling Nikki" and Cyndi Lauper's "She Bop" for the same subject. But it changes the song's meaning and implication dramatically.

There are no women or women's bodies in this song. There are only pictures, "artificial lovers"—imaginary, existing only "inside [the speaker's] head." His sexual prowess similarly exists in his mind and the song only. The codpiece on the cover *is* a cover: a ploy, a decoy. It is a symbolic phallus, because the real one is absent or unknowable. The blood surrounding it is obviously, and only ever was, a stage prop as well. Theatre of Cruelty is, in the end, mere theater.

Nevertheless, the saw led to the song being cut from the album. It would be released as a UK import single only, widely unavailable in the United States until 1998. While today "Animal" is just a YouTube click away, and its profanity pales in comparison to songs by, say, WASP's descendants Insane Clown Posse, at the time, the PMRC indeed successfully prevented Americans from being able to hear it. WASP's debut album went gold, and it is impossible to know whether they even benefited from the publicity. Blackie Lawless, for one, didn't think so: "I think a lot of artists thought, OK, this exposure's gonna help us sell more records. But I don't think in reality it did. I know it didn't for us."[8]

What might have been different if the song had been included on the album as intended? After all, Def Leppard would crack the Top 40 with their same-titled song "Animal," the first of what would be a spectacular run of ten consecutive Billboard Top 40 singles on *Hysteria*, which would sell over 20 million albums worldwide. Its lyrics don't have WASP's profanity: "I got to feel it in my blood, whoa, oh, / I need your touch, don't need your love, whoa, oh, / And I want, and I need, and I lust, animal."[9] And as catchy as WASP's "Animal" is, it's not up there with Leppard's big sing-alongs, featuring the classic '80s "Whoa oh!" But the Leppard is even more of an animal than the WASP—the speaker doesn't even need your love, just your lust. And the blood is real. It's a risqué tune that got a pass, maybe because Joe Elliot and the boys eschewed circular saw codpieces for cool blue jeans.

A decade later, on *The Downward Spiral* (1994), Nine Inch Nails—singer/multi-instrumentalist Trent Reznor—would stun the world with "Closer," a hit that would highlight the line "I wanna fuck you like an animal."[10] There were no Senate hearings. No updated Filthy Fifteen. No brandishing NIN album art on the Senate floor. "Closer" would instead be a Top 100 hit single, and its video would, in 2006, be voted by fans as the number one video in a VH1 Classic poll of the 20 Greatest Music Videos of All Time.[11]

Pearl Jam would also have a song called "Animal" (1993), which reversed WASP's sentiment—this time, the speaker is on the receiving end of cruelty, so much so that he'd "rather be with an animal," since an animal would be less abusive to him than his lover is. "Why would you want to hurt me?" our wounded speaker wails. The difference between WASP's "Animal" and Pearl Jam's "Animal" mirrors the moment in *This Is Spinal Tap* when manager Ian explains to rock star Nigel Tufnel, who doesn't know the difference between "sexy" and "sexist," that Duke Fame's (Rough Cutt's Paul Shortino) lurid album cover is acceptable because, unlike their misogynistic *Smell the Glove* album art, "he's the victim. [The record company's] objections were that she was the victim. You see? . . . If the singer's the victim, it's different. It's not sexist." And then, the iconic line: "It's such a fine line between stupid and clever."[12] By this measure, Pearl Jam was clever.

In 2005, Nickelback would have a hit with "Animals," about having sex in a car: "We're just a couple of animals," if animals also had sex in cars.[13] And then, twenty years after "Closer," thirty years after "Animal (F**k Like a Beast)," in 2014, pop rockers Maroon 5 had a hit with "Animal," featuring the lines "Baby, I'm preying on you tonight, / Hunt you down, eat you alive, / Just like animals."[14] It manages to combine what was objectionable in both Judas Priest's "Eat Me Alive" and WASP's same-name song. The video, featuring singer Adam Levine as a stalker amidst slaughterhouse imagery, received some criticism from women's groups, although Tipper Gore was, by then, out of the public eye. Nevertheless, the song made the Top 10 and was used in a Kia car advertisement, presumably after the company decided against Nickelback.

Dichotomies

If WASP's "Animal" is, in the end, a sexual fantasy, what about the songs that are, as much as song is able to be, about real women?

In 1988, Guns N' Roses released *Lies*, their not-quite-a-follow-up to *Appetite for Destruction* as much as a way to keep the party going and buy some time before a proper sophomore album. The side with new material included the acoustic songs "Patience" and "Used to Love Her" back to back. Taken together, they provide an instructive way into thinking about sexuality and representations of women in heavy metal and, maybe, American culture writ large. They demonstrate what the PMRC was concerned with, but also why those fears were misplaced.

"Patience" is a paean to missing and needing one's partner, but as mature love, not infatuation. The chorus is subdued: "Said, woman, take it slow, / It'll work itself out fine," with a minor chord darkening "fine," suggesting that getting through the hard times of a relationship takes effort, that "All we need is just a little patience."[15] The melodic refrain is wistfully whistled, the vocals low until the final verse, different from the previous ones, when singer Axl Rose finally unleashes his usual yowl—"Oh I need you, / Oh this tiiiiiii-ie-ie-ime!" as if in release. It is sincere, pure, and lovely.

The next song is an anti-love satire consisting of a single repeated chorus with minimal variation: "I used to love her / but I had to kill her. / I had to put her six feet under / And I can still hear her complain."[16] Axl implores us at the end, in spoken word, to "Take it for what it is," but for me it's less of an over-the-top, facetiously misogynistic gag than an equal and opposite reaction to "Patience." Perhaps it's a black comic cautionary tale for what happens when the speaker's patience finally runs out, shifting the "you" direct address of "Patience" to the third-person pronoun "her," because the woman in question is no longer around to speak with directly.

Buckcherry would borrow the same conceit (and more) for their 2005 album, *15*, but reversed. Buckcherry isn't an '80s heavy metal band, mainly because they showed up late, well after the party had already wound down, but "Crazy Bitch" and "I'm Sorry" lay out the same dichotomy as "Patience" and "Used to Love Her." "Crazy Bitch" is straightforwardly about sex with a "crazy bitch," the term repeated eleven times in the song. It is sung as a direct address, using the second-person "you" pronoun, which I can't imagine would go over very well as conversation. Repeated name-calling would necessitate an apology.

But then: voilà, the apology! "I'm Sorry" is a ballad, maybe even a power ballad, even though the great era of the power ballads had passed. It is, like "Crazy Bitch," straightforward and literal. Like "Used to Love Her" directly after "Patience," the song order may or may not be a direct response, but I prefer to think that it is. The speaker is sorry is "about all the things I said to you / And I know, I can't take it back."[17] Maybe he called her a crazy bitch, eleven times, in a song everyone heard, and thought it was a compliment. At least the speaker didn't put her six feet under.

These two pairs of songs dramatize heavy metal's dichotomized depictions of women. At first glance, it resembles the famous Madonna/whore complex, originally put forth by (here we go again, going down the only road we've ever known) Sigmund Freud. In his essay "The Most Prevalent Form of Degradation in Erotic Life" (1912), Freud was the first to suggest that men see some women as objects for sex and others as potential partners for love and marriage. That women might be both, or neither, or they might be more complex, was apparently too much for some men to handle, leading to unhappiness, dissociation, and impotence. "Where such men love they have no desire and where they desire they cannot love," Freud wrote in a lyric-worthy quotation.[18] It's unfortunate for the men, and also, very much so, unfortunate for the women.

One could say that heavy metal suffers from its own version of the Madonna/whore complex, with some songs, like "Crazy Bitch," about women to have sex with, and others, like "I'm Sorry," about women to love; "Patience," about long-term love, and "Used to Love Her," about, in the most euphemistic phrase possible, short-term love.

I'd like to imagine it's more interesting than that, though. Again, it seems possible to understand that both songs may be about the same woman, the same undifferentiated "you." If so, taken together, more than a Madonna/whore complex, they chronicle the phases of an unhealthy relationship, or perhaps a particularly male idea of the stages of that relationship: seduction, sex, ambivalence, regret, and acceptance. It's like the five stages of grief if the man going through the stages were a member of Buckcherry and grief were a woman.

Women! According to Def Leppard, men can't live without them. According to Freud, "the sexual life of adult women is a 'dark continent' for psychology," inadvertently managing to be both sexist and imperialist in twelve words.[19] The PMRC's approach to sex is arguably worse; at least Def Leppard and Freud are open to discussing the topic.

The intertwined subjects of sex and love, and representations of women in male-dominated metal, are central to the genre. Song after song, and video after video, focus on images of women. But, beyond the obvious, what do they mean?

Devils and Angels

Most of the songs and videos are less literal and more symbolic than Guns N' Roses' or Buckcherry's dichotomy, which gives them greater potential for literary analyses and other psychoanalytic readings aside from the Madonna/whore complex. Many songs turn to another dichotomy: between depicting women as devils or angels. It goes way back, in music as well as literature. The R&B/doo-wop group the Clovers had a hit with the on-the-nose-titled "Devil or Angel" in 1956:

> Devil or angel, please say you'll be mine,
> Love me or leave, I've made up my mind.
> Devil or angel, dear, whichever you are,
> I love you, I love you, I love you.[20]

In some ways, it's still simple: a woman who spurns our speaker is a devil; one who doesn't is an angel. In other ways, though, the depictions are more nuanced, suggestive at first of Madonna/whore but not the same. The man both wants and does not want the woman to be a devil—sexually alluring but frightening. And he both wants and does not want the woman to be an angel—pure, but unreal and unobtainable. Both are ways of understanding the complexities of desire, and the ambivalence that often comes with it.

In either case, though, the woman is magical. While 1980s videos may feature and focus on women's bodies, at the same time, many times, women are not depicted as completely human at all. They become supernatural, even conceptual, as opposed to human beings. They function as symbols. But not exactly, or at least not just, what we understand through the term popularized in the '80s, "sex symbols."

In the lyrics, then, but more often, in the videos, the singer and band members are teased and tempted by a woman with magical powers. The surrealism of school-turned-strip club in Van Halen's "Hot for Teacher." The woman magically aging, and reverting to youth, in Bonham's "Wait for You." In Ozzy's *Ultimate Sin* album cover and video of the same name, the magical woman can appear and disappear. In his "Shot in the Dark" video, from the same album, a regular human woman transforms into the cover's magical metal mistress. But what does it mean?

The devil woman is part of the adolescent appeal: the videos get to feature the hot (ha ha) woman. She's not out of reach, like the angel, and therefore the cause of the speaker's loneliness; she's out of reach the way the stove is out of reach for the child. She is dangerous, too hot to touch, but the speaker wants to and can't help it anyway. *A la* Crazy Bitch, he wants her *because* she's dangerous.

Alice Cooper's "Poison" has a great guitar intro leading to a quiet verse laying out how cruel and dangerous the woman is, before the chorus puts the sexy/scary/magical woman conceit completely straightforwardly:

> I wanna love you but I better not touch (don't touch),
> I wanna hold you, but my senses tell me to stop,
> I wanna kiss you but I want it too much (too much),
> I wanna taste you but your lips are venomous poison.[21]

Yes, poison and venom are not the same: cue joke that Poison is glam metal and Venom is black metal. But it's an image of stasis and ambivalence, packaged in Alice Cooper's catchiest song, complete with call-and-response backing vocals, as though the band is there to support the speaker in his sexual sobriety—*don't touch!*, they chant in unison, like a group of parents to a child. Musically, it's a pop-rock departure from Alice Cooper's '70s work but also completely in keeping with the teen torment and contradiction of "I'm Eighteen": "I'm a boy and I'm a man," "I don't know what I want," "I got a / Baby's brain and an old man's heart."[22] The video for "Poison" features a back-and-forth between scantily clad magical women who want to poison Alice and a conclusion where Alice successfully poisons the woman who transformed herself into him, the man who took a woman's name, as the band rocks on in the background. The doubling and gender configurations are complicated, to say the least, but the point is simple.

Mötley Crüe's "Looks That Kill" develops the idiom "if looks could kill" from dangerous contempt to dangerous beauty. Women, as Alice Cooper also warns us in "Poison"—"One look, could kill"—are dangerous. "She's got the looks that kill," Vince Neil shrieks; she's "razor sharp," "She'll slice you apart," "She's a number thirteen," yet, at the same time, "She's going to turn on our juice, boy."[23] The video depicts more post-apocalyptic *Road Warrior* and carceral imagery, featuring images of both the band in a cage and women in a cage, and a final battle between the band and the ultimate magical woman warrior. Except she quickly disappears (they do that in videos), leaving only a flaming pentagram behind.

In *The Dirt*, Nikki Sixx shares the anecdote that, upon seeing his estranged mother for the first time in years, she immediately asks, "Did you write that song about me?"

"What song?" I asked, confused.

"'Looks That Kill.'"[24]

The question raises what is possibly Freud's most famous, and infamous, idea: the Oedipal complex. And that the magical women change, appear, and disappear raises another Freudian concept connected to the Oedipal complex: separation anxiety.

Castration and Separation Anxiety

Based on the Greek myth, as depicted by Sophocles' play *Oedipus Rex* (c430 BCE), the Oedipal Complex describes the psychodrama of the young boy who sees his mother as his first love object but fears reprisal from his father in the form of castration, leading to his unconscious wish to kill the father and replace him by marrying the mother.

It's tricky, dangerous, and wrong to treat real people as fictional characters ripe for literary analysis, but I'm going to do it anyway. The primal scene of heavy metal is the image of Tony Iommi, guitarist of Black Sabbath, vying to escape his Birmingham factory-work fate through the power of heavy music. On his last day of his industrial job, before the band was to record their album and potentially become famous, Iommi was working on an unfamiliar machine and accidentally severed two of the fingertips on his fretting hand. For most guitarists, this would be a catastrophic, career-ending injury. But it was not for Iommi. It was the beginning.

If that event, with that imagery, were in a novel, it would be a too-on-the-nose signifier of castration. That he was, more specifically, from Handsworth, Birmingham, strains belief. Iommi lost his fingers, which are, for Freudians, phallic symbols, and, with them, he lost his phallic power—his ability to play the guitar, which is also a phallic symbol.

But, as all fans know, Iommi fashioned prosthetics for himself and relearned to play his instrument. He swapped in lighter strings, used more distortion, tuned his guitar down to ease the string tension for his new wax tips, and thus heavy metal was born from blood-letting, bodily tragedy—not from phallic power, but from the accident that threatened to take it away. The subsequent decades of obsession with power, the body, and women is not, in this analysis, surprising.

The other half of Freud's Oedipal drama is not just the castrating father, but the anxiety caused by separation from the mother. It is a normal part of childhood development, but if it persists, it is still considered a disorder by the American Psychological Association. Damn Yankees' "High Enough" (1990) is an almost word-for-word explanation of separation anxiety, even down to the speaker, an adult man, being called "baby":

> I just made one mistake,
> I didn't know what to say
> When you called me "baby."
> Don't say goodnight,
> Say you're gonna stay forever.[25]

But, alas, the woman—his lover, the substitute for his mother, if one is a Freudian, and one is—cannot stay forever, which is lyrical hyperbole, to be sure, but also impossible, as people have things to do. The separation anxiety begins because the speaker seems to rebuff commitment, and then he panics when, as a result, the woman actually leaves.

Similarly, Journey's mega-hit "Separate Ways" (1983) turns the dichotomies into the separation between the man and the woman and the classic image of the broken heart:

> Here we stand,
> Worlds apart, hearts broken in two, two, two.
> Sleepless nights,
> Losing ground, I'm reaching for you, you, you.[26]

Sleepless nights? Reaching for you? The speaker sounds like . . . an actual baby.

"Reaching for you" is a good way to put it, though. Most of metal's lyrical women, then, are indeed out of reach. They are devils, who are desirable but should be out of reach because they threaten or reject the speaker. Or they are angels, who are out of reach because they float, non-corporeally, above.

In addition to the unconscious wish for the young boy to kill his father and marry his mother, however, the boy must lose this struggle, realize that his mother and father are a couple, and begin to emulate his father as a result. It's when the boy never stops feeling spurned, or never stops vying to replace the father, that the psychological troubles begin.

Evil Women

It's a quick pivot from the mother/lover who will not stay forever to the spurned boy who now sees her as a devil, pentagram and all, or as a monster. Maybe Nikki Sixx's mother was on to something. In keeping, one of the main images of women in metal songs and videos is not just the dangerous woman, or even the devil woman, but the evil woman, the monstrous woman. In mythology, folklore, and literature, many of the famous monsters are male: Dracula, a seducer with a castle full of undead brides; Frankenstein's creature, with, as Def Leppard would put it, "a need for a mate" (more on the song "Women" soon); King Kong, who has the masculine "king" in his name and, like Tommy Lee, a thing for blondes; and the Wolf Man, whose name even has "man" in it. (The "were" in "werewolf" also means "man," so there's no way around it.)

Yet there are many monsters who are specifically female, seductresses who are part animal (that word again), ready to kill men. The siren, a beautiful woman/fish-or-bird hybrid (this isn't science) who, in *The Odyssey*, would sing in order to lure sailors to their deaths. Odysseus's crew only survived because they plugged their ears and, as instructed, tied Odysseus to the ship's mast because their song was irresistible. The lamia, a woman/snake hybrid who eats children and was the subject of a poem by John Keats in 1819. Harpies? Deadly bird women sent by the gods to punish King Phineus. Medusa? A woman with snakes for hair who killed everyone who looked at her by turning them to stone, reversing and weaponizing the male gaze. The sphynx? A deadly woman/bird/lion who would ask men a riddle and kill them when they couldn't answer correctly. She was defeated by Oedipus. This feels significant.

Songs about devil or monster women, then, can serve as warnings, like "Poison" and "Looks That Kill." Songs about evil women do as well, but they also serve as macho boasts: this is my ex, we had sex, something bad happened between us, and now she's evil. Or she was evil in the first place, a variation on "Crazy Bitch." One of the first of these was "Evil Woman" by Crow, in 1969. But it is better known to metal fans in its cover version as the first-ever single by the first real metal band, Black Sabbath, in 1970. (The song did not appear on the American version of the album.)

> I've seen a look of evil in your eyes,
> You've been filling me all full of lies,
> Sorrow will not change your shameful deeds,
> Do well best, someone else has better seen,
> Evil woman, don't you play your games with me.[27]

What is the look of evil? What are the lies? What are the shameful deeds? The later verses are more revealing: "You want me to claim that child you bore." Whoa. "Wickedness lies in your moistened lips, / Your body moves just like the crack of a whip." Ah. Shameful deeds indeed. *Don't play your games with me, even though you're still sexy.*

Shortly after, the Eagles had a hit with "Witchy Woman," also on their debut, eponymous record. She's another ex—"She held me spellbound in the night"—but the song is more concerned that she sleeps around overall. She's not an evil woman, or even an actual witch, as much as she's a "witch-y," my hyphen, woman: "Raven hair and ruby lips"; "She's a restless spirit on an endless flight." Sabbath's song is sung *to* the evil woman, but the Eagles, we learn in the final verse, are singing their warning to another dude: "Well, I know you want a lover, let me tell you, brother / She's been sleeping in the Devil's bed / . . . She can rock you in the nighttime 'til your skin turns red."[28] The warning is also the enticement. The switch to "witch" from "evil" makes sense now—like the witch hunts, as chronicled in Arthur Miller's play *The Crucible*, the song is a kind of indictment, revealing the guilt and vice of the man at least as much as that of the accused woman.

Electric Light Orchestra put out their song, also called "Evil Woman," just a few years later, in 1975, also about an evil ex: "Hey, woman, you got the blues/ 'Cause you ain't got no one else to use."[29] Even worse than "sleeping in the devil's bed" is, coming full circle, back to angels and devils, being so evil that she's a devil. Enter Cliff Richard and "Devil Woman," in 1976, featuring another scary seductress: "I drank the potion she offered me, / I found myself on the floor / . . . She's just a devil woman / With evil on her mind."[30]

Black Sabbath were back again, this time with Ronnie James Dio, for another stab at an evil woman, and not a cover, with "Lady Evil" in 1980: "Cause there's a lady I know who takes your vision, / And turns it all around, / The things you see are what to be, lost and never found. / Lady evil, evil,/ She's a magical, mystical woman."[31] This song, unlike all the others, doesn't suggest anything about sex at all. Sometimes a song about an evil woman is just a song about an evil woman, as Freud did not say.

The Cult combined the hot woman/devil woman into "Fire Woman," in 1989. It's another great song, with a mysterious, chime-y twelve-string guitar intro, and in between, some excellent bluesy-metal playing. Billy Duffy leaned into the look and sound of the guitar hero, while Ian Astbury did his best Glen Danzig doing his best Elvis impression. The lyrics start as a tone poem, with fleeting images of "T-t-t-twistin' like a flame in a slow dance, baby" with the obligatory slant rhyme with "You're driving me crazy," and also "Prancing like a cat on a hot tin shack," as Tennessee Williams did not write.[32] Eventually, the lyrics capitulate to the usual devil woman accusations, repeating "Fire woman, you're to blame" four times before the hot final guitar solo takes us out for the return of that cool, swooshy, chime-y twelve-string.

By the 1990s, the trope was familiar enough for bands to have some fun with it, including Type O Negative, fronted by bassist/vocalist Peter Steele. Steele himself looked like a less-confused version of Frankenstein's monster—and, at a purported 6'8", nearly as tall—as illustrated on the frontispiece of 1818's *Frankenstein*. The band's hit "Black No. 1," in 1993, is less about an evil woman than a woman who is trying too hard to look evil, hence the hair color of the title.

> Well, when I called her evil
> She just laughed,
> Well, cast that spell on me
> Boo bitch-craft.[33]

And so, with the coining of "bitch-craft," we can close the circle from "Crazy Bitch." Almost—I'd be remiss in leaving out the parody by Flight of the Conchords, the New Zealand duo with an HBO series of the same name. Their song "Demon Woman" satirizes the goofy, hapless male passivity of all these songs, where the man is bewitched, blameless, and helpless—Richard's "I found myself on the floor," etc.—before the evil woman's feminine charms: "Demon woman, / You cut puppies' toes off, / Pull an animal's nose off, / How'd you magic my clothes off?" As "Demon Woman" concludes, "Your breasts are balls of flame / And I'm burning my hands / Playing these ball games."[34] Fire woman indeed.

Angels and America

Then, there is the opposite: the woman is an angel. First, the women are monsters, devils, evil—that is, the men are mad because they want to have sex with them but are too scared to. Or they did have sex with them, and now they're mad anyway. But other women are angels—that is, the men still want to have sex with them, but they can't, because the women are too good for this world. Unlike the generality of the devil women, who are not usually directly equated with any of the female monsters mentioned, these women are very specifically angels. (Angel Witch's 1980 song "Angel Witch" miraculously manages both images.) While metal certainly doesn't have a monopoly on "angel" lyrics ("Earth Angel," "Angel of the Morning," Sarah McLachlan's "Angel"), it has enough examples that it's practically a subgenre. Unlike the devil songs, though, the angel can signify many different, and even contradictory, ideas about women:

- Aerosmith, "Angel": in the video, the magical woman is a shadow, mist, a transparent, noncorporal angel, before, in the end, becoming a literal angel hovering over the bed, as singer Steven Tyler sings, "What can I do? I'm sleepin' in this bed alone."[35] Scenes of the angel woman are intercut with the requisite concert clips, where Tyler wears all white. The song repeats the refrain "Come and save me tonight." Despite the potential for double entendre, it's chaste, especially for an Aerosmith song.

- Poison, "Fallen Angel": While Poison were positioned in opposition to Guns N' Roses in the late '80s, "Fallen Angel" is their version of "Welcome to the Jungle." Here, it's not young hayseed Axl stepping off the bus into predatory LA; it's a young woman and the creepy older men trying to take advantage of her right after she "stepped off the bus" from somewhere that needed a bus to get there. It's a protective, even preachy song, warning about exploitation, with both the woman and Los Angeles as the opposing angels. "Where's the girl I knew a year ago?"[36] singer Bret Michaels wonders. He's not just the narrator, but a participant, as C.C. DeVille's whammy-bar-inflected guitar solo cries for her. Here, the fallen angel is not a devil, like Milton's Satan (more on him later), even as she is "caught between Heaven and Hell," but her experiences have caused her to fall in the speaker's estimation, even as she has his empathy. Great White's "The Angel Song" professes something similar.
- The Black Crows, "She Talks to Angels": at first, like "Fallen Angel," we meet a young woman who is worldly, who has lived a full life despite her age and, by implication, taken drugs; the opening line, "She never mentions the word 'addiction' / In certain company," creates an entire portrait in nine words. We then immediately learn that, bluntly put, she's a liar: "Yes, she'll tell you she's an orphan/ After you meet her family."[37] But she is not fallen, or bad, or a monster. She is still pure, even divine. It's a more mature portrait of a complex woman's spirituality, which the speaker can only describe and even aspire toward.
- Slaughter, "Fly to the Angels": a throwback to the 1950s and 60s songs about dead and therefore idealized girlfriends and lovers. In addition to The Clovers' song, the 1950s and 1960s feature a whole wave of women as angels, but it was less an image of their wholesome lovability than that they were also out of reach, because they were actually dead. "Last Kiss," originally performed by Wayne Cochran in 1961 and covered by Pearl Jam in 1999, is the exemplar of the genre despite never even using the word "angel."

And yet, having said all that, the most magical woman of all in 1980s heavy metal videos, hands down, was Tawny Kitaen, and she was neither an angel nor a devil. As Kitaen herself noted, "Girls weren't the focus of videos—the bands were the focus. I came along and changed all that."[38] She arguably made Whitesnake's career along with her own by dancing on the hood of a Camaro, the apotheosis of American adolescent male fantasy, in the "Here I Go Again" video, subsequently reappearing in "Still of the Night" and marrying, and later, divorcing, singer David Coverdale, who is not even American.

Unlike the songs about other magical women, "Here I Go Again" is not about longing, separation anxiety, or danger. The speaker is not bitter that he's lost his girl, who is now evil, a devil, poison, or razor sharp; or, alternately, an angel, who has come to save him tonight but remains out of reach. He didn't used to love her, she's not a crazy bitch, and he's not sorry. Every frame of the video reaffirms that David Coverdale is in a relationship with the preternaturally and possibly supernaturally lovely Tawny Kitaen, and, by all accounts, it's just as awesome as it seems it would be. While the lyrics and video appear only tangentially related, as is typical, even the song reveals a resigned maturity, not adolescence: "I don't know where I'm going," Coverdale croons, in his best smoky voice, "But I sure know where I've been."[39]

As a 15-year-old listening to that song in 1987, I too did not know where I was going, and I also had not given any thought to where I've been, because I had not been anywhere except Brooklyn. But I believed that David Coverdale had. The proof? Tawny Kitaen. He claims that "Like a drifter, I was born to walk alone," a revision from the previous version on 1982's *Saints & Sinners* where he was "like a hobo" (good edit). But he is not walking. He is driving. The *Sturm und Drang* of the bridge, where Coverdale repeats "Here I go ah-geh-eee-eh-ah-en," this time stretching "again" over five syllables before hitting a trademark stratospheric screech of "Here I GOOOOO-OOOOOAH" is big drama, but the guitar solo by Adrian Vandenberg is melodic and reassuring, and so are the subsequent repetitions that round out the rest of the song. Yet for all its hyperbole of Kitaen's pole dancing without a pole, on the hood of a car, and all the visible tongue kissing, in retrospect, it seems much healthier, and amazingly, more attainable, than singing about women who are angels—non-corporeal, unreal, dead—or evil— tantalizing, scary, dangerous. The song and video prove that Coverdale does, in fact, "know what it means / To walk along the lonely street of dreams." Except he's not lonely at all. He's with Tawny Kitaen. And he's not walking. He's driving a Camaro.

Def Leppard's Women

For Def Leppard, women themselves, not as devils or angels, are already imbued with a kind of innate paranormal quality stemming from their mystical origin. The opening guitar lick of "Women"—a single-note melody, as opposed to chords or a riff—is otherworldly, vast, echoing, epic, jumping up an octave as the big drums enter at a slower tempo than listeners were used to for most of *Pyromania*.

The lyrics provide a take on the Biblical creation of women. But, in many ways, despite borrowing the most famous first line in literary history, "Women" seems closer to John Milton's retelling in *Paradise Lost* than the canonical version of Genesis (the first book of the Bible, not the progressive rock band):

> In the beginning, God made the land,
> Then He made the water and creatures,
> Then He made man.[40]

Def Leppard definitely left out a few things, mainly "Let there be light." But the song isn't about the universe, or light, or God. It's about women, but even with elisions it's going to take two verses and a pre-chorus to get to them. Man, they sing, "was born with a passion, love and hate, / A restless spirit with a need for a mate." That's not what happens in Genesis at all. At this point, Man seems content with the rivers and the animals he's named and the trees he can eat the fruit from—all except that one particular tree. All God says at this point is that "It is not good that the man should be alone; I will make him a helper as his partner."[41]

The mood of the song shifts, and the guitars get about as dissonant as Def Leppard gets, when we arrive at the pre-chorus: "One part love, one part wild, / One part lady, one part child." It's almost a rewriting of the "Sugar and spice and everything nice" (more on sugar up next), but with substitutions in the recipe, leading into the chorus's proclamation of "Women, Women / Lots of pretty women," allowing the leap from the singular Eve to the plural "women." I can't say myself how women feel about being an equal combination of love, wild, lady, and child—different and unparallel categories. Yet to their credit, the song eschews the much more common refrain of "girls" (see: Mötley Crüe) for a more mature term, and the song isn't a sex romp (see: Mötley Crüe) as much as a kind of tribute to, rather than fear of, women's overall sexual power over men.

Before concluding "Women," let's thematically compare it with Def Leppard's biggest hit, "Pour Some Sugar on Me." "She fed him with a hunger, an appetite" is, of course, sexual—this is not a song about actual apples. While "Pour Some Sugar on Me" was said to be inspired by a real-life banal conversation about putting sugar in tea—how British—it would not have been the hit it became unless audiences heard in it something a bit more symbolic.[42]

As in the Garden of Eden, the sins of gluttony and lust become intertwined in "Pour Some Sugar on Me": "You got the peaches, I got the cream," Joe Elliot and company yell-sing, decades before emojis would make this sexual imagery commonplace. The verses, sung in almost-rap style, are similarly free-associative, with a focus on rhythm and rhyme rather than the quasi-narrative of "Women." And the song is meant to be heard and played in a group, where crowds dance and listeners understand "pour some sugar on me" as an opportunity to seduce, and be seduced. There is a gender-egalitarian aspect to the seduction, and it's "in the name of love."

Back to "Women." The bridge moves on to use synecdoche, metal's favorite literary device for describing women. Synecdoche uses a part as a way to understand the whole—say, using "blonde" to mean an entire woman who has the singular noticeable feature of blonde hair. Here's Def Leppard's version:

> I give you
> Hair, eyes, skin on skin,
> Legs, thighs
> What's that spell? What's that spell?

Technically, it spells H-E-S-L-T: Hair/ Eyes/ Skin [on skin]/ Legs/ Thighs. But this is not the time to quibble. Def Leppard have, in many ways, written the quintessential male perspective love and sex song. The video, in keeping with the long tradition of videos having only a tangential relationship to the lyrics, is still about women, but with a science fiction and metafictional twist. I'm reluctant in principle to cite Wikipedia, but its summary of the "Women" video is golden:

> The music video for "Women" focuses on a boy who reads a comic book outside an abandoned warehouse while the band performs inside. The comic book, titled "Def Leppard and the Women of Doom!", [sic] features a skateboarding protagonist named Def Leppard, who travels to a distant planet and battles evil aliens to liberate female robots.[43]

Except, as the video progresses, we—and superhero "Def Leppard"—discover that *the robots aren't really robots*—they're real women under the metal! The women are real! It's in the '80s tradition of *Weird Science* and *Mannequin*, where young men can turn a simulated woman into flesh through the power of love, as opposed to the '70s tradition of *Stepford Wives* and *Westworld*, where simulated women are first subservient and then dangerous. In any case, the robot women-who-are-real-women are freed in the comic book, which is in the video, which is loosely based on the song, which is loosely based on the Bible. This postmodern stew of signifiers could represent objectification, or women as subjects; liberation, or oppression; the power of simulation, or the power of the real. It's a lot for a song that is, at bottom, an attempt to celebrate the simple fact of "lots of pretty women."

"Women" also includes a verse describing the biblical fall, what for Milton is the main event, the bite of the fruit from the forbidden tree: "And in the garden, lust began, . . . She fed him with a hunger, an appetite, / And filling with emotion, he took a bite." They don't mention the actual apple, but it's the apple that introduces the sin of lust to Adam and Eve, leading them to the first moment of shame. After eating the fruit, Milton writes, "Then the eyes of both were opened, and they knew that they were naked; and they sewed fig leaves together and made loincloths for themselves."[44]

On the one hand, Def Leppard's version of the fall, like Milton's, is in the literary spirit of the *felix culpa*, the fortunate fall. Eating the fruit defied God and got Adam and Eve expelled from the Garden, but it also led to all that we understand about humanity and history. We have the anxiety and sadness, but also the joy and anticipation, of our appetites and emotions, which Def Leppard celebrates. Adam and Eve have been cast out of Eden, but as Milton's angel tells them, "then wilt thou not be loth / To leave this Paradise, but shalt possess / A paradise within thee, happier far."[45] Their fall is tragic, but the paradise they have within themselves is even better. As Bon Jovi sagely understood, they've got each other, and that's a lot.

On the other hand, from that point on, Man and Woman would never have the same innocent love, with Eve herself becoming the unwitting prototype for all those Evil Woman songs, eventually leading to "Used to Love Her." And they would have to leave the Garden: "The world was all before them, where to choose / Their place of rest, and providence their guide."[46]

That is: where would they go now?

Where Do We Go Now?

Even though they provided the easy way in, it's *not* really so easy for Guns N' Roses. "Sweet Child O' Mine" is, with "Home Sweet Home," and "Every Rose Has Its Thorn," one of the great power ballads of the era, even though, with its note-y, noodle-y guitar intro, heavy-ish chorus, multiple lead guitar breaks plus long, two-part guitar solo, final extended breakdown, and big rock ending, it may not be a ballad at all. But it's a ballad in sentiment, and, of all things, a love song.

It's not like there's any shortage of love songs. From anyone else, a love song wouldn't be surprising. But Guns N' Roses' other songs are gritty and dirty. Take "It's So Easy," not to be confused with the Buddy Holly song of the same name, where "It's so easy to fall in love." Guns N' Roses have a very different idea of what is easy, and even what "easy" means: "It's so easy, easy / When everybody's tryin' to please me, baby," with this remarkable third verse:

> You get nothin' for nothin' if that's what ya do,
> Turn around bitch, I got a use for you,
> Besides, you ain't got nothin' better to do,
> And I'm bored.[47]

Axl takes Alice Cooper's anti-rhyme gag from "School's Out" ("And we got no intelligence, / We can't even think of a word that rhymes") even further: in his boredom, rhyming isn't worth the effort.

"It's So Easy" isn't an easy celebration of how easy it is to get sex and drugs, or a superficial sex, or maybe sexist, rollick. There's something Axl Rose—or at least the persona he assumes throughout the songs—loves even more than sex, drugs, and rock & roll. And that is grievance. It's not only *so* easy. It's *too* easy. It's terrible to be a woman who is objectified, nameless and used. But, amazingly, the song suggests, it's not fun to be the one doing the using or objectifying, either.

"It's So Easy" sounds like a party: fast bass, fast drums, raunchy guitar. An angry, angsty party, but still a party. But the words tell another story, as words so often do. Guns N' Roses weren't even rock stars when *Appetite for Destruction* was recorded, but Axl's low-range delivery on this song is already paunchy and tired. The vocal is doubled almost throughout by an overdubbed, bitchy high octave. It sounds cool, sure, but it speaks to the song's duality and split personality—illustrating decadence; lamenting decadence.

Mötley Crüe proclaimed the 1980s the decade of decadence, but it wasn't by any means the first. Among others, there was also the '90s—by which I mean, the 1890s. Axl is like a straight, twentieth-century Oscar Wilde (great rock name, as Zakk knew), capable of depicting, celebrating, and critiquing decadence simultaneously. Wilde's *The Picture of Dorian Gray* is the classic *fin de siècle* novel about a character as close to a rock star as one could be in 1890. Like metal musicians a century later, Wilde—flamboyantly dressed and long-haired—was unfairly conflated with his character and writing, so much so that he would be sentenced to prison for gross indecency (although, unlike most 1980s rockers, for a relationship with a man).

It's so easy (I'm done now) to focus on the novel's supernatural element: Dorian Gray commits a litany of debaucheries, most of which aren't named but that include opium and presumably sex, including gay sex. But, in further shades of rock stardom, he does not age, like Keith Richards; in addition, his many vices do not cause his death, also like Keith Richards. A magical portrait of him hidden in his attic grows old and ugly in his stead, in keeping with the ugliness of his deeds, while Dorian Gray stays young and beautiful. It's a Gothic wish fulfillment—related to heavy metal's own interest in the Gothic, obsession with youth, and deals with the devil—but, like all wishes, it has a cost. In this case, it's Dorian's soul, which he understands too late. It took Dorian Gray eighteen years of excess to recognize the limits of hedonism. Axl seems to get it almost right away: "So easy, / But nothin' seems to please me, / It all fits so right, / When I fade into the night."[48]

The song is almost punk in its simplicity and ferocity, staying on E (or E flat, since they're tuned down a half-step) for almost the whole time, except to use that Black Sabbath-inflected scary tritone for the verse. Yet while rock stars' actual lives usually can't help but glorify hedonism and excess, many songs warn against rock stardom, or even mock it, going all the way back to The Beatles and "Help." For every "Rock and Roll All Nite," there is a "Life's Been Good" (Joe Walsh, sarcastic, as usual), a Bob Seeger, sad on the road in "Turn the Page," or a David Bowie, bemoaning "Fame," all before G N' R. Later, Cypress Hill would have "(Rock) Superstar" and Nickelback would use the same idea in "Rockstar" to stage this astonishing rhyme: "I wanna be great like Elvis without the tassels, / Hire eight body guards that love to beat up assholes."[49] Elvis himself, arguably the first rock star, also had the first rock song lamenting rock stardom, with "Fame and Fortune": "Fame and fortune, / How empty they can be . . . They're only passing things," in contrast with "the touch of your lips on mine," or true love.⁵⁰

The contrast between the emptiness of rock life and the fullness of rock love that Elvis sang of in 1960 animates the tension between "It's So Easy" and "Sweet Child O' Mine." It's not "Crazy Bitch" vs. "I'm Sorry," Madonna/whore, or angel/devil. It's not Tawny Kitaen, although it is Erin Everly, who appears in a thong and bondage gear in the "It's So Easy" video, with Axl dressed to match in his assless chaps. While the video complicates the complaint of boredom by being filmed live in front of a rowdy crowd, Everly's presence creates the parallel to "Sweet Child O' Mine," since Rose said the lyrics to that song were written for her. "Sweet Child O' Mine," in contrast with "It's So Easy," instead develops a different version of a magical woman alluded to in Def Leppard's "Women": the woman as child.

Psychoanalyst/visionary Carl Jung was a student of Sigmund Freud. He went on to develop the ideas of introversion and extroversion, eventually revised (and, arguably, degraded) by Myers and Briggs into their personality test. Jung also pioneered the idea of the archetype. One of his main four archetypes is The Child. For Jung, the recurrence of the Child image throughout myth and religion provides a way of understanding our stories and therefore ourselves. As he writes in "The Psychology of the Child Archetype," "the child motif is a picture of certain *forgotten* things in our childhood," and further, "the child motif represents the pre-conscious, childhood aspect of the collective psyche."⁵¹ It's like W. Axl Rose read C.G. Jung himself. What the speaker of "Sweet Child o' Mine" loves about this woman is not the woman herself, exactly. It's what she represents to him. And what she represents is something the speaker, and, maybe also, the collective psyche, has forgotten: "She's got a smile that it seems to me, / Reminds me of childhood memories, / Where everything was as fresh as the bright blue sky."⁵²

A delay repeats "sky...sky...sky...," as though to emphasize its distance in the past. The sky, like the past, the sky *as* the past, is innocent, unblemished, like the speaker's lover's smile. The next verse continues in this vein: "Now and then when I see her face, / She takes me away to that special place, / And if I stare too long, I'd probably break down and cry."

As Jung continues, as though analyzing "Sweet Child O Mine" and not the archetype of the child, "Backwardness may be closer to naturalness, but in its turn it is always menaced by painful awakenings"⁵³—that is, he'd probably break down and cry. And then: "Her hair reminds me of a warm safe place, / Where as a child I'd hide, And pray for the thunder and the rain to quietly pass me by." Although repeatedly called a child, the subject of the song is not the only one. The speaker also becomes the Child, through the woman's beauty and reassuring presence. Her innocence takes him back to where he was before he entered the jungle, to the safe place in his past and now, in his mind.

The post-solo extended bridge repeats the refrain "Where do we go now?" Supposedly, Axl asked this question during the songwriting process and producer Mike Clink thought it was just the way into, and out of, the rest of the song, in the spirit of Led Zeppelin's "The Crunge" and its non-ending ending, where singer Robert Plant asks, "Where's that confounded bridge?" (That itself was an allusion to James Brown, but now we're too deep into music's collective unconscious.) But the line is not a gag, throwaway, or homage. The magical woman, in the form of the Child archetype, has led our speaker into the safe recess of the past. But once we've entered the past, where *do* we go?

So many of Guns N' Roses' lyrics from different songs wonder about where you're going. With "Sweet Child O Mine," throughout *Appetite for Destruction*, Axl also poses versions of the same existential and postmodern problem:

- "You know where you are?"—"Welcome to the Jungle"
- "Said where you going / What you gonna do . . . I've been looking everywhere"—"You're Crazy"
- "Sometimes it's easy to forget where you're goin'"—"Out Ta Get Me"
- "Ridin' the nightrain, never to return"—"Nightrain"
- "It's such a lonely place for you, for you to be"—"Rocket Queen"
- "So far away, so far away, so far away"—"Paradise City"

That last one, "Paradise City," reiterates the powerful, plaintive childhood wish of "Sweet Child O' Mine": "Oh won't you please take me home." Axl Rose, and Adam and Eve, are not the only ones who feel this way.

Home Sweet Home

Heavy metal songs about sex and love keep coming back to Freud's separation anxiety. And, for me, the biggest and greatest ballad of the era comes from its first and worst bad boys, Mötley Crüe.

Mötley Crüe didn't include a ballad on either of their first two albums, *Too Fast for Love* and *Shout at the Devil*. Their first ballad didn't appear until *Theatre of Pain*, the album recorded after Vince Neil killed Razzle from Hanoi Rocks and injured two others in his drunk driving fiasco, and the other band members, especially Nikki Sixx, struggled with addiction. Their very first single, "Toast of the Town," before even the first album, already was an anti-rock stardom warning *a la* "It's So Easy," about the fragility and precariousness of fame, again before Crüe had even achieved it: "You know it"—that is, "it" being "the toast of the town"—"won't last too long."⁵⁴

But it did, and it has, and now, after being underdogs and, indeed, the toast of the town, Crüe were ready for their ballad. It would not be a traditional love song. After the years on the road and the personal tragedies, by now, the idea of home—a kind of idyllic, platonic ideal of home—started to look better than the wish of the first album, to "Take Me to the Top." In that song, after repeating "take me to the top" eighteen times, at that point more of an incantation for a wish than a proper chorus, the final recitation adds (parenthetically on the lyrics), "Take me to the top (to the top and throw me off)."⁵⁵ They had made it to the top. They were, then, arguably, thrown off. And now, what was left was this: to go home.

Comedian George Carlin humorously contrasted baseball with football. "In football," Carlin states in stentorian baritone, "the object is for the quarterback, also known as the field general, to be on target with his aerial assault, riddling the defense by hitting his receivers with deadly accuracy in spite of the blitz, even if he has to use the shotgun. With short bullet passes and long bombs, he marches his troops into enemy territory, balancing this aerial assault with a sustained ground attack that punches holes in the forward wall of the enemy's defensive line." Switching voices to a high-pitched kid, Carlin concludes, "In baseball the object is to go home! And to be safe! I hope I'll be safe at home!"⁵⁶

"Home sweet home": Vince Neil repeats the well-worn phrase, associated more with embroidery kits for hanging on paneled walls than glam and pentagrams. And yet, it rings true. We believe him. I believe him. Home sweet home is the wish of a child, of Dorothy, relieved, returning to Kansas from Oz. But after what Mötley Crüe had been through in just a few years, going home, being set free—"just set me free"—is an appealing, humble wish.

The problem is that the speaker never gets there. Like "Livin' On A Prayer," the wish, the prayer, remains ever in the present, ever in motion, ever unfulfilled. "I'm on my way, / I'm on my way..." But the speaker never makes it home. The video opens with each band member receiving a phone call and answering it by saying "I'm on my way."⁵⁷ But they are on their way to perform at the Mötley Crüe concert that is the video, and the video ends with a shot of the tour bus. Maybe it's going home. But they're still on their way. They are still not home.

Vince Neil and Axl Rose had a famous feud in the 1980s. But they had the same longing—like the object of Carlin's joke-that-is-not-a-joke, to be safe at home. The openness of the yearning—"My heart is an open book / For the whole world to read," from the same band that sang PMRC-target "Bastard" just two years earlier—is intended for the listener, the implied "you" of "[you] just set me free." We would if we could. But we all loved Mötley Crüe too much to let them go. At least until they left us first, when Vince parted ways from the of the Crüe in 1992.

Then, in the mid-1990s, Mötley Crüe languished. They got a new singer, John Corabi, and recorded an actually pretty good album, the self-titled *Mötley Crüe* (1994). But the album and tour flopped. Tommy Lee became more famous for his tumultuous marriage to magical woman Pamela Anderson, among other things with Pamela Anderson, than for his drumming.

A decade-plus later, though, Mötley Crüe had become a generational touchstone. The movie *Hot Tub Time Machine*, in 2010, would conclude with a loving parody of the "Home Sweet Home" video. It was not just the butt of a joke, though. It was the pinnacle of living the '80s metal dream. Then, in 2022, "Home Sweet Home" would reappear in the HBO-MAX series *Peacemaker*. This time, it wouldn't be funny, or even cool. Instead, former wrestler turned actor John Cena plays a heartfelt instrumental rendition on the piano as a way for the audience to realize the heinous childhood abuse his character suffered at the hands of his father. Despite *Peacemaker*'s many gags, including a hug from a trained eagle named Eagly, "Home Sweet Home" demands to be taken seriously, the yearning for a home the ironically named Peacemaker never had. In baseball, but, maybe, also in life, the object is to go home. And to be safe. I hope I'll be safe at home.

Every Rose Has Its Thorn

Rather than playing the piano opening of "Home Sweet Home," singer Bret Michaels opts for a portable, practical instrument appropriate for a campfire ballad, his acoustic guitar, and begins strumming his sad, sad song:

> We both lie silently still
> In the dead of the night,
> Although we both lie close together
> We feel miles apart inside.[58]

The speaker is not on his way. He is not coming home. He is already home. Home is where the trouble begins. "Every Rose Has Its Thorn" is a broken home song, a breaking-up song, a broken heart song. He and the woman were together, they touched, and now they don't anymore. The opening verse begins with the palpable image of the bed, while poetically showing that proximity does not mean intimacy. After a verse of self-doubt–"Did my words not come out right"—we get to the chorus, still revolving around the same two simple alternating chords. It's a G chord—the most basic beginner's chord—to C add 9, which is just a C chord—and maybe even easier to play than a regular C—with the high D from the G chord held over and ringing on, like the memory of the previous chord won't go away even when the chord changes. Sadness lingers. Sadness isn't complicated. Neither are similes:

> Every rose has its thorn,
> Just like every night has its dawn,
> Just like every cowboy sings his sad, sad song,
> Every rose has its thorn.

It's in keeping with Shakespeare's Sonnet 35:

> No more be grieved at that which thou hast done:
> Roses have thorns, and silver fountains mud,
> Clouds and eclipses stain both moon and sun,
> And loathsome canker lives in sweetest bud.[59]

Shakespeare's speaker tells the listener not to be upset at what he's done, citing beautiful phenomena that nevertheless hold flaws. Like Shakespeare, Bret Michaels (a phrase that delights me) looks to the contradictions of nature for solace. He's not singing to forgive his lover, who, like the "thou" in Shakespeare, has presumably transgressed in some way. It's a simple acknowledgment of the vicissitudes of life. In keeping, the song goes up and down dynamically. After the first softer chorus ends, the whole band kicks in, and the song rocks on. C.C.'s guitar gently weeps, and then not so gently weeps, then rings out and turns to feedback. The band drops out, the drums and bass perform a tremendous fill to come back in, the song rocks another pre-chorus and chorus, and the acoustic guitar, alone again, like the singer, lets its final chords bookend its introduction.

It's tempting to chastise Bret Michaels for fudging his analogy for the sake of the rhyme. If the rose is sweet and the thorn sharp, shouldn't the following line read "Just like every dawn"—something positive—"has its night"—something negative? But the shift, inadvertent or not, makes a different point. Beauty contains the possibility of danger. Love makes us vulnerable. The potential to be hurt lies latent in any relationship. And then, just the opposite: hidden in darkness, the possibility of light. The speaker's sadness already holds the possibility of redemption. That redemption is not for the relationship, which can't be saved. The redemption comes in the form of the song itself. Bret Michaels is singing that sad, sad song for us. He is that cowboy. We know this, because he's wearing a cowboy hat.

This chapter has largely understood representations of women in these songs as binaries, as either/or's. By eschewing precise Shakespearian analogy, "Every Rose Has Its Thorn" deconstructs those binaries between women who are evil or angelic, and between passion and pain. Both possibilities always exist within the other. Everyone who has experienced heartbreak followed by self-recrimination implicitly understands this, but Poison found a way to play it to thousands of people. Juxtaposed against other Poison songs about "a girl on the left of me, a girl on the right" and "like gasoline you want to pump me" (a very different simile), "Every Rose" blooms. It turned out to be the perfect arena lull to break out the lighters and feel the sad feelings before getting back to talking dirty.

The Hair in Hair Metal Part II

Pearl Jam singer Eddie Vedder decided that 2022 was finally the year to share his feelings about Mötley Crüe:

> You know, I used to work in San Diego loading gear at a club. I'd end up being at shows that I wouldn't have chosen to go to—bands that monopolized late '80s MTV. The metal bands that—I'm trying to be nice—I despised. Girls, Girls, Girls and Mötley Crüe: [expletive] you. I hated it. I hated how it made the fellas look. I hated how it made the women look. It felt so vacuous.[60]

For anyone looking for a case-in-point of rock misogyny, Mötley Crüe might be the perfect poster boys, if WASP hadn't already been displayed on the PMRC's actual poster. "Live Wire"'s "Break her face or take down her legs," cited by Tipper Gore in the same opinion piece attacking "Under the Blade."[61] "Use you up, throw you away" in "Piece of Your Action." And, of course, Eddie Vedder's example, "Girls, Girls, Girls." On the one hand, "Girls, Girls, Girls" is a case study of the male gaze, where women exist as objects for male attention, as opposed to having their own autonomy. This song is the hair metal and groupie ethos in its purest, most concentrated strain, from the title through the subject matter, which is strippers. Vince Neil sings, "I'm such a good, good boy," but he's being facetious. Being bad boys was Mötley Crüe's *raison d'être*.

At the same time, the focus on the female body obscures the song's—and hair metal's—real focus: the male body, the "good boy," including the hair. It's not just the strippers in the video who are performing burlesque. The real burlesque act is, and always was, the members of Mötley Crüe themselves.

Mötley Crüe make themselves the focus of visual attention with their elaborate costuming, physicality, and elaborate, three-dark-brunettes-and-a-blond coifs. As a result, they, and many of the hair metal bands, were derided as looking and acting like women, which, everyone was supposed to understand, was bad. The androgyny and misogyny were intertwined. (Alice Cooper and later, Marilyn Manson and many others, adopted feminine names or styles as bastions of rebellion and got the predictable reaction.) The misogyny of the era wasn't limited to sexual portrayals of women in videos or the explicit lyrics Tipper Gore crusaded against. In an extension of systemic misogyny, the worst insult a man could receive was that he was like a woman. This strategy only works if women are something people—men, yes, but, paradoxically, women, also—should not want to be in the first place. And this line of criticism didn't come from outsiders like Tipper Gore, either; it can from the rifts in the fragmented '80s metal community. Kerry King of Slayer put it bluntly, and he wasn't alone: "Before we came out, what was popular? Glam. Men looking like women. I knew that's what I didn't want to be."[62]

The condemnation of men looking like or displaying themselves in the way that women stereotypically display themselves—as objects to be gazed upon—goes back at least to Elvis Presley. As Trent Hill writes, *Life Magazine* and the *New York Times* "both agreed that Elvis's signature stage mannerism—his wild, grinding, abandoned hip movements—were not so much suggestive of a new masculine sexuality as they were reminders of the old spectacular presentations of the female sex: the burlesque, the bump-and-grind, the hoochy-koochy."[63] Elvis's sexuality was dangerous because it was attractive *to* women, who were not supposed to express any sexual agency in the 1950s, but also because to be a man on display was seductive *like* a woman.

"Girls, Girls, Girls" becomes a form of self-defense, a way of saying that the Crüe, too, like Slayer, are tough guys. The song's first verse, the title's repetition to the contrary, isn't about girls at all. It boasts how threatening the male speaker is: "Friday night and I need a fight, / My motorcycle and a switchblade knife," at which point in the video Tommy Lee throws a switchblade knife, in case we missed it.[64] "Handful of grease in my hair feels right": not hairspray. Grease, like a real man, like Elvis, even as he was accused of effeminacy in his own time. The imagery, the use of "girls," like the sexuality, is deliberately retrograde. It is, in keeping with Judith Butler and Queer Theory, less an affirmation of Mötley Crüe's heterosexuality than it is an attempt at homosociality; "Girls, Girls, Girls" allows men to bond with other men, not with women. Women are the means, the conduit, of that male bonding.

That Mötley Crüe turned to motorcycle fashion—along with Slayer, who adopted black leather, studs, and spikes—is all the more ironic considering that the look was popularized in metal by Judas Priest's Rob Halford. Halford took it from gay male subculture and eventually, in 1998, came out of the closet as gay himself, the first metal star of his stature to do so, although, in fairness, maybe no one else was of Halford's stature. The two seemingly opposite pillars of metal fashion, hairspray and spandex vs. leather and studs, lie on foundations of androgyny and homosexuality.

Looked at from this lens, the Filthy Fifteen seems less a reaction to X for Explicit than a 1950's style moral panic about the state of heterosexuality itself. In that *Newsday* editorial, in her first foray into the Filthy Fifteen, Tipper Gore said that "sadomasochism, bondage, incest, and rape are out of the closet and into the lyrics." She was referring to Mötley Crüe and Judas Priest (and Twisted Sister, certainly no strangers to androgyny). "Out of the closet," then, meant exactly what it sounded like.

The homosocial bro bonding of "Girls, Girls, Girls" didn't work for Eddie Vedder and others. But the spectacle of androgynous male display did work for Mötley Crüe's and other hair metal bands' many women fans. That these bands were attractive to women did not staunch the male disparagement, the accusations that the musicians were like women, from groups like Slayer. They were also disparaged *because*, not despite that, women liked them, a line of criticism often unfairly aimed at artists who are popular with women, going back to Elvis through decades of boy bands. That so many women responded positively to "Girls, Girls, Girls" could be a form of false consciousness, to be sure. But maybe they were also responding to Mötley Crüe's own Elvis-esque burlesque performance, providing an opportunity not just for the male gaze of the "Girls, Girls, Girls" video, but, at the same time, the opposite as well: the chance for women to look and leer themselves.

The Female Gaze

So far, these representations of women have only been from male musicians' points of view. That most of the perspectives are male is one of the genre's shortcomings. It is also, for the same reasons, a shortcoming of much of literary history, and much of the Western canon of literature itself. Literary critic Harold Bloom's 1994 book *The Western Canon* assembled his list of the twenty-six greatest writers of all time, and only four women appeared on it.[65] The decades since the 1980s, in both heavy music and literature, have attempted, and achieved, far greater inclusion.

At the same time, two major artists during the 1980s provide a counterpoint to the male perspective. Consider Lita Ford, the queen of 1980s heavy metal. And yet her means of balancing male rock-star behavior was, in many ways, to participate in it. Ford lived the sex, drugs, and rock & roll of her male counterparts. She wore the black leather, performed the big stage shows, and toured indefatigably. Most importantly, after leaving The Runaways, her successful 1970s all-female rock band, Ford became her own bandleader, took over singing, and moved her lead guitar playing to the forefront of her sound.

Ford's hit "Kiss Me Deadly" (1988) captures all of the seemingly male-gendered elements of the lifestyle: "I went to a party last Saturday night, / I didn't get laid, I got in a fight uh-huh, / It ain't no big thing."[66] And for Lita Ford, it ain't. But for anyone else, it would be. "Kiss Me Deadly" *was*, in fact, written by a man, Mick Smiley, which might explain the perspective. And yet, Lita Ford has no trouble taking on the outlook and the cultural practices of rock & roll usually associated with men, easily and casually. The title comes from a 1955 Mike Hammer film noir about a murdered woman, but Ford turns the film—and the usual rock conventions of the song and '80s rock generally—around. After all the songs about an evil woman, a devil woman, and a dangerous woman, here is another one, but this time the singer *is* that dangerous woman: "Come on pretty baby, kiss me deadly." It's hard now to picture a man singing the line. The supposed truism, stated overtly in Noel Monk's book about Van Halen, that managing a rock band means "We want the girls in the audience to want to be with the boys in the band, and we want the guys in the audience to wish they were in the band," becomes irrelevant.[67] Everyone wants to be Lita Ford. And certainly, a lot of people wanted to be with her. Ford seemed in control of her sexuality, her metal goddess image, in the same way as her male contemporaries. Throughout *The Dirt*, Nikki Sixx refers to Lita Ford reverentially and respectfully. She is the only person to receive this treatment. She had romantic relationships with Sixx, Eddie Van Halen, Richie Sambora, and Tony Iommi, not as a groupie, not as a *girl*, but as a fellow rock star.[68]

Lita Ford's former bandmate in The Runaways, Joan Jett, was even more iconic in the 1980s and beyond, having toured with Mötley Crüe and Def Leppard as recently as 2022. Joan Jett embraced the black leather and heavy guitars, but she was cool against Lita Ford's deadly hotness. Jett broke big earlier than Ford with a huge hit, "I Love Rock 'n' Roll," in 1982. It too reverses the usual male gaze of the heavy metal song, opening with the lines "I saw him dancin' there by the record machine, / I knew he must've been about 17."[69] With its self-referentiality, a rock song about listening to rock songs, and Jett's deadpan delivery and catchy "Ow!" at the end of the chorus, the song would become a rock radio staple.

Like Lita Ford's "Kiss Me Deadly," Joan Jett didn't write "I Love Rock 'n' Roll," or even record it first. The song belonged to a forgotten group called The Arrows. Their version proves to be a very different song, despite that the lyrics, aside from swapping male pronouns for female pronouns, are identical. And, for that matter, so is the music, with Jett's version a half step higher and better arranged and produced. When sung by a guy, "I Love Rock 'n' Roll" is a typical homage to the joys of jailbait, and the references to dimes and jukeboxes sound dated even by the 1970s. Even more than "Kiss Me Deadly," the gender inversion of "I Love Rock 'n' Roll" is revealing and powerful. A song about some fella in his 30s hanging out in a juke joint hoping to score with a high school girl seems sad at best and predatory at worst in the twenty-first century.[70] Conversely, Joan Jett sounds tough, in control, and able to breathe new life into the phrase "I Love Rock 'n' Roll." It's a cliché for The Arrows but believable and, for all her coolness, sincere from Joan Jett, even as her MC jacket and black bangs suggest a singer with a wry ironic sensibility. We don't take her interest in the 17-year-old seriously, either. It's a love song for rock & roll, not boys. Her invitation to "come and take your time and dance with me" is not for him. It's for the listeners. It's for everyone.

Post Script: Just Give It Up

"Take It Off" (2002) by The Donnas, provides a flipside to many of the songs chronicled in this chapter, but especially Mötley Crüe's "Girls, Girls, Girls." Taken together, "Take It Off" and "Girls, Girls, Girls" allow the listener to consider what changes when women play and sing a song that objectifies men, where they're the rockers and the subjects of the sexual chase. The lyrics turn Mötley Crüe inside out:

> Need your love 1,2,3,
> Stop starin' at my D cup,
> Don't waste time, just give it to me,
> C'mon baby, just feel me up.[71]

The song was used in a Budweiser commercial, perhaps the ultimate dude compliment. Yet it's less a tribute to Mötley Crüe than it is to Lita Ford and Joan Jett, more than a decade after they broke the rock ceiling. Reversing the male gaze doesn't seem demeaning to The Donnas, or to men, or to anyone. Their songs and lyrics reaffirm the spirit of sexual performance that the PMRC wanted to label explicit, and develop Elvis's sexuality to its final stage: The Donnas perform Mötley Crüe who were performing Elvis who was performing female burlesque. The video for "Take It Off" emphasizes their playfulness with gender even further. The Donnas are playing a high school battle of the bands, but then, in obvious costumes, they also appear as a Joan Jett-esque punk band, the judges rating the bands with Olympic-style number cards, and even themselves in male drag. The Donnas play post '80s hard rock, but they also play on (male?) viewers' latent biases and expectations of what women in rock are supposed to look and act like.

Or, at least, *were* supposed to act like. 2002 is a long time ago, too. Another twenty years later, in 2024, Skid Row announced that, with the departure of not-Sebastian-Bach singer Erik Grönwall, they would conclude their tour with singer/guitarist Lzzy Hale, of Halestorm. When Lzzy Hale sings "Youth Gone Wild," there will not be any dichotomies. No angels, no devils; no Madonnas, no whores. Hale will not dance on the hood of a Camaro. She will be David Coverdale, not Tawny Kitaen. When she sings, "We are the youth gone wild," her "we" will include everyone who believes it, young or not. In her statement, Hale, indifferently, unceremoniously, used non-gender-specific language: "We are all just astronauts cut from the same cloth, worshipping the same magic that is this music. I'm so grateful for their support of me in my career, and as a fellow human."[72]

The same magic that is this music. It is a lovely egalitarian twenty-first-century coda to the '80s.

As it turns out, though, in the actual 1980s, the PMRC was against magic, too.

5

O for Occult

Figure 10 An engraving by the French printmaker Gustave Dore of Satan Smitten by Michael, a scene from John Milton's Paradise Lost. (Photo by Chris Hellier/Corbis via Getty Images).

> I AM THE WAY INTO THE CITY OF WOE.
> I AM THE WAY TO A FORSAKEN PEOPLE.
> I AM THE WAY INTO ETERNAL SORROW.
> SACRED JUSTICE MOVED MY ARCHITECT.
> I WAS RAISED HERE BY DIVINE OMNIPOTENCE,
> PRIMORDIAL LOVE AND ULTIMATE INTELLECT.
> ONLY THOSE ELEMENTS TIME CANNOT WEAR
> WERE MADE BEFORE ME, AND BEYOND TIME I STAND.
> ABANDON ALL HOPE YE WHO ENTER HERE.
>
> Inscription on the gates to hell, Inferno, Canto III,
Dante (c. 1314, trans. John Ciardi)[1]

> *Welcome to hell,*
> *Welcome to hell,*
> *Welcome to hell,*
> *Welcome to hell.*
>
> "Welcome to Hell," Venom (1981)[2]

During her 1985 Senate testimony, Susan Baker, the other founder of the Parents Music Resource Center, said, "While a few outrageous recordings have always existed in the past, the proliferation of songs glorifying rape, sadomasochism, incest, the occult, and suicide by a growing number of bands illustrates this escalating trend that is alarming."[3]

It's a disconcerting list, but one item stands out as categorically unlike the others: the occult. What does it mean for a song to glorify the occult? Maybe more importantly, what does Baker mean by "the occult" in the first place? Glen Danzig, whose songs include "Heart of the Devil," "Devil's Plaything," "Devil on Hwy 9," "Devil's Angels," and "Am I a Demon," reasonably wonders the same. "People like to use the word occult like it's going out of style. It can cover parapsychology, witchcraft, Satanism, black magic—everything. It's an unfair word."[4]

The ambiguity is worth analyzing, and clarifying. After all, descriptions of Satan, hell, and aspects of what might be called the occult are central to the Western canon of literature. And where Baker sees "occult," I see powerful acts of the imagination—and even more powerful metaphors for rebellion, nonconformity, and the wisdom of youth, three of heavy metal's dearest values. And where Baker was ostensibly concerned with teen welfare, efforts like hers not only failed to protect anyone—they actively caused harm.

Descent to Hell

Danzig's own song "Mother" warns against parents overly meddling in their children's lives: "Mother / Can you keep them in the dark for life? / Can you hide them from the waiting world?" Not surprisingly, Danzig said that the song was about Tipper Gore and the PMRC.[5] But the language turns dark, threatening, and violent: "But if you wanna find hell with me / I can show you what it's like / 'Til you're bleeding."[6] The ambiguity of "find hell with me," the overall menacing tone, the sacrificed chicken in the original cut of the video (no real chickens were harmed), and presence of one Glen Danzig can't help but make the song sound like an invitation to the occult, or at least, *a* cult. And, in a sense, it is. The cult is the metal culture. The initiation is simply listening.

Mercyful Fate's "Into the Coven" and Venom's "Possessed," the two songs the PMRC put on their Filthy Fifteen list labeled "Occult," are, in keeping with Glen Danzig's criticism, not really about "the occult" at all, but rather straightforward invitations to a fuzzy form of Satanism but a concrete form of metal. Metal offers its fans an invitation to its community, its subculture: "Come, come into my Coven / And become Lucifer's Child," sings King Diamond, Mercyful Fate's face-painted, falsetto-voiced singer.[7] (Insane Clown Posse should pay him royalties for stealing his makeup.) Similarly, Venom commands the listener to "Look at my eyes and you will see / Fire is burning inside of me . . . Look at me Satan's child / Born of evil thus defiled."[8] It's a heightened version of the grandfathers of face paint Kiss and their fan club, the Kiss Army. Kiss was also accused of Satanism; the urban legend was that Kiss stood for "Knights In Satan's Service." It didn't. But like all religious proselytizers, Kiss was trying to recruit and grow the base. They succeeded.

Unlike Paul Stanley and Gene Simmons, who knew great marketing when they saw it, King Diamond seems to have been an actual Satanist, but in the tradition of Anton LaVey, where Satan is a metaphor and figure of rebellion—that is, a Milton's Satanist, as we will see. Venom singer Chronos, presumably named after the Greek mythological father of the gods who ate his children, never shared King Diamond's true belief: "'I don't preach Satanism, occultism, witchcraft or anything,' Cronos said in 1985. 'Rock & roll is basically entertainment and that's as far as it goes.'"[9] Instead, Venom's "Possessed" went for greater shock value and a surprising level of specificity: "We drink the vomit of the priests, / Make love with the dying whore, / We suck the blood of the beast, / And hold the key to death's door." Not everyone will agree on its entertainment value, but Venom had its fans.

Satanism certainly works as well for shock value alone as it does for genuine rebellion. But hell and the devil do more. As Venom understood, the imagery of hell and the damned is an excellent vehicle to depict horrors as entertainment, although traditionally, it was couched in the language of religion and so was considered acceptable, even moral. In this way, hell can be used to demonstrate a just and fair universe, even if the representations themselves are violent and shocking. Good is rewarded and evil punished, and good people watching evil people get punished is perfectly fine. Heavy metal hell, then, provides additional metaphorical language for justice and revenge, plus more metal themes like pride and rebellion. In doing so, it follows a long literary and folkloric tradition.

American Faust

Metal's roots are American blues and European classical. It might sound like an odd, transcontinental marriage on paper, but it's easy enough to hear. Once again, Black Sabbath provides the way in. Sabbath began as a blues band—Ozzy himself said so, and sometimes he remembers things. They took their name from the 1963 Italian horror film featuring *Frankenstein*'s Boris Karloff, and the rest is history, or maybe self-made mythology. But while never intended as a racial descriptor, the *Black* in Black Sabbath is revealing and takes on multiple meanings in practice. Ozzy explained that at least some people thought Black Sabbath would, in fact, be Black on their first American tour: "One guy, a big tall fella with a massive Afro, spent the whole gig sitting up on a high window ledge, and every few minutes he'd shout out, 'Hey, you—Black Sabbath!' . . . [I asked him,] 'What is it, eh?' And he peered down at me with this puzzled look on his face. 'You guys ain't *black*,' he said."[10] More recently, Black Sabbath's official online store began selling t-shirts that use the Black Sabbath logo but spell out *Black Lives Matter*, with the proceeds donated to the movement.[11]

Black Sabbath's debut album opens with its eponymous title track, the metal trifecta of band name/album name/song name, and, according to a thousand critics and millions of fans, the sound of heavy metal was born. It was birthed from a classical lineage on one side. The riff and song revolve around the tritone, also known as the diminished fifth interval, the famous *"diabolus in musica."*

You know it when you hear it. It just *sounds evil*. The album and song open with spooky bells and lightning crashing, before the guitar, doubled by the bass and accented by Bill Ward's wild drumming, comes booming in. Then, it calms down, but tensely, for the most famous opening line in metal: "What is this that stands before me?"[12] It's the same question anyone listening for the first time might ask of the song itself.

"Black Sabbath" has no sung chorus; the diabolical riff simply returns *fortissimo*, and in its sublimity, it is enough. Near the end, the song speeds up, Ozzy gets agitated, and the lyrics conclude, "Is it the end, my friend? / Satan's comin' 'round the bend." We knew from the tritone that he was on the way all along.

Composer/guitarist Tony Iommi and bassist Geezer Butler had been listening to Gustav Holst's "Mars, The Bringer of War" from the suite *The Planets*.[13] (That song would also influence Diamond Head's "Am I Evil?" [1980]. The answer to the title—"Yes I am"—comes in the chorus, but the tritone had already told us.) The heavy brass tritone, about four minutes into "Mars," sounds powerful and menacing, portending violence. The classical use of the tritone goes back further, though. Camille Saint-Saëns's "Danse macabre, Op. 40," from 1874, based on a poem describing Death calling for skeletons to dance on Halloween, with its devilish violins, would not sound out of place in a movie like *The Nightmare Before Christmas*. Franz Liszt's Dante Sonata, from 1849, and separately, his Dante Symphony, from 1857, take the listener through medieval Italian poet Dante Alighieri's *Divine Comedy*, beginning with *Inferno*, or Hell, which is represented, naturally, with the tritone. (Dante, as we'll see, will prove to have a complex relationship to metal.)

And yet, the next two songs on *Black Sabbath*, while heavy, are more clearly offshoots of the blues. "The Wizard" revolves around, of all things, a big honkin' harmonica, and Ozzy's voice sounds smokier and more bluesily melismatic than on the previous track, or, maybe, any other Ozzy track. The next song, "Behind the Walls of Sleep," is even bluesier, a cousin to Led Zeppelin's "Heartbreaker," which, like many of their heavy, riffy songs, is based on the pentatonic, or blues, scale. The coincidental resemblance to the word "pentagram" comes from the prefix *penta-*, meaning five: a five-note scale; a five-pointed star.

Similarly, Led Zeppelin themselves are part classical, part blues, plus a dose of folk, music that, like the blues, is rooted in orality rather than classical music's emphasis on score and musical literacy. We can chart Zeppelin's influences through two of the many lawsuits filed against them. Blues artist Willie Dixon sued in 1985, contending that Zep's "Whole Lotta Love" plagiarized his song "You Need Love," recorded by blues singer/guitarist Muddy Waters in 1962. Then, in 2016, Zeppelin was sued by the estate of the rock band Spirit, alleging that Zeppelin's most famous song, "Stairway to Heaven," plagiarized Spirit's song "Taurus." Jimmy Page countered that "Stairway" was built around a common classical progression, and he got expert support: "Lawrence Ferrara, a music professor at New York University, said 17th century Venetian opera singers and Mozart used music techniques which feature in both 'Stairway to Heaven' and 'Taurus' as he played both songs on a keyboard in the courtroom."[14] Dixon's suit was settled out of court; Spirit lost.

Deep Purple also combines classical and blues, especially in the same song. "Highway Star" (1972) starts as a fast, heavy blues—another pentatonic-based verse guitar and bass riff, this time doubled by keyboardist John Lord's overdriven Hammond organ. But then, the keyboard and guitar-doubled and -traded solos are positively neo-classical, Baroque-inspired note-fests employing the harmonic minor scale that launches into the kind of fast arpeggios that would later become associated with guitar wunderkind Yngwie Malmsteen. As though to signal that the classical break is over, the band runs up and down a blues scale, and screamer supreme Ian Gillan comes back for another verse, before it's time for—why not?—another round of solos.

If metal is the musical descendant of the blues and classical, it's no wonder, then, that it has such a strong relationship to the devil and the occult. The devil sits at the center of both their founding musical—and, it would seem, lyrical—influences. Along with the musical juxtaposition of styles, and despite the disparate continents, time periods, racial differences, and historical associations, European classical music and American blues share a significant *ur*-narrative: they tell, retell, and remix, the story of a man's bargain with the devil.

Faust provides the storyline for at least twenty classical music pieces and, separately, twenty operas, composed by, among many others, Beethoven, Schubert, Wagner, Mendelssohn, Berlioz, Liszt, Rachmaninoff, and Stravinsky. In each, the story remains the same: a man named Faust sells his soul to the devil, sometimes named Mephistopheles, in exchange for something. Hence, the phrase "Faustian bargain": trading one's values, one's very self, for knowledge, magic, youth, power, or pleasure in life, with subsequent suffering in the afterlife.

Classical—including literature also based on the Faust story, by literary heavyweights like Christopher Marlowe, Thomas Mann, and, most famously, Johann Wolfgang von Goethe—was never stigmatized for its preoccupation with the devil. But the blues was. It was always clear that Faust was a story, featuring characters, and had a moral that warned against bargaining with the devil.[15] Blues, and later, rock & roll and heavy metal, blurred the lines between the artist and the character, the person and the persona, as well as complicated the moral. This conflation, as we've seen, causes confusion and controversy for critics looking for it. But it is not itself a bad thing. Fans find it fun and entertaining, as fans should.

The American Faust story has become inextricably tied to one person: blues singer/songwriter/guitarist Robert Johnson (1911–1938). Johnson, supposedly a mediocre musician, disappeared for a few years. When he returned, he was the best guitarist anyone had ever heard. According to stories, he went to the crossroads and sold his soul to the devil for the musical ability. In folklore, people who committed suicide were buried at the crossroads to prevent them from coming back undead, as the intersection would confuse their vampiric form. Alternately, a burial at the crossroads was the closest that an unconsecrated death could come to a cross-like grave marker. Still other folktales say that the crossroads is the place to make a deal with the devil. In every case, it's a powerful metaphor about choice and human free will. Which path will we take in life—and in death? And even after death?

When Johnson died a few years later, at the age of 27, he was the first of the so-called "27 Club" that would later include Brian Jones of the Rolling Stones, Jim Morrison, Janise Joplin, Jimi Hendrix, Kurt Cobain, and Amy Winehouse, all of whom died at 27. Johnson died under what can only be called mysterious circumstances. He may have been poisoned by the jealous husband of a potential love interest, a fatal cocktail of, if not sex, drugs, and rock & roll, then maybe sex, booze, and blues. Also, poison. And so, in his death, even more than in his life, Robert Johnson's mythos was secured.

Johnson's preternatural playing, seeming to pull off two and even three guitar parts at once, his sometimes-spectral voice, and his mystical lyrics, in the twenty-nine songs he recorded in 1936, seem to support the case for the supernatural. His catalogue includes songs like "Cross Road Blues," "Hellhound on My Trail," and, most damningly, "Me and the Devil Blues," where Johnson sings, "Early this morning / When you knocked upon my door / And I said, 'Hello Satan / I believe it's time to go.'"[16] ("Door" and "go" rhyme if you're Robert Johnson.) Black Sabbath's debut would echo Johnson in their song "NIB": "My name is Lucifer, please take my hand"—although, Sabbath being Sabbath, the song appears to be about the devil falling in love.[17] In both songs, the use of the first person "I" to tell the story conflates the real-life singer with the song's speaker. Johnson's speaker is part of the devilish adventure, and the listener is a confidante, an ear-witness.

In true proto-metal spirit, Johnson, even in the 1930s, appeared to be cultivating a musical persona for himself. While it's tempting to imagine a literal pact with the devil, it's better to imagine Johnson, in the infancy of recording technology and before anything we consider modern media, already understanding that singing "me and the devil" was a quick way to earn notoriety. The song concludes with the speaker's death, but then, in Dickinsonian fashion (both Emily and Bruce), the continued life of the spirit: "You may bury my body, ooh / Down by the highway side, / So my old evil spirit / Can get a Greyhound bus and ride."[18]

Johnson didn't have to have a pact with the devil. He learned and practiced for years, under the tutelage of the great Son House. Thanks, though, in part to the mythologizing—furthered still by the blues-rock musicians who would later idolize him like Keith Richards and Eric Clapton, both of whom would have their own hellish songs—Johnson's spirit would indeed live on, through his lineage in the blues, rock & roll, and eventually heavy metal.

Johnson—and, later, heavy metal—displayed a powerful literary ambiguity when it comes to the devil and the occult. His songs greet the devil at the door, invoke the legend of the crossroads and the power it confers, and summon the magic and mystique. And yet, Johnson's lyrics in other songs contradict the supposedly satanic alliance. In "Cross Road Blues," Johnson sings, "I went to the crossroad, fell down on my knees, / Asked the Lord above, 'Have mercy, now, save poor Bob if you please.'"[19] As Robert Johnson's grandson Steven Johnson says, "I often tell people to listen to the lyrics themselves to the song 'Crossroad Blues.' Why would you go to the crossroad to sell your soul to the devil and be asking God to save you at the same time? The two just don't go together."[20]

He's right. These lyrics are not the language of a man making a pact with the devil and losing his soul, the Faust story. This is the Christian story of sin and redemption. And while "Hellhound on My Trail" sounds like someone being chased by the devil—"And the days keeps on worryin' me, / There's a hellhound on my trail, hellhound on my trail"—Johnson's gigging schedule as a traveling musician renders the hellhounds metaphorical and the song a predecessor to the rock and metal on-the-road genre, including Scorpions' "Rock You Like a Hurricane" ("I've got to leave, it's time for a show"), Bon Jovi's "Wanted Dead or Alive," and Mötley Crüe's "Home Sweet Home."

More troublingly, Robert Mugge suggests that the "hellhounds" are the musicians and scholars that just won't leave the deceased Johnson alone.[21] And most troublingly, the documentary "ReMastered: Devil at the Crossroads" (2019) wonders whether the "hellhound" is a thinly disguised version of the very real bloodhounds used historically to track runaway slaves or any Black people suspected of any infractions.[22] In each case, the seemingly satanic reference codes additional, metaphorical significances.

If madness in metal is best understood as a metaphor most of the time, the devil—and, as we'll see, other representations of hell and the occult in metal—is best understood as a metaphor all of the time. Perhaps no metaphor is as powerful as the devil, which is why it's so pervasive, including in Christianity. Yet the devil—Satan, Mephistopheles, Lucifer, Beelzebub, Baphomet; as they say, the devil goes by many names—has stood for more than just Christianity's version of evil throughout literary history. John Milton's version of Lucifer, in the epic (because it's a story, not because it's awesome, although it is awesome) *Paradise Lost*, is a fallen angel, a rebel, and an anti-hero, written during an age of political revolutions, who gets all of his poem's best lines. Going back even further, in his *Inferno*, Dante creates a Satan who is a traitor and sad convict, weeping tears that turn to ice from his own wings beating in attempted escape, ironically further trapping him. Hell is his prison, not his kingdom, and he suffers, surrounded by fellow sinners. But in describing hell, Dante gets to have wicked fun in his representations of graphic violence and revenge fantasies.

Together, Milton and Dante popularized many people's contemporary images of hell and the devil, ideas that were never scriptural. In the Hebrew Bible, Satan is more of a devil's advocate than a devil himself, raising questions about Job's faith that God is willing to test. Robert Johnson's devil, then, seizes the idea of power for someone who was shut out of political and economic power during his short life. The deal was never with the devil. The deal was with everyone who wanted to believe it. It's the same deal, the same rules of the contract, to recall Don DeLillo's phrase, that rock stars make today. It is still sometimes fatal.

Satan Rocks

Like the topic of madness, the devil holds a special place in metal, in its representation of power and freedom, and in Satan's rebellion against a conventional, overbearing Parent. While the Faust story dominates classical music's storytelling, versions of *Paradise Lost*'s satanic hero, rather than the devilish antagonist, is more widespread in metal songs and iconography. Ghost, Marilyn Manson, and The Police (not metal) reference Mephistopheles on their songs, but in the 1980s, only Sabbat's "A Cautionary Tale" (1988) seems an actual retelling of Faust. The closest we have to a metal Faust is arguably the uber-'80s movie *Crossroads* (1986), starring *The Karate Kid*'s Ralph Macchio and Jami Gertz. In a plot directly revolving around the Robert Johnson myth, Macchio's Eugene has a guitar duel with the devil's own shredder, played by former Frank Zappa, then-Alcatrazz, and future David Lee Roth virtuoso Steve Vai. Despite all of the music throughout the film being blues, the contest is metal, which, by 1986, was clearly the devil's musical idiom.[23] The play *The Book of Mormon* features an excellent number, "Spooky Mormon Hell Dream," replete with distorted guitars. Needless to say, Satan rocks its metal-style shred guitar solo.

The Tenacious D movie *The Pick of Destiny* (2006), like *Crossroads*, ends with the protagonist beating the devil. This is, it is worth emphasizing, not supposed to be the end of *Faust*. It's certainly not much of a warning against dealing with the devil with this revision. Both seem more indebted to Charlie Daniels's 1979 country hit "The Devil Went Down to Georgia" than *Faust* itself. At the end of "Devil Went Down to Georgia," Johnny comes away with a golden fiddle, as opposed to, say, losing his immortal soul.

Maybe that's because Faust was never quite in keeping with metal's idea of the devil in the first place. *Faust*'s Mephistopheles is a part of Christian storytelling in the sense that he is evil and manipulative. In the end, *Faust* is a cautionary tale against making deals with the devil. In Goethe's *Faust Part Two*, Faust even goes to heaven, earning redemption through God's grace. Milton's Satan, though, is more complex—and interesting. That he is beyond redemption, too proud to change, is, for a certain kind of person, part of his symbolic appeal. He, like Adam and Eve, has free will. He decides to rebel, and then decides to rebel again. Satan chooses his actions, regrets them, but carries on anyway, leading Adam and Eve to the temptation that costs them paradise.

At the end of the song "Black Sabbath," on the album *Black Sabbath*, by the band Black Sabbath, the speaker seems to summon the devil, but he ultimately regrets it. In the end, Ozzy wails, "Oh, no! No! Please, God, help me!" Robert Johnson does not open "The Cross Road Blues," as one might expect, with a pact with the devil, but, as Johnson's grandson noted, with a plea to God. Maybe both are closer to *Faust* than I'd led you to believe. Johnson's speaker even ends with a lament, but it's not about missing God, or, for that matter, losing to the devil: "I went to the crossroad, baby, I looked East and West, / Lord, I didn't have no sweet woman, ooh well, babe, in my distress."[24] It's why Adam chooses to eat the fruit and be expelled from paradise with Eve: because he loved her, and he didn't want to abandon her.

The PMRC missed all of the literary aspects of "the occult" in its easy, blanket dismissal and fearmongering. Not just its prominent place in symbolism, storytelling, and spirituality. But that, most of the time, its use is a metaphorical call to consider one's choices, freedoms, and responsibilities. That's what Satan, Adam, Eve, and all rock & roll rebels do. We're still waiting on Susan Baker.

My Friends Are Gonna Be There Too

If we look at some of the biggest metal hits, like Van Halen's "Runnin' with the Devil" or AC/DC's "Highway to Hell," it's clear that the devil and hell continue to be powerful metaphors for rebellion and freedom—that is, for the markers of adolescence itself. It's fitting that Led Zeppelin saw the path to heaven as a stairway—something one must climb, with effort, one step at a time. Langston Hughes used the image in his poem "Mother to Son" (1922), writing, "Life for me ain't been no crystal stair. / It's had tacks in it, / And splinters, / And boards torn up, And places with no carpet on the floor— / Bare."

But the poem becomes a paean to perseverance, of "a-climbin' on, / And reachin' landin's, / And turnin' corners."[25] Hell, though, does not require determination. It is eminently drivable, convenient, and fast, as AC/DC is happy to share: "No stop signs, / Speed limit, / Nobody's gonna slow me down."[26] It sounds like much more fun than taking the stairs, and it is. AC/DC may not be American, but they resonate here so well because the car and the highway are America's favorite symbols of freedom and of the self, as Whitesnake understood. Plus, it's all tongue-in-cheek. Or it would be, if singer Bon Scott hadn't died, in 1980, of alcohol poisoning at the age of 33. He was not 27, but 33 seems an equally portentous age to die. In spite of his death, the song never became a cautionary tale, ending up on at least thirteen television and movie soundtracks when filmmakers needed to signal adventure, including cues for actual descents into hell in both *Little Nicky* (2000) and *Percy Jackson and the Olympians: The Lightning Thief* (2010).

Similarly, Mötley Crüe's *Shout at the Devil* (1983), with its all-black album cover featuring the pentagram, becomes a symbolic way of fighting cultural norms. Some parents panicked. The album was featured on an episode of *20/20* called "The Devil Worshippers" in 1985, another example of the since-debunked panic of satanic murders that inspired the *Stranger Things* Season 4 ending.[27] "Shout at the Devil"'s verse's lyrics are unintelligible when listened to, but the song affords fans the opportunity to shout "Shout!," the one understandable word, no less than sixty-five times, which is some workmanlike defiance. By contrast, The Beatles' "Twist and Shout" clocks a paltry three "Shout"s, although in fairness, that song is more about shaking, by which they mean sex.

Reading those verse lyrics, though, reveals a cascade of vivid and violent images: "He's the wolf screaming lonely in the night, / He's the blood stain on the stage"; "Well, he's the razor to the knife, oh, lonely is our lives"; "He'll be the love in your eyes, he'll be the blood between your thighs"; leading into that shouty chorus.[28] But the listener is not exhorted to shout *with* the devil, but to shout *at* the devil. In the collective Crüe memoir *The Dirt*, Tom Zutaut, who signed the band to Elektra, says, "Nikki was getting heavily into satanic stuff and wanted to call the record *Shout with the Devil* . . . Nikki must have realized [that he tapped into something evil], because he decided on his own to change the album title to *Shout at the Devil*."[29]

Parents seem to have missed this distinction. Or maybe they were focused on the black leather pants and Nikki Sixx's penchant for setting those pants on fire during the shows. The devil's in the details. In a way, it doesn't matter. The song traffics in satanic imagery. That alone was a call for parental protest, but it should not have been. Satanic imagery is a powerful rallying cry for metal fans to feel like individuals and also a way to shout together with thousands of other individuals who feel just as they do.

Paradise Lost

The idea of Satan as a rebel is rooted in one of literature's greatest Christian poems, John Milton's *Paradise Lost*. *Paradise Lost*, as an epic, begins *in medias res*—in the middle of things—with Satan and his fellow fallen angels/current demons in hell after losing their rebellion against God. Milton's Satan (from here on, just "Satan") is upset about the loss but immediately starts hyping his fellow devils to rebel again. He's an excellent motivational speaker, convincing his followers that hell isn't their prison, but rather their new kingdom: "Hail, horrors! hail. / Infernal world! and thou, profoundest Hell, / Receive thy new possessor—one who brings / A mind not changed by place or time. / The mind is its own place, and in itself / Can make a Heaven of Hell, a Hell of Heaven . . . Here at least/ We shall be free."[30] It sounds like a grounded teen rationalizing that "I wanted to go to my room ANYWAY," but it's effective rhetoric.

The metal band Paradise Lost's song "Paradise Lost," on their album *Lost Paradise* (*so* close to the Black Sabbath trifecta), does not attempt to capture Milton's point or spirit. That song opens with the lines "Claws of death grip my life, / Empty my mind and my knowledge is deceased, / Mindless and dumb instincts gone."[31] But for Milton, Satan doesn't feel that way at all. Satan's "The mind is its own place, and in itself / Can make a Heaven of Hell, a Hell of Heaven" is a proto-version of the self-help mantra, "Wherever you go, there you are," in the good sense.

The rest of the story may be familiar to many readers. Milton, as the title reveals, is leading toward retelling the story of Adam and Eve and the fall, from Genesis in the Bible, as I discussed in the previous chapter. Yet unlike the Biblical telling, in this version, Satan—who takes over the serpent's body in order to tempt Eve—is the hero, if by hero we mean protagonist, as opposed to good guy. Milton throws a taunt to other poets almost immediately. He boasts that his poem "pursues / Things unattempted in Prose and Rhyme," a seventeenth century version of Eminem's "All you other Slim Shadys are just imitating" or AC/DC's "'Cause I'm T.N.T . . . / Watch me explode."[32] Sure, Milton is writing Bible fan fiction, but he's planning on surpassing the original in scope and style, and, by taking on a Big Story with Big Themes, claiming the mantle of greatest poet. To do so, though, he must vastly expand the relatively short story of Genesis. And the way he does it is, in part, to vastly expand the part of Satan, who is now much more than a talking snake on a forbidden fruit tree.

Satan convinces the devils that their best plan is for him to infiltrate this new place, the Garden of Eden, and destroy God's new favorites, Adam and Eve. Now it sounds like that grounded teen is also the older sibling. To get there, Satan has to get past Sin, his own daughter, who sprouted from his head when he rebelled against God. Previously, we learned that Satan also raped this daughter, and she gave birth to the monster Death.

This is where I should point out that *Paradise Lost* is, among other things, an allegory. That is, we can take it as a story in and of itself, but we should also learn that each of its components is representational. Satan's mind created sin, lower case, the concept, by rebelling, so in *Paradise Lost*, his head literally gives birth to Sin, the monster, capital S. And then, Satan coupled with Sin creates Death.[33]

But it's also where I get to point out that *the classics are bonkers*. Classics are often seen as conservative (small c), and, to the extent that *Paradise Lost* is a Christian poem, maybe it is conservative. Yet here, and in Dante (up next), or Shakespeare, or most of Greco-Roman mythology (Oedipus, anyone?), the goals may be lofty. Some of the language is stylized and unfamiliar to current readers. But, quite simply, there's just not much in '80s (1980s, I should specify) metal lyrics to compare, in terms of V for Violence, X for Explicitness, and O for Occult, with what Milton casually tosses out in *Paradise Lost* Book II. After Sin gives birth to Death, already bad enough, Death rapes his mother, and then Sin can't ever stop giving birth to disgusting monsters that "howl and gnaw / My bowels, their repast, and then, bursting forth / Afresh, with conscious terrors vex me round, / That rest or intermission none I find."[34] Slayer lines like "Zombies' screaming souls cry out to you, / Satanic laws prevail, your life is through" are kid stuff in comparison.[35] *Read the classics*, anti-rock polemicists like Allan Bloom said in books like *The Closing of the American Mind* (1987). I agree, but not for the same reasons. The classics remind us that people have always had powerful and bizarre imaginations and have always found violence, sex, and the occult endlessly entertaining. Milton also writes that, in Eden, Adam doesn't shit. His only waste is "temperate vapors bland." I guess if he did shit, it just wouldn't be paradise. Satan is also credited with inventing gunpowder. Why not?

Satan's most famous line, the soundbite of the whole epic, comes when he declares, shortly after the quotation above, "Better to reign in Hell, than to serve in Heaven."[36] I'm sure Dave Mustaine said something similar upon forming Megadeth after being kicked out of Metallica. Satan has chosen hell—and maybe he's rationalizing, or maybe he believes it—because he'd rather rule the worst place than be subservient in the best place. After all, hell, in Milton's coinage, is "pandemonium"—not chaos, as we've taken the word today, but literally *the place of all demons*. In addition to introducing Satan, Book 1 also introduces us to his fellow fallen angels Moloch, Chemos, Baalem, Ashtaroth, Astarte, Astoreth, Dagon, Rimmon, Osiris, Isis, Orus, Mammon, and Belial. "Highway to Hell" gets Milton exactly right: hell can't be bad, since "My friends are gonna be there too." "Better to reign in Hell, than to serve in Heaven" is Satan's "We're Not Gonna Take It," his "Killing In the Name Of": "Fuck you, I won't do what you tell me." Maybe strangely enough, it's his "Shout at the Devil." He's Marlon Brando's Johnny in *The Wild One* (1953): "What are you rebelling against?" "Whadda you got?"³⁷

The grounded teen comparison isn't really a gag. Satan turns out to be the perfect icon of adolescent rebellion. Even after getting kicked out of the house, he's still rebelling against his Father.

As the epic goes on, rebellion alone starts to feel like an empty choice. The negative flipside of "The mind is its own place, and in itself / Can make a Heaven of Hell, a Hell of Heaven" is Satan's realization that, like that teenager, he isn't happy:

> Me miserable! Which way shall I fly
> Infinite wrath and infinite despair?
> Which way I fly is hell; myself am hell;
> And in the lowest deep a lower deep,
> Still threat'ning to devour me, opens wide,
> To which the hell I suffer seems a heaven.³⁸

Ozzy Osbourne, Prince of Darkness, uses similar language in "Bark at the Moon" (1983):

> Howling in shadows,
> Living in a lunar spell,
> He finds his heaven,
> Spewing from the mouth of hell.³⁹

In the end, hell isn't all it's cracked up to be, even for Satan, but that hasn't stopped artists from writing about it. Just the opposite: writing and then reading about it becomes our way to understand the complexities of power and choice.

Metal Monsters

In addition to *Paradise Lost*, Ozzy also channels another more modern classic, Robert Louis Stevenson's *Strange Case of Dr. Jekyll and Mr. Hyde* (1866). While the novella does not suggest the occult or the supernatural, Ozzy's transformation of it does. In the "Bark at the Moon" video, Ozzy and the band begin in stately Victorian garb, working in a Dr. Jekyll-ish laboratory before he, Ozzy, is thrown into—in another example to match "Mad House," "Institutionalized," and "Metal Health"—

an insane asylum. But he's not mad—he's really a werewolf! Ozzy transforms into a beast, a kind of Mr. Hyde-meets-the-wolfman monster mashup. Then he dies. Then he comes back to life. Then he and the monster are somehow separate when now-alive Ozzy looks up and sees wolfman Ozzy in his Victorian window. It looks cool and doesn't need to make sense.

And yet here, the seemingly occult transformation recalls one interpretation of *Strange Case of Dr. Jekyll and Mr. Hyde* alluded to by the video's potions and test tubes. In the story, Dr. Jekyll drinks a liquid, and it turns him into a different person—cruel, criminal, sadistic. But we come to understand, unlike the usual pop cultural readings of the story, that Jekyll is not all good and Hyde all evil. Rather, Jekyll, like all people, is a mix of good and evil. Hyde is Jekyll minus the goodness, therefore just evil, and so also smaller in stature, unlike, again, some film depictions where he is Incredible Hulk-like. That is, Hyde is not a new personality, but Jekyll's own concentrated, nascent evil, which, as a conventional Victorian, he attempts to conceal—to hide.

While the story has been treated allegorically (there's that word again) for its Good and Evil themes, in Ozzy's hands, the comparison is much clearer: the transformation is less about morality or magic than a straight-up metaphor for alcoholism. He's smiling English Ozzy, then he drinks something, and then he's bad Wolfman Ozzy, no doubt about to bite the head off some innocent creature. They're the same person, yet also separate and distinct. Building on the earlier imagery of "Suicide Solution," and leading toward the more explicit imagery of "Demon Alcohol" (1988), "Bark at the Moon" becomes less occult or supernatural and more representative of Ozzy's own personal transformations, between "I love you all" Ozzy and the raging, black-out drunk who tried to strangle his wife, Sharon.

It's also clear that Ozzy is able to draw upon familiar, readymade horror images and tropes—no one is seeing a Jekyll and Hyde or lycanthropic film transformation for the first time in his video, so he can elide all of the narrative elements. It's a mini-fantasy, a movie short, a supercut. Many of metal's occult lyrics are similar, and indebted, to horror films. By the 1980s, metal and horror had become an ouroboros, each feeding off of and being fed by the other. Metal became the go-to soundtrack, and sometimes even the subject, for horror. *Trick or Treat* (1986) featured a teen metalhead protagonist named Eddie, backwards messages on records, and an appearance by Ozzy himself as a preacher against metal! *Nightmare on Elm Street 3* (1987) featured Dokken's song "Dream Warriors." Stephen King's *Maximum Overdrive* (1986) had an all-AC/DC soundtrack. Many of the advertisements during MTV's *Headbangers Ball* were, not surprisingly, for horror movies.

What the PMRC thought of as occult was, by that point, simply popular culture itself, which is steeped in battles, monsters, and devils. Black Sabbath's name, as mentioned, came from a horror movie; so did White Zombie's (1932, starring *Dracula*'s Bela Lugosi). The video for Iron Maiden's "Number of the Beast" juxtaposes the usual live band clips with scenes from classic and camp monster movies: *Nosferatu* (1922), *One Million Years B.C.* (1940), *How to Make a Monster* (1958), *Mothra vs. Godzilla* (1964), and more. We don't need a story because the images are enough to create their own collage-like impressions. Metal and monsters are a little scary, but mostly, they're fun together, collisions of Freudian signifiers, of wishes and fears.

The lyrics to Iron Maiden's "The Number of the Beast" are more serious than the video. They present another of Maiden's odes to madness, but rendered more ambiguously. As we are poised to wonder at the beginning of "Bark at the Moon," is this version of madness occult-induced or hallucinated? It is, naturally, in the first person, another unreliable narrator. The speaker begins by saying, "I left alone, my mind was blank." He is suffering and seeing shapes and faces, but "Was all this for real or just some kind of Hell?" Maybe he stumbles onto some kind of ceremony: "Torches blazed and sacred chants were praised . . . In the night, the fires are burning bright, / The ritual has begun, Satan's work is done."[40] The ending, like "Powerslave," threatens retribution from beyond the grave: "I'm coming back, I will return, / And I'll possess your body and I'll make you burn."[41] But he, and we, are left unsure about what is inside versus outside of his head. Maybe it doesn't matter. Iron Maiden's lines between violence, madness, and the occult are porous, by design, as they are in life. And life does not come with a warning label.

Satan and the Romantics (The Poets, Not the Band)

Consider the image of Satan that *Paradise Lost* inspired at the beginning of this chapter, from artist Gustave Doré (1866). Then consider the sculpture "Le génie du mal," installed 1848, about 200 years after *Paradise Lost*, translated as "The Genius of Evil" but known in English as "The Lucifer of Liège," by Belgian artist Guillaume Geefs. There's no other way to describe it: Satan looks hot, and not from flames. Or consider the painting by James Barry, "Satan and His Legions Hurling Defiance toward the Vault of Heaven" (c.1792–95), where Satan looks like a muscled hero, even a king. And finally, consider the gorgeous watercolors by poet/artist/visionary William Blake, whom we'll get to shortly, illustrating specific scenes from *Paradise Lost*.

They would all make excellent album covers. It's not surprising. In addition to being the ultimate underdog, Milton's Satan emblemizes human pride and desire, in the positive as well as negative senses of the words. Artists, and then heavy metal lyricists, saw this version of Satan as a Romantic figure—that is, with a focus on human inspiration and the agency of the individual, which overlaps rock and metal themes.

Poets William Blake and Percy Shelly, writing later, couldn't help but notice that *Paradise Lost* was an epic that rendered God boring and Satan fascinating, just as heavy metal later would. Even the Christian-metal band Stryper titled their most successful album *To Hell with the Devil* (1986), and not, say, *To Heaven with God*. As Blake put it in the Dio-esque-titled *Marriage of Heaven and Hell*, "The reason Milton wrote in fetters when he wrote of Angels and God, and at liberty when of Devils and Hell, is because he was a true Poet and of the Devil's party without knowing it."[42] Or, as Shelley later elaborated,

> Nothing can exceed the grandeur and the energy of the character of the Devil, as expressed in *Paradise Lost*. He is a Devil, very different from the popular personification of evil, and it is a mistake to suppose that he was intended for an idealism of Evil ... Milton's Devil, as a moral being, is as far superior to his God, as one who perseveres in a purpose which he has conceived to be excellent, in spite of adversity and torture, is to one who in the cold security of undoubted triumph inflicts the most horrible revenge upon his enemy—not from any mistaken notion of bringing him to repent of a perseverance in enmity, but with the open and alleged design of exasperating him to deserve new torments.[43]

Scholars, particularly Stanley Fish, have come to understand that Milton, a religious Puritan, saw the poem as an opportunity to demonstrate how persuasive evil can be, and, ultimately, that we must ward against it.[44] In Fish's reading, Milton was not of the Devil's party, and he knew what he was doing. He made Satan seductive to the reader in the same way he was to Eve because he's Satan, and that's what Satan does: he seduces through his words. It is up to the reader to reject those charms as false. Fair enough. But the experience of reading

Milton's Satan is thrilling. Songs like "Cross Road Blues" and "NIB"—and, for some listeners, "Into the Coven" and "Possessed"—are thrilling, too.

The label "Occult," then, does grave injustice to images and lyrics that use mystical, even satanic, elements. These images and narratives provide ways of having cosmic stakes to otherwise mundane adolescent rebellion. They gave Black Sabbath and Robert Johnson the language they needed to exercise their freedoms and exorcize their demons when a post-war industrial Birmingham and a segregated American South did not. Heavy metal did the same for teens who needed even more potent symbols than murderers and madhouses. In the end, maybe ironically, the threats, scapegoating, and labels only gave metal fans more reasons to rebel, and the PMRC hearing elevated the stakes even higher. Then, once the advisory stickers were affixed, they became a way to take sides once again. Better to reign in metal than to serve the senate.

Inferno

Going back even further than Milton, Dante Aligheri wrote his famous poem, *Inferno*, in the early 1300s in Italy. Like *Paradise Lost*, *Inferno* is an epic—a poem with a plot. *Inferno* is one third of the larger poem *The Divine Comedy*, featuring *Inferno*, *Purgatory*, and *Paradise*, thus "comedy," not because it's funny, but because it ends well. Dante was interested in nothing less than exploring—somewhat literally—the afterlife, a vast expansion of what *his* predecessor, Virgil, provided in *his* epic, the *Aeneid*, in about 19 BCE. And Virgil was riffing on Homer, from all the way back to the ninth or eighth century BCE, predating writing itself. Literary and artistic interest in the afterlife and some version of hell is older than heavy metal. It's older than Christianity. It's practically older than *actual metal*, or at least human use of it.

Writing in the first person ("I" pronoun again) and under a persona using his real name before it was a rock-star convention, Dante takes a walk through hell, and there, he describes Hell's different levels, or "circles": who is being punished, what their punishments are, and how their punishments are symbolically appropriate for their crimes. While Dante's time and place are obviously different from ours, his concerns about what happens after we die, whether there is divine justice in the afterlife, and what that justice might look like feel universal to the human experience. It's no wonder that metal asks the same questions.

The epic begins when Dante finds himself lost in a dark forest, where he is menaced by three scary beasts. He is rescued by none other than Virgil! Or at least Virgil's soul, referred to as a shade. Virgil explains that the only way to avoid the beasts is to go through hell, which is unfortunate. But Virgil, who has already written about the underworld, will be Dante's perfect guide. Like the Marvel Cinematic Universe, Virgil also mentions the upcoming sequels, where Dante will visit Purgatory and eventually Paradise, and his true love, Beatrice, will have to take over as guide.

Hell, it turns out, is like a complicated country, composed of nine circles, and later on, *bolgias* (Italian for ditches) within those circles. Dante and Virgil make their way through, where, more often than seems statistically likely, Dante meets the tormented shades of people he has heard of or known in real life, along with lots of monsters, mostly drawn from Greco-Roman mythology. At the end, he winds his way down to the lowest circle, where he meets Satan himself. That's metal, or would be if Dante weren't so scared through the whole thing.

It's worth emphasizing that we—and maybe Tipper Gore—should be cautious about taking Dante's descriptions of the afterlife too literally, even if Dante presents them as such, or to conflate Dante's vision of hell with the Bible, which has far less to say about the specifics of hell than Dante does. Like Milton, Dante is composing an elaborate allegory, with more of it coming from his imagination than any actual scriptural text. And most of what people think about hell comes from Dante and Milton, and not the Bible, anyway.

If hell is metaphorical in heavy metal, and it is, that's because it is derives from the tradition that Milton and Dante established. Virgil is not exactly a character, and certainly not just a guide, but a *symbol*. He's human reason. Beatrice, whom we don't see much of in *Inferno*, is also a symbol, of divine grace and love. The dark forest, as we know from the many fairy tales that would follow, is a way to show that Dante is lost spiritually, by using a visual image associated with being lost physically. Those beasts? Clearly labeled, in translator John Ciardi's rendering, as the leopard of malice and fraud, the lion of violence, and the she-wolf of incontinence, which refers to a lack of self-restraint, especially regarding the body and its functions.[45]

In allegorical fashion, one story—about a literal journey—needs to be understood as another—about a metaphorical journey, or, as we say today, a spiritual journey. Otherwise, it's just an adventure, much like the 2010 video game *Dante's Inferno*, which turns the scared poet into a warrior and ignores the allegory in favor of kills and thrills. Not that there's anything wrong with that, but that's not what the poem is after. We can appreciate the poem as a poem and story even if we don't see or believe in the religious allegory.

Dante's poem, then, is at least as personal as it is religious, which takes us to the poem's biographical elements. With the spiritual allegory, Dante is also using *Inferno* as a chance to settle all kinds of personal scores and vendettas. Dante was on the losing side of a political conflict and was banished on pain of death from his home in Florence. Many characters Dante meets are based on real people, and he uses his poem as a way of extracting revenge on those who wronged him politically—including Popes, whom Dante places in hell! Nuclear Assault's "Hang the Pope" (1986) pales in comparison.

In a way, it's a little juvenile—imagine writing a story about all the people you're mad at, where you imagine them all suffering in hell. Actually, Steel Panther comes pretty close in "Death to All but Metal," opening with "Fuck the Goo Goo Dolls, they can suck my balls" and going downhill fast from there.[46] But on the other hand, the stakes were high. In his middle age, Dante found himself banished, broke, alone, and helpless—except for the power of poetry, which he used to even the score for posterity. And it worked! I'm not sure what the Goo Goo Dolls ever did to Steel Panther.

Symbolic Retribution

Hell is not just a place of punishment, but *ironic* punishment. We can think of this practice of metaphorically appropriate or ironic punishments as *symbolic retribution*. It is a metaphysical version of the punishment fitting the crime, not in the American sense of proportion, but in the poetic sense of representation. Just as the beasts, Virgil, and Beatrice are part of the allegory, so are the penalties. Sometimes, the symbolism of the punishments is relatively straightforward, symbolically speaking: in the seventh circle, those who were violent against others are placed in a river of boiling blood; how deep depends on how violent they were in life. Blood, as in "bloodshed," is associated with violence, and we still use the expression "made my blood boil" to refer to anger. This symbolism makes the punishment of violence against others quite literal.

Many of the other symbolic punishments, however, are more complex and less straightforward, or just downright weird and disturbing. They take some thought, imagination, and understanding on the reader's part to get Dante's imagery and, ultimately, purpose. This is where Dante is at his most metal. In the ninth bolgia, deep into Hell, Dante comes across "Falsifiers of Metal." He doesn't mean Vinnie Vincent Invasion (or pick your favorite example of false metal), although in another sense he does—he means would-be alchemists who attempted to turn lesser metals into superior metals, which also sounds like Vinnie Vincent Invasion. In hell, the falsifiers of metal have leprosy forever, their skin changing to itchy scabs for all time, just as they would have changed and debased true metal. Fortunetellers have their heads on backwards, since they were sacrilegiously looking into the future in life and now can only look back after death. Flatterers are submerged shit, the thing they spewed and were full of in life.

Suicides are there, too. Although they're placed in hell, in keeping with church doctrine, Dante's imagined punishment, for me, is similar to the idea of songs like "Fade to Black." The suicides are turned into trees, and, as John Cardi explains, "they are permitted to speak only through that which tears and destroys them. Only through their own blood do they find voice."[47] That is, as trees, they are silent, but when their branches are broken, they bleed, and when they bleed, they can also speak, to share their grief and woe. This idea of pain giving rise to feeling, and feeling giving rise to one's voice, is powerfully moving. "I hurt myself today / To see if I still feel"—and, in hurting, and feeling, Trent Reznor of Nine Inch Nails transmutes the pain into the language of the song "Hurt," popularized by Johnny Cash.[48] Similarly, Papa Roach sings, "I tear my heart open just to feel" in "Scars."[49] But again, it's not the tearing, or the feeling—it's that the pain gives the speaker, like the trees, the ability to speak. Here, one's voice is literally derived from suffering, a depressing idea that for many people rings true.

Seeing things in a different light, in addition to creating the prototype for the first video game, and first metal song, Dante also created the prototype for the diss track, a song designed to disrespect a rival and settle scores. Angry at the way his triumphant enemies treated him, Dante did the only thing a poor poet could: he dissed them, by name, hard, for all generations to come, by putting them in hell and airing their sins. It's not very different from the way rapper Ice Cube handled the members of his former group NWA in "No Vaseline" (1991), dramatized in the film *Straight Outta Compton* (2015). How did Ice Cube retaliate against those whom he felt had wronged him? Not with violence. With poetry. Angry poetry, like Dante.

The most famous metal diss track is probably Guns N' Roses, "Get in the Ring" (1991). The opening lines are already belligerent: "Why do you look at me when you hate me, / Why should I look at you when you / Make me hate you too." If there is an opposite to the sentiment of "Sweet Child O' Mine," this might be it. And it gets worse; attempting to make good on the title's threat, Axl Rose, like Dante, names names: "all you punks in the press . . . Andy Scher at Hit Parader / Circus Magazine / Mick Wall at Kerrang / Bob Guccione Jr. at Spin."[50] Even Dante didn't threaten to kick anyone's ass. Better yet, Megadeth's "Hook In Mouth" (1988) features lyrics that form the acrostic "FREEDOM," and the song takes aim at a specific target: "This spells out freedom, it means nothing to me / As long as there's a PMRC."[51]

It's also worth remembering that there wasn't much in the way of entertainment in Dante's day. And lest they be condemned as sinners themselves, Dante's audience had to be careful about what they found too entertaining in the first place. So a poem like *Inferno*, as well as the artistic renderings of hell before *Inferno* and then inspired by it, allowed people to experience the prurience of depicted sex and violence—a demon actually farts in *Inferno*—not ostensibly because they enjoyed seeing it, which, being people, they did, but under the auspices of spiritual guidance and cautionary tales. One can find something similar in the magnificent painting "The Garden of Earthly Delights" by Dutch painter Hieronymus Bosch from 1515. The final panel, depicting hell, predates Surrealism by centuries, and it allows the artist's imagination to run wild with grotesqueries—but under the safe mantle of religion. Too bad Slayer didn't have the same cover story.

Hell on Earth

Dante's symbolic retribution suggests that we as individuals bring our punishments on ourselves, but Bosch implies something perhaps even more frightening: all of his tortures in hell are human-made, derived from the atrocities that humans, as a group, perform on earth. Once again, Ozzy Osbourne puts it most succinctly in an under-examined lyric from "Suicide Solution": "Then you ask from your cask, 'Is there life after birth?' / What you saw can be Hell on this earth."[52] The suffering of life is enough for the speaker to question not just life after death, but after *birth*; that is, whether he's already in hell now. Hell can be used as a means to describe not just the imagined horrors of the supernatural, but the very real horrors that humans have managed to perpetrate here. And the idea that hell is here and now has a long literary history as well.

Slayer's *Hell Awaits* (1985) may be metal's most overtly *chthonic* album; that is, having to do with the underworld. Like Metallica's not-quite-a-concept concept albums, many of the songs on *Hell Awaits* hang together to paint a violent picture of the afterlife. The opening/title track greets us with the screams of the damned, or maybe demons, in what turns out to be backward masking of "Join Us," repeated sixty-six times, presumably since 666 times would have taken up too much space on a vinyl LP. "Join us" is their version of Mercyful Fate's "Come into my Coven" and Venom's "Look at my eyes."

Slayer is, for me, the *thrashiest* thrash band of the Big Four, which included Metallica, Megadeth, and Anthrax. Bassist/vocalist Tom Araya's angry singing mostly eschews melody and genuinely sounds like he's either inflicting or receiving pain. Kerry King's and Jeff Hanneman's guitars can only be described as brutal, the leads more interested in evoking noises and moods—or, just the one mood, anger—than the technical mastery of, say, Megadeth's Marty Friedman. And drummer Dave Lombardo sounds like he might actually be having fun slamming the drums and changing tempos, but in an angry way.

The lyrics to "Hell Awaits" seem to draw equally from Milton and Dante, almost a mashup of both of their ideas of hell, in a timeless realm where everything seems to be happening at once. That, plus a dose of good old-fashioned horror. The beginning depicts the scene Milton decided not to go with, although he gets to it later, through a retelling, in Book VI: the first battle between Satan and the demons against God and the angels. In Slayer's case, as witnessed by a priest: " . . . The priest had never known, / To witness such a violent show, / Of power overthrown."[53]

But then, immediately, *katabasis*, Greek for the descent into hell. Is it for the fallen angels? For human sinners? Probably not. Is the "I" Virgil, guiding Dante? Probably not. Charon, the ferryman of souls across the river Styx? Styx—not to be confused with the band of the same name who have songs called "Come Sail Away" and "Boat on the River" that are inexplicably *not* about hell! More likely but still probably not. Could it be . . . Satan?[54]

Probably Satan. But then it switches to third person and sounds more Dante-esque in its descriptions of "seven ways to go," an oddly heavenly number choice when six or nine are more in keeping. But of all the horrors, slaving "eternally" stands out. In some ways, the most hellish part of hell is that it lasts forever. Even

Dante underplays this aspect with his outrageous imagery and clever wordplay. Arguably, anything unchanging would eventually become a version of hell. Even pride aside, it helps to explain why Milton's Satan is quick to leave hell and attempt revenge on God so soon after losing the battle: he's already bored.

Another song on *Hell Awaits* develops this idea further. On "Crypts of Eternity," we're treated to more images seemingly pulled from *Inferno*. Slayer bellows, "Perish to the sand," as Dante's violent against God walked on burning sand; "Master of the blackened arts" as Dante would see magicians in hell; "Thieves amongst the Seven Gates"—the Seven Gates are back! Dante's punishment for thieves is especially dark and clever: they were made into snakes and reptiles, forced to steal a limited number of human forms from amongst themselves. "Sorcery spite"; "Decay to powder"; "ashes to dust," with the reminder that these punishments are forever.[55]

"Hell Awaits" has more lines and lyrics than most of the metal songs of the era, or maybe any era. They go by fast, too, alluding to "seven kingdoms," before settling into a near ending: "The Gates of Hell lie waiting as you see, / There's no price to pay just follow me." This is not a Faustian bargain. It's more nihilistic than that. Milton's understanding of the universe revolves around freedom, but with consequences: Satan chooses to rebel, inevitably loses, and falls. Adam and Eve choose to disobey God, are exiled, but still have a chance at love and redemption. Dante's denizens are punished in what he feels are symbolically appropriate ways, but the reader can learn from them. It's horrific and scary, but it represents a moral universe of reward and punishment. For Slayer, there is no trade-off, no magic or even guitar skills in exchange for the soul. Hell awaits—for everyone.

And it gets worse. On "Praise of Death," we learn that life isn't any better than death: "Stricken to live, Hell on Earth, / Shackled and bound we lie, / Praise of Death life's a dream, / We're only living to die."[56] We're pretty far from "I wanna rock and roll all night and party every day." These are not escapist lyrics, songs of wish fulfilment. Yet they are, once again, a different kind of fantasy, and a kind of coping mechanism. The song dispenses brutal lyrics, accompanied by brutal music, to deliver what fans—especially in 1985, as the Cold War crescendoed and many teens were themselves feeling nihilistic—believed to be brutal truths.

They weren't alone. Metal-adjacent singer Pat Benatar released "Hell is for Children" (1980), five years earlier, about child abuse:

> And you know that their little lives can become such a mess,
> Hell, hell is for children,
> And you shouldn't have to pay for your love,
> With your bones and your flesh.[57]

It's harsh in its own way, and much less of a horror fantasy than Slayer. Benatar provides a visceral reminder of the abused children's damaged bodies, "your bones and your flesh," turning the use of "you" as direct address into powerful, forced empathy. Similarly, the novel *Linden Hills*, by Gloria Naylor, published the same year as *Hell Awaits*, in 1985, presents a quasi-update on Dante's *Inferno*, structured the same way. It opens with a context-free, italicized conversation between a child and grandparent:

> *Grandma Tilson, I'm afraid of hell.*
> *Ain't nothing to fear, there's hell on earth.*[58]

Going back further, existentialist Jean-Paul Sartre published his play *No Exit*, best remembered for its final reveal: that the hotel room the three main characters inhabit is hell, and that they are there to punish each other, because "hell is—other people!"[59] Sartre had been a French prisoner of war during World War II. He had witnessed the worst. There was little hell could offer that humans had not already done to each other.

In the end, the devil serves as many symbols: of rebellion, as a cautionary tale against Faustian bargains—which is, of course, the very lesson of Faust itself—and as a way to think about evil and hardship. Not in the afterlife, but here, now, on earth. That was true in the 1980s, and it remains true now. So-called party band Van Halen ushered in the 1980s with their symbolic Satan of "Runnin' With the Devil," but there is nothing symbolic about that song's own harsh truths:

> I found the simple life ain't so simple,
> When I jumped out, on that road.
> I got no love, no love you'd call real,
> Ain't got nobody, waitin' at home.[60]

It's the same lesson Robert Johnson learned if we look beyond the legend and go straight to the end of "Cross Road Blues": "Lord, I didn't have no sweet woman, ooh well, babe, in my distress." The devil was human loneliness all along.

Heavy metal was a balm for that loneliness. And the PMRC absolutely could not see it for what it was.

"I cry out for magic!": Ronnie James Dio

That was a rough way to end that section. But it's not *the* end. The ending is just the beginning, according to the poet and prophet Ronnie James Dio.[61]

The PMRC was so focused on their imagined satanic indoctrination that, in addition to everything else it misunderstood, it was also blind to the flipside of occult imagery, the same thing critics missed about *Dungeons & Dragons*: its channeling of the imagination. Its gift of fantasy. And no one in metal celebrated imagination and fantasy more than Dio. Dio's songs didn't end up on the PMRC's Filthy Fifteen, but he too was attacked for trafficking in occult imagery. And more than Venom and Mercyful Fate, Dio is arguably more concerned with the meaning of hell than its mere imagery. Dio, like Milton and Dante, is especially interested in hell's contrast with heaven, the way we need each other in order to understand either. In Dio's lyrics and music, we get the range of human feeling, from cynicism to hope. While it's tempting to ask Dio why are there so many songs about rainbows, he does not sing about rainbows and sunshine. He sings about rainbows in the dark— contraries, and how, together, oppositions create our experience of the world. For every "Hold on, good things never last" and "Bloodied angels fast descending," we get a "Circles and rings, dragons and kings / Weaving a charm and a spell," all from Black Sabbath's "Neon Knights" (1980).[62] Even that song has the contradiction of light and dark in its title's pun, as well as a clash of modern and medieval.

Dio replaced Ozzy in Black Sabbath, and he brought with him not just an entirely different approach to singing—virtuosic, melismatic, operatic, on key— but a different view of life, and the afterlife. Ozzy's heaven and hell resemble a traditional Church of England duality of good and evil. On "Sabbath Bloody Sabbath" (1973), Ozzy sings, "Dreams turn to nightmares, / Heaven turns to hell, / Burned out confusion, / Nothing more to tell, yeah."[63] Life has its ups and downs, its vicissitudes, with heaven at the top and hell at the bottom. It can be good, or bad. It can be good and turn bad, or be bad and turn good. It's not complicated. Heaven and hell, in their obvious differences, represent the opposites of the good and the bad.

But, as Dio would sing in "The Last in Line" (1984), we're the "light inside the darkness that it needs, yeah"—not counterparts, but interwoven. Then, developing further, and more pointedly, "Two eyes from the east, / It's the Angel or the Beast, / And the answer lies between the good and bad."[64] While for

Milton, Dante, and Ozzy, God and Satan might be positioned as opposites, for Dio, humans lie and shift across a fuzzy spectrum.

In his insistence on looking between the contrasts, Dio's heaven and hell resemble that of another poet and visionary, William Blake (1757–1827). In his own collection of poems, proverbs, and images, Blake used heaven and hell to argue that "Without contraries is no progression. Attraction and repulsion, reason and energy, love and hate, are necessary to human existence."[65] Blake's *Marriage of Heaven and Hell* (completed in 1793) predates Sabbath's *Heaven and Hell* by almost two centuries, but Blake's understanding was prescient. The artist uses the deceptively simple divine images of heaven and hell in his attempt to understand human complexities. It's not that heaven and hell are opposites, good and bad; it's that we must have both, and understand both, in order to understand the world.

In his own "Heaven and Hell," with Sabbath, Dio begins, "Sing me a song, you're a singer, / Do me a wrong, you're a bringer of evil."[66] So far, the world is straightforward. Things are, tautologically, what they are: not "singers sing," but "you're a singer." Essentialist. Singing isn't something one *does*; being a singer is something one *is*. And yet, the next lines seem to continue this idea about the inherent nature of things, except that the line spills over, enjambed, already messing with the first two lines' sense of order. "Singer" rhymes with "bringer," but the line can't contain the crucial feature, "*of evil*." We get to "Heaven and hell," but the usual, meaningless rock glossolalia, the rhyme with "hell" of "Oh, well," along with the additional spillage of "yeah," here is critical. It dismisses the portentous binary of heaven and hell casually. Heaven and hell? Oh well, yeah.

After all, as the song continues, life is more than essentialisms, more than just dichotomies:

> Well, if it seems to be real, it's illusion,
> For every moment of truth, there's confusion in life,
> Love can be seen as the answer,
> But nobody bleeds for the dancer.[67]

The assurance of "Sing me a song, you're a singer" is gone. The rhyme of "illusion/confusion" once again is disrupted by the spillage of "in life." Love is treated to a passive voice construction: love *can be seen* as the answer. But by whom? The missing grammatical agent implies skepticism that love is even the answer at all. And if love is, or can be seen as, the answer, we get the contrast, "But nobody bleeds for the dancer." Near the end, the bass kicks the mid-tempo song into *presto*—very fast—Tony Iommi comes back for another melodic guitar solo, and Dio begins anew, that "they'll tell you black is really white, / The moon is just the sun at night," and more.[68]

The certainties of the beginning—or is it really the ending?—have completely reversed themselves. Or have they? As *love can be seen as the answer, but is it?* black is not really white, but *they'll tell you* black is really white. The most fundamental point is not even what heaven and hell represent, their dichotomy, or their possible interchangeability. Like Milton, Dio suggests that we must be free to choose, but that we know that choices are based on illusion, people make mistakes, and authority figures can lie. It goes on and on and on. And, as Dante wrote, heaven and hell depend on one's choices on earth.

The reemergence of this image, "Nobody bleeds for the dancer" transformed into "You've got to bleed for the dancer," now imperative, becomes the most important point: commitment to art comes from the body, not the soul, or at least not just the soul. Or, as William Blake wrote in *The Marriage of Heaven and Hell*, "Man has no Body distinct from his Soul. For that called Body is a portion of Soul discerned by the five senses, the chief inlets of Soul in this age."[69]

Singers sing because they are singers; dancers dance because they are dancers. But the rest of us cannot be a passive audience. Incorporeal love is not enough. Love comes from the blood, the body. Music, like heaven and hell, is ethereal and otherworldly, but our response must come from the flesh. By listening, we embody the music. The PMRC dismissed songs about hell with "occult," wielding the word like an epithet. But Dio is engaging in real theology.

In that sense, Dio is reflecting on a particularly Catholic idea of belief: the idea of sacrament. The body, the blood, is the vessel through which we express the spirit. The song seems to condemn the state—"The world is full of Kings and Queens / Who blind your eyes and steal your dreams"—but also the theological certainties of organized religion: "The closer you get to the meaning, / The sooner you know that you're dreaming." Instead, it pleads for personal, physical divinity. Or, at least, the attempt: "Fool, fool, / Look for the answer."[70] We're trying, Ronnie.

Dio's poetic worldview, then, like Blake's, might be best understood as a series of contraries. It's no surprise that, in addition to "Neon Knights," Dio rhymes "night" with "light" in "Turn Up the Night," "I Speed at Night," "Evil Eyes," "Sacred Heart," "Rainbow in the Dark," "Breathless," and probably more, while "Shame on the Night" includes "light" midline. If you've got a perfect contrary that rhymes, well, use it. And not just night and light, or heaven and hell, but more. "Heaven and Hell" sets up a series of parallels and opposites, mostly using rhyme: the singer vs. the bringer (of evil), the maker vs. the taker, the lover of life vs. the sinner (although he rejects this opposition), the ending vs. the beginning, meaning vs. dreaming, truth vs. confusion, love (spiritual) vs. bleeding for the dancer (physical), black vs. white, moon vs. sun. Through these contraries comes progression—and poetry.

Dio would revisit the same contraries in "Hungry for Heaven" (1985), but more accessibly, both musically and lyrically: the dancer, the dreamer, the seeming contradiction that "You're hungry for heaven . . . But you need a little hell."[71] The "you" wants the rewards of goodness, but, in order to do that, even in order to understand it, one needs to have all kinds of experiences. In keeping, one of Blake's other books of illustrated poems was called *Songs of Innocence and of Experience* (1795), in order to show "Two Contrary States of the Human Soul." Not good and evil. Not even innocence and guilt, but innocence and *experience*.

These contraries, though, do not contradict each other. They *complement* each other. Only together can they lead to progress, to understanding. That they're presented in Dio's heavy metal songs only furthers Blake's proto-metal point that "The road of excess leads to the palace of wisdom."[72] Even 200 years later, Blake's point would have gotten him a parental advisory sticker. Excess, under traditional morality, is supposed to lead to ruin and punishment. Blake and every heavy metal band understand that it leads to experience.

And yet, the excess of metal can also lead to lyrics like these, from Dio's, "Holy Diver," the title track of his first post-Sabbath 1983 solo album:

> Holy Diver, you've been down too long in the midnight sea,
> Oh, what's becoming of me?
> Ride the tiger, you can see his stripes but you know he's clean,
> Oh, don't you see what I mean?[73]

Not everyone sees what Ronnie James Dio means. It's actually pretty cryptic. But William Blake certainly would. In *The Marriage of Heaven and Hell* once again, Blake writes, "The tygers of wrath are wiser than the horses of instruction." The wild animal knows things that the domesticated, useful animal cannot. "Holy Diver"'s tiger is equally indebted to Blake's most famous poem, "The Tyger":

> Tyger Tyger, burning bright,
> In the forests of the night;

What immortal hand or eye,
Could frame thy fearful symmetry?

The tyger is beautiful but dangerous. It is not good, or evil. Later, the poet wonders, "Did he who made the Lamb make thee?"[74] The universe is filled with contraries, with energy. Dio would echo that line, too, in "All the fools Sail away" (1987): "Hunted by the lion and the lamb." As humans, we can only do our best to understand them, separately but preferably together.

But even Dio's channeling of Blake needs balance and contrast. And that contrast comes from the side of Dio that is hidden in plain sight. Ronald James Padavona, Italian American, chose "Dio," Italian for God, as his stage name. And we thought Milton's Satan had hubris. But with his name, Dio also brings with him what seems to me to be the Catholic idea of divine mystery. Dio has a song called "Mystery" (1984), with its second verse extoling the power of fantasy: "Just imagine, will you try? / I can see that you've opened your mind." That verse leads into a chorus equally extoling the concomitant power of mystery itself: "It's always a mystery, / Not what it seems to be, . . . / Just like you and me . . . "[75]

"Mystery" is perhaps Dio's most pop-sounding song, and "you and me" in pop usually means a relationship. Here, that would suggest that romantic love is a mystery, and the speaker and his partner are mysteries to each other. Which is fine. But in the larger Dio cosmology, "you and me" doesn't represent differences between people, but that we're together, representing the human side of the universe. *Everything* is a mystery, even human beings. Especially human beings. In 1868, the Vatican Council of the Catholic Church explained that the idea of mystery was central to one's faith: "If any one say that in Divine Revelation there are contained no mysteries properly so called (*vera et proprie dicta mysteria*), but that through reason rightly developed (*per rationem rite excultam*) all the dogmas of faith can be understood and demonstrated from natural principles: let him be anathema."[76]

That's another way of saying, *It's always a mystery*. And while it's tempting to see "Shame on the Night" (1983) as the corollary—not Catholic mystery, but Catholic guilt—it too confirms the idea of mystery, if also in its frustrations rather than joy: "Shame on the night / For places I've been and what I've seen / For giving me the strangest dreams / But you never let me know just what they mean."[77] "Shame on the Night" exists as a tautology with "Heaven and Hell": "the closer you get to the meaning / The sooner you'll know that you're dreaming." The song and album *Sacred Heart* confirm the stakes of dreaming, connecting the disembodiment of dreams with the Catholic idea of embodiment: "Whenever we dream / That's when we fly, / So here is a dream / For just you and I, / We'll find the sacred heart / Somewhere bleeding in the night."[78] The Catholic Sacred Heart represents God's love—and God's mystery. Dio would never get there, though, without a little hell.

But even more than night and light, fools, tigers, and dreams, Dio loves rainbows. His first band, Elf, had a song called "Rainbow" in 1974. He would subsequently join the actual band called Rainbow, with Deep Purple's Richie Blackmore, and write lyrics for "Catch the Rainbow," "Stargazer" ("I see a rainbow rising"), "Kill the King" ("Fly like the rainbow"), and "Rainbow Eyes." He would then join Black Sabbath, writing lyrics for "Wishing Well" ("Then think of a rainbow and I'll make it come real") and "The Sign of the Southern Cross" ("There's a rainbow that will shimmer"). Then he would found Dio and write lyrics for "Breathless" ("There could be hell or rainbows"), "Evil Eyes" ("Oh do you ever think about the way I caught the rainbow?"), "Egypt (The Chains Are On)" ("They had rainbows in their eyes"), "Sacred Heart" ("You run along the rainbow and never leave the ground"), "Hide in the Rainbow," "Dream Evil" ("Don't go to the edge of rainbows"), "I Could Have Been a Dreamer" ("I've heard about a rainbow"), "Born on the Sun" ("There's a crack in the rainbow"), "My Eyes" ("The color of rainbows"), "Otherworld" ("Rainbows and blue skies"), and, most famously, "Rainbow in the Dark."[79]

Dio himself, in a handwritten note, wrote, "A rainbow is one of the most fantastic phenomena of our natural experience. It symbolizes our insignificance and our dreams of fulfillment. There can be gold at the end of our Rainbows."[80]

But it seems like it is much more than natural experience alone, as Dio immediately references the Celtic legend of a pot of gold. Although scientifically explainable, the rainbow has been an expression of magic, numinousness, and mystery from the beginning of mythology across cultures. In both Greek and Norse mythology, the rainbow is a bridge between the human and the divine. Similarly, Buddha uses a rainbow for his return from heaven. The Vietnamese and Inca saw the rainbow as a fantastic serpent. In the Bible, after flooding the earth, God tells Noah, "I have set my rainbow in the clouds, and it will be the sign of the covenant between me and the earth," promising never to flood the world again.[81]

So too is the rainbow Dio's covenant with his fans. And maybe even more than a promise, the rainbow is a spectrum.[82] It is the full range of color and hue. And while discrete colors are certainly visible, there are also the infinite gradations in between. It is the ultimate rejection of binary, either/or thinking. And while we can see and appreciate its colors, we also know there is much more to the spectrum that is invisible to us, beyond our human senses. It's always a mystery.

While William Blake painted several images of the rainbow, it is more strongly associated with a different Romantic poet. William Wordsworth (great poet name), in the 1802 poem titled for its first line, and sometimes called, simply, "The Rainbow," writes,

> My heart leaps up when I behold
> A rainbow in the sky:
> So was it when my life began;
> So is it now I am a man;
> So be it when I shall grow old,
> Or let me die!
> The Child is father of the Man;
> And I could wish my days to be
> Bound each to each by natural piety.[83]

Wordsworth could be referencing Noah's rainbow. His heart leaping up feels different from Blake's idea of progress through contraries and overall distrust of anything that could be called natural piety. Here, the rainbow is constant, unchanging, even as the poet himself, and all people, change and age. But childhood and adulthood—like light and dark, and heaven and hell—are not opposites, but rather, again, contraries, ways of experiencing the world. The idea that "The Child is father of the Man"—that children have wisdom that adults lack, or lose, that the wise man is not always right and may play the fool (from Dio's "Mystery," recalling "Heaven and Hell" and "All the Fools Sailed Away")—is a doctrinal metal belief as well, inherited from the Romantics. We're not gonna take it. We are the youth gone wild. We don't need no parental guidance here.

On the other hand—and with Dio, there is always another hand—the rainbow is not in the sky. You're a rainbow in the dark. There's no sign of the morning coming. The child is father of the man, but man, childhood is terrifying.

Say Your Prayers: Enter Metallica

Unlike other heavy bands of the era, Metallica is not known for occult or satanic lyrics. If anything, as we've seen, they have a strong social conscience when it comes to violence, war, and death, as opposed to co-opting mortality for mere entertainment. And yet, their biggest hit song, "Enter Sandman," from their biggest album, *Metallica*, usually known as *The Black Album* (no Black Sabbath, Black Sabbath, "Black Sabbath" trifecta here), deserves inclusion and analysis alongside their contemporaries' Romantic, satanic, and occult offerings. "Enter Sandman" is straightforwardly about sleep, but, as Hamlet understood, "To die, to sleep; / To sleep, perchance to dream —ay, there's the rub: / For in that sleep of death what dreams may come."[84] Or, as Wayne Isham, the director of the "Enter Sandman" video, said, "For 'Enter Sandman,' we all sat around a hotel room talking about our worst nightmares."[85] And we get a short list of nightmares, later in the song: "Dreams of war, dreams of liars, dreams of dragons' fire / And of things that will bite, yeah." It wouldn't be Hetfield without the "yeah."

But that's not how the song begins. The lyrics open innocently, innocuously, a parent-child bedtime routine:

Say your prayers, little one, don't forget, my son
To include everyone,
I tuck you in, warm within, keep you free from sin
'Til the Sandman, he comes.[86]

So how do we know there's evil afoot? And supernatural evil at that? Go back to the beginning and listen to the music. It opens with a clean guitar, but there it is in the riff: the tritone. The devil in music returns. The same interval that promised the arrival of occult evil in "Black Sabbath." Before long, the drums enter and build, and Kirk Hammett's guitar—with wah-wah pedal in tow, naturally—enters like a snake into paradise. The song builds further before bursting free, a triumph of metal but, at the same time, musical malevolence.

After the contrast between the verse's lyrics with the music, as well as Hetfield's vocal delivery, which is, as usual, threatening, the pre-chorus arrives. The clean opening riff returns, but now distorted, heavy, and moved up a step, escalating the menace to match the new lyrics: "Sleep with one eye open, / Gripping your pillow tight." This is equally the mantra of the scared child and the adult paranoiac, but it's delivered in the gruff voice of the adult paranoiac for sure. And, finally, the chorus, which concludes with "off to never-never land."[87]

Like the opening verse, the printed lyrics, out of the song's context, don't sound scary, which is precisely the point. Never Never Land evokes childhood, where Peter Pan and the Lost Boys live in the novels and plays of J.M. Barrie, later adapted by Disney. Dreams are the place of eternal childhood. If the Sandman—

the figure from European folklore who puts children to sleep and leaves sand in their eyes—is benign, then perhaps all is well. But we can hear in the song that all is *not* well, because it's Metallica. Other folkloric versions of the Sandman are frightening, just as sleep itself can be frightening, to children and adults alike. Night can be many things, but it is, for many people, scary, synecdochal of death, a reminder of our mortality.

The guitar solo repeats the song structure in miniature, but with wah-wah pedal. The iconic wah brand is called the Cry Baby, which, in this song's context, is further evocative. Hammett's squealing guitar mimics the visceral fears and tears missing from the ironic lyrics and Hetfield's husky delivery. And then, coming down from the solo, instead of a last verse, we get the famous bedtime prayer, spoken back and forth between the child and father:

Now I lay me down to sleep [repeated by child]
Pray the Lord my soul to keep [repeated by child]
If I die before I wake [repeated by child]
Pray the Lord my soul to take [repeated by child].[88]

The prayer is intended to invoke the peace and safety of God's protection, of heaven, so that children sleep more soundly. The delivery here, though, is off kilter, out of time, rendered disturbing by the tritone and drums rumbling beneath.

Then, there it is, not comforting at all: "If I die before I wake." And more: "Pray the Lord my soul to take."

It is a stark reminder of how central death and the afterlife are to this Puritan, Calvinist version of Christianity, where heaven is not based on a good life or good deeds, or even prayer, exactly, but rather, whether one has already been chosen by God. The individual's death and eternal fate are God's predestination. Gone are Milton's free will and Dante's sense of divine reward and punishment based on actions on earth. To the child, and maybe some listeners, the threatener of death, the monster under the bed, isn't Satan at all. It's God.

In its dynamics, wah solos, growling vocals; its inclusion of benevolent-seeming prayer turned sinister; its conflation of childhood, sleep, beds, nightmares, monsters, and death; in its invocation of the Sandman, together with its use of the tritone, the song evokes a specific but ineffable feeling: *the uncanny*. That is, our uneasiness when something is frightening but drawn from initial feelings of safety and familiarity. Not the devils, monsters, and slashers common through much of horror and metal. Instead, the home, childhood, and even God become the sources of menace. Beneath it all is the song's dramatic situation: the parent, who cannot protect the child from the realms of sleep, nightmares, and death. In fact, "Enter Sandman" began explicitly as a song about Sudden Infant Death Syndrome before being revised into the more uncanny, ambiguous, and, in my mind, superior recorded version we know and love.[89]

Even the idea of the uncanny is itself unnerving. Images of the home are meant to elicit feelings of safety. Why should they also be upsetting? One thinker who was especially interested in this question was, yet again, Sigmund Freud. Freud analyzed the idea in an essay called—what else?—"The Uncanny." The German word he used was *"Das Unheimliche,"* which literally translates as "un-homely," with "homely" referring to something cozy, like being at home. If ballads are ultimately about going home—*home sweet home, oh won't you please take me home?*—the uncanny proposes the further problem of what happens when one gets home, but it turns out to be frightening anyway.

Freud says, "The 'uncanny' is that class of the terrifying which leads back to something long known to us, once very familiar"; his essay attempts to explain how "this is possible, in what circumstances the familiar can become uncanny and frightening."[90] And what story will Freud analyze to develop this idea of the uncanny?

"The Sandman" ("Der Sandmann") by E.T.A. Hoffmann (1817). Uncanny.

Let's look at Hoffman's story before discussing Freud's interpretation of it. It opens with Nathaniel, who is thinking about his childhood and how he didn't spend much time with his father. He remembers his mother telling him and his siblings to go to bed, because the Sandman is coming. When he has questions, his mother assures him that "'There is no Sandman, dear child . . . When I say the Sandman's coming, I only mean that you're sleepy and can't keep your eyes open—just as if sand had been sprinkled into them.'"[91]

Dissatisfied, he then asks his nanny, who replies, "'He is a wicked man, who comes to children when they won't go to bed, and throws a handful of sand into their eyes, so that they start out bleeding from their heads. He puts their eyes in a bag and carries them to the crescent moon to feed his own children, who sit in the nest up there. They have crooked beaks like owls so that they can pick up the eyes of naughty human children.'"[92] Let me remind you that this is a German story.

As Nathaniel gets older, he understands the Sandman to be a folktale, but he is now scared for the rest of his life. It's also becoming clearer that Nathaniel may or may not be entirely sane. Much more ensues, including a thwarted marriage, a real-life Sandman bent on stealing eyes, and, of all things, an "automaton"—a living doll who passes for human, a further example of the uncanny in its resemblance yet ultimate difference from ourselves.[93] But the specter of the Sandman hangs over the rest of the story and all of Nathaniel's actions.

Metallica's Sandman keeps the father/son subtext—after all, the Sandman folktale would presumably be told from parent to child as a bedtime story. That, not surprisingly, is also crucial for Freud, who, again, also not surprisingly, sees the idea of losing one's eyes as a terrifying fear in its own right, but also a form of metaphorical castration, going back to Oedipus tearing his own eyes out when he understands that he has killed his father and married his mother. In that sense, perhaps the real menace of Metallica's "Enter Sandman" is not the nightmares or dark prayers, but the scary voice of Hetfield, playing the father. The way he sings, from the beginning's "Say your prayers, little one," is the scariest part of the song. And fear of the supernatural is displacement of the much more real fears of parental power.

"Mr. Sandman," the song from 1954 popularized by the Chordettes and the Four Aces, acts as a flipside to Metallica, with its focus on dreams as wishes, rather than nightmares as fears. And yet, the wish is explicitly for a lover: "Mr. Sandman, bring me a dream, / Make him the cutest that I've ever seen," and with a particular focus on the eyes: "Mr. Sandman (yes) bring us a dream, / Give him a pair of eyes with a 'come-hither' gleam."[94] Eyes again. Eyes connected to manhood again. Freud was on to something.

Monsters in Your Closet vs. In Your Head

The final lines of the bridge in "Enter Sandman" evoke another childhood form, the lullaby, but it too turns dark:

> Hush, little baby, don't say a word,
> And never mind that noise you heard,
> It's just the beasts under your bed,
> In your closet, in your head![95]

Again, Hetfield's guttural "hush little baby" is a far cry from the comforting lullaby of the same name popularized by Joan Baez and Regina Spektor. "In your closet, in your head," though, is the bridge back to the occult as metaphor. It's also a great example of a figure of speech called zeugma, where the objects of a verb or preposition come from two different senses of the word. In the end,

Hoffman's "Sandman" is less about literal monsters or devils, or even nascent parental threats, and more about fear and madness—shades of Ozzy and Iron Maiden. Beasts under your bed and in your closet are monsters in the world—scary, but ultimately, containable. Milton's Satan is banished back to hell. Dante's Satan never even escapes. The devil appears at the end of "Black Sabbath," but in the next song on the album, the blues-metal "The Wizard," the Wizard banishes him: "Evil power disappears, / Demons worry when the wizard is near."[96] "The Wizard" is practically a reversal of Faust. Sabbath's wizard doesn't make a deal with the devil for more power, but uses the power he has to fight him, like Gandalf against the Balrog in *The Lord of the Rings*, or any good wizard against any monster in *Dungeons & Dragons*.

But the monsters in one's head are much harder to banish or vanquish. Those are the ones Metallica and Freud are interested in. When detractors of metal in the '80s focused on the occult and images of Satan, they were looking for monsters in the closet—those different from and outside of themselves. In a sense, they found them, and tried to label them accordingly. Yet the occult was never a threat—it was another form of escapism and a marker, not of the beast, but of imagination and subcultural inclusion.

The more we look at metal's use of Satan—and, by extension, what Susan Baker called the occult—the more metal demonstrates that, as I suggested of Hieronymus Bosch's painting, *Linden Hills* by Gloria Naylor, *No Exit* by Jean Paul Sartre, and Slayer's entire catalogue, there is nothing in hell that's not already on Earth, nothing that a poetic or lyrical rendition of Satan can do to punish anyone that humans have not already done to each other, or are not doing to each other, somewhere, right now. Maybe that harsh reality is what the PMRC wanted to protect children from. But probably not. It was certainly not satanism.

Just the opposite: the panic, not the music, not *Dungeons & Dragons*, was what, in the end, caused real harm to teens, at least a few of them. Along with Milton's epic and the metal band of the same name, *Paradise Lost* is the name of a 1996 documentary film, with the subtitle *The Child Murders at Robin Hood Hills*. The film chronicles the trials of the West Memphis Three, teens who were accused of the murder and mutilation of three children in 1993. The film demonstrates that the surrounding community believed the murders to be part of a satanic ritual, and the accused teens' interest in heavy metal was used against them during their trials. They were convicted, with two sentenced to life in prison, and the third sentenced to life plus 40 years, despite what would later prove to be uncertain evidence.[97]

Metallica became interested in the case and granted permission for their music to be used in the documentary. "It was the least we could do," says Lars Ulrich. "They were outsiders who didn't fit into what that community wanted. I could definitely identify with them. We all could." Other musicians became interested as a result: Ozzy Osbourne, Henry Rollins, Eddie Vedder, Patti Smith, and more. Eventually, in 2010, the three teens were released on an Alford plea—they would plead guilty although maintain their innocence. "The state used our personal preferences for music to destroy us," one of the Three said. "I find it telling that, in the end, some of those very same artists helped us gain our freedom."[98]

The monsters were not in their closets. They were in their heads. The accusers' *own* heads, just as Dee Snider said of Tipper Gore seeing the potential for real-life harm in the fantasy of "Under the Blade." Dr. Thomas Radecki, who, in 1985, testified on behalf of the PMRC that song lyrics indeed cause teens to be violent, who appeared on *60 Minutes* to make the same argument about *Dungeons & Dragons*, is now in prison for prescribing opioids to female patients after taking sexual advantage of them.[99] One might even wonder if it was the PMRC who made a deal with the devil.

Post Script: Who Cries for the Children?

There was one more song with lyrics written by Ronnie James Dio to feature a rainbow: "Stars" (1986), the collaborative single by the collective Hear 'n Aid: "We can be strong, / We are fire and stone, And we all want to touch a rainbow."[100]

In 1984, Band Aid, organized by Bob Geldof and Midge Ure, featuring members of Duran Duran and U2, Phil Collins, George Michael, and other British pop megastars, had a hit with "Do They Know It's Christmas?" in order to raise money to fight the ongoing famine in Ethiopia. They raised £8 million within a year.[101] Inspired, musical juggernauts Harry Belafonte, Quincy Jones, Lionel Richie, and Michael Jackson created USA for Africa in 1985. Their single, "We Are the World," brought together the biggest names in rock, pop, and R&B, including a few legends: Stevie Wonder, Tina Turner, Billy Joel, Diana Ross, Bruce Springsteen, Bob Dylan, and Ray Charles, plus many more. They raised an astonishing $80 million.[102]

It feels bad to heckle a good cause. Geldof, in particular, had his heart in the right place and did a lot of good. But as a song, "Do They Know It's Christmas?" hasn't aged well, and it might never have been good in the first place. It's bland and goofy, sure, but it's also ethnocentric. "Well tonight thank God it's them instead of you" is not, perhaps, the Christian sentiment it was presumably intended to be. That it was sung by U2's Bono, who was by then developing a reputation for condescension, surely didn't help.[103] Ethiopia is more than two-thirds Christian. Ethiopians definitely knew it was Christmas. Non-Christians also definitely know when it's Christmas. It's hard to miss.

"We Are the World" is only a little better. The title, while intended to foster affinity, reads as egotistical, to put it mildly. The "we" does not necessarily feel inclusive of everyone. It feels, and, in fact, just straightforwardly sounds, like the pop stars alone think they are the world. The refrain that "We're saving our own lives, / It's true we'll make a better day, just you and me" is patronizing.[104] The song is treacly, and several of the vocal performances, especially Springsteen and Dylan, verge on self-parody. Again, apologies for jeering a cause that indeed raised money and awareness.

Dio guitarist Vivian Campbell, who would later join Whitesnake and Def Leppard, was inspired to create a fundraising song from the metal community, which had been shut out of USA for Africa. He and Dio bassist Jimmy Bain brought in Ronnie James Dio to write the lyrics.[105] What would Dio do? In the documentary "The Greatest Night In Pop," Lionel Richie says, "Michael and I decided from the beginning that ['We Are the World'] should be an anthem."[106] But *of course* the song Dio wrote, "Stars," is an anthem. It had to be. "We Rock"? "Stand Up and Shout"? "Rock and Roll Children"? All of Dio's songs are anthems.

And then? They brought together some of metal's greatest singers and pit them against each other, which is what happened in "We Are the World" anyway. Dio, assuming the role of vocal director, but also Quiet Riot's Kevin DuBrow, Judas Priest's Rob Halford, Queensrÿche's Geoff Tate, and Don Dokken. Many more would bray the giant backing vocals on the chorus: Mick Mars and Vince Neil of Mötley Crüe, members of Rough Cutt and Blue Öyster Cult, and even members of WASP, including Blackie Lawless, taking time off from f**king like a beast.

And then? Record a 7:20-minute song and spend almost four of those minutes on guitar solos, featuring some of metal's greatest players, and pit *them* against each other, too. Nothing against Twisted Sister's Eddie Ojeda, but he must have needed a moment to collect himself when he realized that he would be alternating licks with George Lynch, Brad Gillis, and Yngwie fucking Malmsteen.

As though poking fun at USA for Africa, the lyrics offer a nod and a wink folded into the anthem. What's even bigger than claiming "we are the world"? What's even bigger than the world? What does the world revolve around? "We're staaaaaaars!," belted some twenty-seven times, especially with Rob Halford's shrieking high harmony. It was over the top, but clearly tongue-in-cheek. After all, Dio invited "David St. Hubbins" (Michael McKean) and "Derek Smalls" (Harry Shearer) from Spinal Tap to sing along on the chorus. In character, Michael McKean added that, after hearing Malmsteen, he'd be using his guitar "as a coffee table from now on, 'cause I cahn't play the thing like that."[107]

The single, album, and video raised $3 million. It wasn't "We Are the World" money, but it didn't have "We Are the World" coverage, either. Heavy metal also benefited from low expectations. That was $3 million raised by musicians whose videos featured "exceptional savagery with special effects that leave nothing to the imagination," as Tipper Gore continued to insist after "Stars," in 1988, even after the PMRC hearings were over.[108]

In the end, heavy metal was not a force of evil. It was even more than a force for good. It was a show of community from a genre infamous for its individualist ethos. It rallied more than forty metal musicians, some of whom were notorious for their egotism. (I won't say who, but one of their names rhymes with Styngwie fucking Stalmsteen. Also, Vince Neil.) And Ronnie James Dio's sorrowful opening lines, in typical Dio fashion, over a haunting clean guitar before the midtempo heavy rock progression kicks in, are vastly more personal and powerful than "We Are the World"'s haughty, vague "There comes a time / When we heed a certain call." If, in the end, the occult—from the Latin for "to conceal"—seems supernatural, Dio's elegiac words ultimately reveal the most sadly mundane thing imaginable: the everyday suffering of starving children. Real danger, not the danger that existed only in the minds of the PMRC.

"Who cries for the children?" Dio wails, with his otherworldly vibrato.

"I do."

An Ode to Guitar Solos

Figure 11 "Angel Musician", *c* 1520. Found in the collection of the Galleria degli Uffizi, Florence, Italy. (Photo by Art Media/Print Collector/Getty Images).

You can't get the sound from a story in a magazine, as Billy Joel noted. This is a book. As an English professor, I've focused on lyrics. Words alone, though, do not make a song, even as I've tried to include lyrics in conjunction with musical and cultural analyses. The guitar solo, a crucial part of 1980s heavy metal songs that I'd be remiss in ignoring, is a wordless experience. It's also personal—I've been a guitarist for longer than I've been an English professor. It was my Plan A. As I discussed in the Preface, I was going to stay in school until I was a rock star, but then I ran out of school and was still not famous, so I moved on.

"Solo" is the word that's taken hold, but most guitar solos are not true solos, from the Latin word for "alone," strictly defined as "unaccompanied." The guitar solo highlights and elevates the individual player, sure. But the best solos rely on a great song behind the solo, and a great band behind the song. In exchange, the solo makes the group and the song, not just the guitarist, look and sound better.

In *Amadeus* (1984), about a famous long-haired musician's talent, terrible behavior, and premature death—practically an '80s metal movie—the Emperor tells a young Mozart, "Your work is ingenious. It's quality work. And there are simply too many notes, that's all."[1] Mozart was far beyond the conventional sound that the Emperor was comfortable with. '80s metal solos are criticized along similar grounds. Virtuosity for virtuosity's sake. Athletic but without feel. Wanking. "Shred," used disparagingly. Too many notes.

Too many notes? Too many notes? Too many notes *is entirely the point*. As Bon Jovi sang, too much is never enough. The guitar solo acts as a burst of brilliance to take a high-adrenaline song even higher.

"Stars" is a perfect example of how integral the guitar solo is to metal. The song is solidly Dio-esque, almost an alternate version of "Rainbow in the Dark." The vocal ensemble is impressive, sure. But the guitar army is memorable because that kind of cooperative baton-passing is so rare. Most groups have room for one virtuoso. A few—Night Ranger, Iron Maiden, Judas Priest, Megadeth—manage two. So what happens when twelve virtuosos (or eleven virtuosos, plus Twisted Sister's Eddie Ojeda) shred in tandem? For some people, too much. Self-indulgence, excess. Not me. Not metal fans. We love guitar solos. The solos are the best part of "Stars." I'm not alone. Prince wanted to play a guitar solo on "We Are the World" but was rebuffed by Lionel Richie. It would have improved the song, but it also would have shifted the song's spotlight onto Prince for too long—at least for Lionel Richie.

Yes, guitar heroes Eric Clapton, Jimmy Page, Ritchie Blackmore, and Jimi Hendrix predate the 1980s. But with Eddie Van Halen's 1978 eruption, the 1980s perfected the solo. Guitarists were able to attempt, and achieve, what words and the human voice could not: a touch of the sublime. "The beautiful in nature is a question of the form of the object," wrote philosopher Immanuel Kant, in his *Critique of Judgement* (1790), "and this consists in limitation, whereas the sublime is to be found in an object even devoid of form, so far as it immediately involves, or else by its presence provokes, a representation of limitlessness, yet with a super-added thought of its totality."[2] The guitar solo is sublime because it is not limited by beauty, or anything as tedious as tastefulness. Too many notes is still not enough.

The best players are tasteful, too. Eddie Van Halen, Randy Rhoads, Slash, Nuno Bettencourt, Vernon Reid, Vito Bratta, Lita Ford, and many more—and their best solos—"Eruption," "Mr. Crowley," "Sweet Child O' Mine," "Get the

Funk Out," "Cult of Personality" (which is not tasteful and *has* too many notes and I love it), "Wait," "Close My Eyes Forever," and many more—represent a symbiosis between human and instrument. The guitar can sing. It can cry. It dares, it leaps, it surprises. It argues and articulates, using sounds that in some ways resemble the human voice and in other ways surpass it. Singing rendered superhuman, cyborg.

It's no surprise that so many guitarists are also muscle car aficionados. (As it happens, I drive a Honda.) The guitar solo allows the player, and the listener, to race. At my gigs, when I play the solos from "Jump," "Rock You Like a Hurricane," "(You Can) Still Rock in America," "Round and Round," "Turn Up the Radio," or "Bark at the Moon," I feel as close as I ever will to speeding, but without the need of a car. Flying, but without a plane, and taking everyone with me. Safely. The playing is technical and proficient, sure, but it's much more than that. Like the requisite long hair of the '80s, the ability to shred demonstrated an instantly recognizable commitment to the metal cause. No one could play like that without putting in the time. Many aspiring players give up. Progress is slow, and it even hurts. Like "hair bands," the term "shred" didn't exist in the '80s, and it was applied retroactively and sometimes pejoratively. But also like "hair bands," "shred" shed its negative connotations and moved from a neutral description to, maybe, even, a compliment.

And yet, it's more than that, still. The guitar solo is an overflow of human feeling, channeled into an iconic instrument at its beginnings associated with the technology of tomorrow. The Telecaster, at the dawn of popular telecommunications. The Stratocaster, reaching the stratosphere at the height of the Space Race. The guitarist becomes a near-mythic figure, in the lineage of the pioneer, the Olympic athlete, the astronaut. Its combination of physical prowess plus mystical aura explains how the term and subsequent video game Guitar Hero could exist.

While the guitar solo doesn't have the same place in the culture as it once did, consider the contemporary dominance of the rap break. The song needs it so someone other than the lead singer can demonstrate technical excellence about two-thirds of the way through the song, a way to elevate and enhance everything that comes before and after, just as the guitar solo once did, and, for some of us, still does.

The singer may be the cruise director, emcee, secular charismatic, and seducer. But the guitarist alone has a shot at becoming a god.

Heavy metal bands also have bassists and drummers.

Conclusion

Let Me Get It Back

Figure 12 Orpheus. Private Collection. (Photo by Fine Art Images/Heritage Images/Getty Images).

Do I contradict myself?
Very well then I contradict myself,
(I am large, I contain multitudes.)
　　　　　　　—Walt Whitman, "Song of Myself" (1855)[1]

It's alive, afraid, a lie, a sin,
It's magic, it's tragic, it's a loss, it's a win,
It's dark, it's moist, it's a bitter pain,
It's sad, it happened, and it's a shame.

—Faith No More, "Epic" (1989)[2]

We Became the Dinosaurs

Even before there was *Dungeons & Dragons*, for me, there were dinosaurs.

I had a collection of dinosaur books. And dinosaur books, when I was a kid, all ended the same way: with an image of modern city life, and, hovering above it, apparitions of Apatosaurus, Tyrannosaurus, and Triceratops in the sky. Below, brief text along these lines: "No one knows why the dinosaurs disappeared."

As it was happening, in 1991, at least for me and my friends in the heavy metal scene, it didn't feel like an era was ending. It probably didn't for the dinosaurs, either. I suppose it never does.

Decades later, by the time my own children got interested in dinosaurs, all the dinosaur books would still end the same way, but not the *same* same way. Now, it's the dinosaurs looking up at the sky, cluelessly, as a comet approaches. Below, brief text along these lines: "And then, 65 million years ago, a comet hit the Earth, wiping out the dinosaurs."

In 1991, for metal's dinosaurs, that comet had a name: Nirvana.

To quote the most famous and now most cliché opening line in literature, 1991 was the best of times and the worst of times for 1980s heavy metal. On September 5, 1991, the MTV Video Music Awards featured performances by Van Halen, Poison, Queensrÿche, Metallica, and Guns N' Roses. Bon Jovi won the Michael Jackson Video Vanguard Award. Ozzy was flying high again with *No More Tears*. Skid Row and Extreme had explosive, chart-topping albums. It was a great year for heavy metal.

And then, it wasn't. Nirvana released *Nevermind* on September 24, 1991.

- Video director Kevin Kerslake: "'Teen Spirit' crossed the Rubicon. Nirvana became the mold for success, the way Poison had been four years earlier."[3]
- Kip Winger: "I watched 'Smells Like Teen Spirit' and I thought, All right, we're finished. We all knew it. It was obvious."[4]

- Warrant's Jani Lane: "My manager and I flew to New York to say, 'Please play our new video'. . . . And [MTV Vice President] Rick Krim said, 'I can't do it.'"⁵
- Andy Morahan, director of Guns N' Roses' "November Rain" video: "I wanted to cry when I saw 'Teen Spirit.' I thought it was perfect. In a way, Guns N' Roses, myself, we became the dinosaurs, the kind of artists punk rockers hated."⁶

We became the dinosaurs. They're far from the only '80s rockers to feel that way. But I think it's more complicated. Like those dinosaur books, the accepted ending might need a revision.

At the time, and especially in retrospect, the Nirvana-as-metal-extinction-event is overly simplifying. Even without the impact of Nirvana, by 1991, other staples of '80s metal were in crisis. The Moscow Music Peace Festival was anything but peaceful for the bands, who threw temper tantrums—and punches—arguing about lineup, stage entrance, and anything else. It was a movement in its end phase. "Decadence" doesn't only suggest debauchery; a decadent phase also historically signals stagnation, leading to the end. Pretty Boy Floyd and Tuff were not, at this point, elevating the genre.

Van Halen had a successful album with *For Unlawful Carnal Knowledge*, but Eddie Van Halen and Sammy Hagar's partnership was souring, and Eddie was having health and substance abuse problems. Poison had a disastrous performance at that same MTV Video Music Awards, which led to guitarist C.C. DeVille exiting the band. Then, in 1994, singer Bret Michaels would have a serious car accident. Michaels even said, "I don't blame grunge for anything. Poison was imploding anyway."⁷

White Lion broke up in 1991, before *Nevermind*. They would never reunite. Tom Kieffer of Cinderella lost his voice in 1991. It would come back, eventually. Anthrax fired singer Joey Belladonna in 1992. He would come back, eventually. Also in 1992, Vince Neil would leave Mötley Crüe. He would come back, eventually. In the same year, Rob Halford would leave Judas Priest. He would come back. In 1993, Bruce Dickinson would leave Iron Maiden. He too would come back. It's impossible to tell what came first, the move away from metal or these singers' departures. Maybe some of these bands' rifts were caused by the musical shift, as opposed to being part of the cause. Perhaps they spiraled into each other. The effect was the same.

The musicians who could come back often did. Others, however, could not. Def Leppard guitarist Steve Clark died of an overdose on January 8, 1991. Queen singer and rock icon Freddie Mercury died of AIDS-related complications on November 24, 1991. Kiss drummer Eric Carr died of cancer on the exact same day. Ratt went on hiatus in 1991 due in part to guitarist Robbin Crosby's substance abuse problems. Crosby would die in 2002 of a heroin overdose. In 1993, Warrant would be dropped by their record company and Jani Lane would depart. In 2011, he would die of acute alcohol poisoning. In 1993, Badlands' Ray Gillan would die of AIDS-related complications. So it goes.

Meanwhile, in 1992, after highlighting metal on *Headbanger's Ball* since 1987, MTV introduced *The Real World*, filling a New York City apartment with young, pretty, volatile strangers in order to film them fight with each other. Although MTV had experimented with other forms of non-musical programming, *The Real World* signaled MTV's most striking move away from music videos entirely, towards a newly emerging genre, reality TV. It was cheap to produce and helped boost ratings by fighting that bane of cable TV, channel surfing. MTV incited the music video industry, and now it would end it. Video killed the radio star. *The Real World* killed the video star. Or, if that's too simplistic, it at least put a nail in its coffin. *Headbangers Ball* concluded in 1995. *The Osbournes*, the reality TV sitcom starring a newly loveable Ozzy, manager-wife Sharon, and kids Kelly and Jack, would debut in 2002. It would become MTV's most-viewed series.

At the time, though, I hardly noticed. I *still* didn't have MTV. I was nineteen in 1991, and I didn't necessarily want to listen to the bands I loved when I was thirteen. It felt like a lifetime ago. There were newer bands that were plenty heavy for me and my metal friends to love: Alice In Chains, Soundgarden, Pearl Jam, even Nirvana, who no one blamed for ending anything. With their rasping vocals, roaring guitars, and gigantic drum sounds, Nirvana didn't even seem all that different from '80s metal. Apparently, unbeknownst to me at the time, this pained Cobain, who complained that *Nevermind* was "closer to a Mötley Crüe record than it is a punk rock record."[8] As far as I was concerned, that was a good thing. Mötley Crüe was already on to a greatest hits album by then.

Twisted Sister's "We're Not Gonna Take It" morphed into the refrain of Rage Against the Machine and "Killing in the Name Of," but more explicit and rebellious than the PMRC could have imagined: "Fuck you, I won't do what you tell me!," repeated sixteen times. Did it matter that the verse pointed towards systemic police racism? That "some of those that work forces / are the same that burn crosses"?[9] For me it did. I was in college majoring in Political Science. I admired Rage's aspirations and agreed with their sentiments. Others didn't notice or didn't care, which was surprising, but fine, at least with me, although not with Rage guitarist Tom Morello. He didn't get to decide.

As Gen X waxes nostalgic for the 1970s and 1980s, Millennials instead fondly remember the 1990s: Nickelodeon, Furbys, plastic neon phones. A *New York Times* editorial declared, "The Best Decade Ever? The 1990s, Obviously": "It was simply the happiest decade of our American lifetimes. This isn't (mainly) fogeyishness on my part. No. It is empirically, objectively, broadly true."[10] Gen X memories of Pac Man, Pez, and Poison mask the cultural reality of the '80s: labeling albums for song lyrics, false accusations of satanism, the failure of the War on Drugs and Just Say No, exaggerated fears of missing children and valid concerns of rising poverty, the beginning of unproven abstinence-only sex education, and the possibility of nuclear annihilation. Millennial memories are no different. Cultural recollections, like decades themselves, are fragile, fickle things.

What Rage Against the Machine—and many others—understood was that, at the time, 1992 felt bleak. At the risk of sounding like "We Didn't Start the Fire," released three years earlier, in 1989, in 1992 four police officers were acquitted in the videotaped beating of Rodney King. Mass violence erupted in Los Angeles. Iran-Contra. Unemployment. Recession. The Gulf War (the first one). George Bush (the first one), President of the United States of America, unloved and unliked, running for reelection. Bill Clinton, with Al Gore, would beat him on the very same day that the Rage Against the Machine album came out, thanks in part, coming full circle, to MTV.

Those images of confinement and captivity of '80s heavy metal videos like "Rock You Like a Hurricane," "Metal Health," and "Foolin'" didn't go away. They were updated, even elevated. Soundgarden's Chris Cornell, who would die by suicide in 2017, screaming his wish "to break my rusty cage."[11] Alice In Chains' Lane Staley, who would die of a drug overdose in 2002, solemnly intoning, "I'm the man in the box!"[12] Pearl Jam's Eddie Vedder, yowling, "Release me! Release me! Release me!"[13] (Vedder is, as his song goes, still alive.) Smashing Pumpkins' Billy Corgan howling, "Despite all my rage, I am still just a rat in a cage."[14] No wonder '80s metalheads were quick to adapt. It was a new decade of young, angry, long-haired white males with guitars who still, nevertheless, felt trapped, and they were making great music.

At the same time, other heavy alternative bands from the '80s were now poised for mega-stardom, and some of them even achieved it: Jane's Addiction, the Red Hot Chili Peppers, Faith No More, Primus. Jane's Addiction singer Perry Farrell would launch Lollapalooza, a festival for the road, ostensibly for alternative rock that nevertheless leaned on heavy bands, in—guess when?—1991, before Nirvana broke. Between these groups, plus Guns N' Roses and Metallica (who would even join Lollapalooza in 1996), and all those MTV Video Music Awards metal artists, in many ways, 1991 may have been heavy rock and metal's very best year of all time.

And then, it wasn't. Not right away. By the turn of the millennium, heavy metal had been eclipsed in sales and popularity by pop and rap. It would continue to be from then on.

Not just heavy metal, but even the broader genre of rock & roll itself. Yes, rock had been declared dead plenty of times, with reports of its death greatly exaggerated. As early as 1957, it died when Elvis was drafted. The Day the Music Died, in 1959, when Buddy Holly, Ritchie Valens, and The Big Bopper were killed in a plane crash. The same year, when Chuck Berry was charged with transporting a minor across state lines. It died again in 1969 at the free concert in Altamont, headlined by the Rolling Stones, when the Hells Angels, hired to run security, fatally stabbed a concertgoer. It died in 1980, with John Lennon's murder, and again, in 1994, with Kurt Cobain's suicide. And again, after Woodstock '99, with its riots, rapes, and three fatalities.

Rock and metal, though, live on, every time anyone listens to them. Heavy metal did not end in 1991, even as this book concludes. The dinosaurs are still with us, as birds. '80s metal survives in a wieldier form as well. AC/DC, Metallica, Guns N' Roses, Bon Jovi, Def Leppard, and more together sold hundreds of millions of albums. But that's over. Today, they've had *billions* of views on YouTube. Gen Xers who complain that MTV doesn't play videos anymore are waxing nostalgic. Anyone can watch any video they want, when and where they want. And they do. But the complaint is the point. The experience is different now, even though the songs remain the same, because everything else has changed. The medium is the message, Marshall McLuhan famously wrote, and the medium now is a phone, not a TV. The screens, like the dinosaurs, are littler. It's the pictures that got small. But the music continues, not by virtue of new technology, but something older and more ephemeral: nostalgia.

But that kind of life, that *after*life, has its own perils.

It's Been a Long Time Since I Rock and Rolled

In 1948, George Orwell imagined 1984 as the distant future. In 1982, Prince imagined 1999 as the distant future. I'm writing in 2024. It has been a full 40 years since Van Halen's *1984*. In 1989, political philosopher Francis Fukuyama published an essay called "The End of History?" revised as a book in 1992 sans question mark, suggesting that the conclusion of the Cold War left only Western-style liberal democracy as a viable form of government, and, thus, the end of dialectical history. For anyone who listened to music in the 1980s, we're not living in the future. We're beyond the future. At least we're not up to Rush's 2112 yet.

Yet as much as rock songs have looked ahead, even more often, they have looked back. Sometimes, it was, in keeping with William Blake, with a sense that experience is constructive. In 1973, The Faces sang, "I wish that I knew what I know now / When I was younger" in "Ooh La La."[15] Bob Seger felt exactly the opposite way in "Against the Wind" (1980): "Wish I didn't know now what I didn't know then."[16] Experience can be adverse, in the spirit of William Wordsworth's previously-cited idea that "the child is father of the man." That line would lend its title to a song by the Beach Boys and an album by Earth, Wind, and Fire. Seger's speaker is nostalgic for innocence, even ignorance. "Against the Wind" is a lamentation of lost youth, where "It seems like yesterday / But it was long ago." Bob Seger was 35 when that song was released. In 2024, he's 78 and still singing it, now presumably about being as young as 35.

Poison would echo Seger in "Something to Believe In" ten years later, in 1990: "Sometimes I wish to God I didn't know now / The things I didn't know then."[17] With its crooked preacher, suicidal Vietnam veteran, homeless man, and the speaker's own sense of loss, the song is a plea against the disillusionment that comes with age, more than it is a wish for youth itself. Bret Michaels was 27 when the song was released. At least he made it past that age. In 2024, he's 61 and still singing it. Similarly, Poison's "Cry Tough" opened nostalgically, even then: "Remember the nights we sat / And talked about all our dreams, / Well little did we know then / They were more distant than they seemed."[18] They're way more distant now.

On the other hand, "Talk Dirty to Me," with its drive-ins, make-out cellars, and "old man's Ford"—to say nothing of its doo-wop, '60s, goofy pop chord progression and Chuck Berry-esque guitar solo, is its flipside: happy reminiscence. The 1960s were twenty years earlier than the '80s; the '80s are forty years earlier than the 2020s. Chuck Berry's hope that rock & roll would "Deliver me from the days of old," back in 1957's "School Days," seems as quaint as 1957 itself.[19]

Nostalgia can be both the disenchantment of "Something to Believe In" and the joy of "Talk Dirty to Me." Don DeLillo has a character in *White Noise* (1985), Murray J. Siskind, opine, "I don't trust anybody's nostalgia but my own. Nostalgia is a product of dissatisfaction and rage. It's a settling of grievances between the present and the past. The more powerful the nostalgia, the closer you come to violence. War is the form nostalgia takes when men are hard-pressed to say something good about their country."[20] Like all of Murray's lines, it's hard to tell if that's how it goes or he's going off the rails on a crazy train, but the key words are not "dissatisfaction," "rage," or even "violence." They're "I don't trust anybody's nostalgia *but my own.*" Everyone else's nostalgia is wrong, he suggests. *But mine is right!*

Even rock songs not explicitly about the past are often nostalgic, or at least aware of the passage of time. The many self-referential rock songs, rock songs about rocking and rolling, inadvertently raise the problem of whom they're singing about, and when the rocking is actually taking place. In 1971, the year of my birth, Led Zeppelin opened their song "Rock and Roll" already lamenting, already looking back:

> It's been a long time since I rock and rolled,
> It's been a long time since I did the stroll,
> Ooh let me get it back, let me get it back,
> Let me get it back, baby, where I come from.[21]

My dear Robert. Are you not rocking and rolling *right now*? The song's 12-bar blues form suggests that Zeppelin may have been thinking of *rock & roll* specifically in its early, original 1950s incarnation, as I've historicized "heavy metal." But it doesn't matter. Kiss sang, "I want to rock and roll all night and party every day." They *want to*? But *aren't they*? Scorpions want to "rock you like a hurricane." Helix wants to "rock you." Great White wants *you* to "rock *me*." Is this metal or meta?

There are fewer live-in-the-moment directives along the lines of Poison's "I want action tonight" or Van Halen's "Don't want to wait 'til tomorrow, / Why put it off another day?" in "Right Now" than one might think.[22] More often, we get versions of Queen's declaration that "We will, we will rock you." You *will*? But, when? Because *aren't you rocking us right now*? I guess, according to Van Halen's Sammy Hagar era, "only time will tell if we stand the test of time." As if there were another way.

The problem runs all the way back to rock's inception. I discussed this song at the beginning of the book in its anti-school context, but once again, arguably the very first rock song, "Rock Around the Clock," from 1955, claims they we're going to—future tense, as though we'll get to it as soon as this song is over—rock every hour of the day, from one to twelve, at which point "we'll cool off then / Start a rockin' 'round the clock again." That's a lot of rocking, too much even for Autograph, who, in "Turn Up the Radio," admit that "The only time I turn it down / Is when I'm sleepin' it off."[23] No sleep for Bill Haley & His Comets!

It's possible to take "rock and roll" in its initial slang meaning, for sex, rather than music, which certainly changes the meaning of a song like "Rock Around the Clock." That version is somehow even more rockin' than actual rockin'. But for seventy years, we've taken "rock & roll" to mean music, and that definition has stuck. In the end, even more than violence, substances, sex, or the occult, rock's favorite subject has been itself, since it encompasses all of those, and much more. Yet, somehow, it's always been a long time. As Led Zeppelin continued, "Let me get it back." We always want it back. To *go* back.

One can want to rock and roll, even if one is already rocking and rolling. Consider the famous haiku by Matsuo Bashō (1644–94), where the sound of the cuckoo makes the poet nostalgic for Kyoto, even though he is in Kyoto! It is possible for the speaker to long for the city in the speaker's past, even though he is there in the present. Music, even by a bird, is a powerful lure and trigger. The speaker can never again, however, occupy the Kyoto of his memory. Even in my city, I long for my city. Even though we are rocking right now, I wanna rock. The unfulfilled ache is inherent to nostalgia. Listening to the sounds of the past can tamp down the longing but not extinguish it. It doesn't need to, and it shouldn't. Music can be its own form of longing. That longing doesn't even need a specific object. It's been a long lonely, lonely, lonely, lonely, lonely time.

In *Midnight in Paris* (2011), Owen Wilson's character travels back to his favorite era of literature and the arts, the 1920s, only to discover that his heroes also wish they could travel back to their own historical golden ages. *Stranger Things* similarly transports its viewers. Some of them, like me, were the characters' ages during those years of the 1980s. Others, like my kids, are closer to the characters'—and the actors'—ages now. For all of the show's dangers, some fantastic—mind control, monsters—and some real—the anti-metal, anti-youth satanic panic, the threat of the Cold War—*Stranger Things* is a wish. It is the same wish as all nostalgia: *let me get it back*. It can even produce the perverse, phantom, would-be nostalgia of wishing to have experienced the '80s for viewers too young to have been there in person.

Taylor Swift, arguably the most popular musical artist of any genre in the 2020s, released her album *1989* in 2014. 1989 was the year she was born. It is possible to be nostalgic for a time one has not personally experienced. *1989* doesn't sound to me like the actual music of 1989, but, with its '80s-era synths and samples, I suppose it resembles a 2010s idea of what an '80s album might sound like. And then, in 2023, Swift went back again, this time to 2014, rerecording *1989* as *1989 (Taylor's Version)*. *Let me get it back.* Or, as Swift would put it, "Was it over then? And is it over now?"[24] "It's never over," Damn Yankees sang in 1990, so close to the perfect symmetry of 1989. "And yesterday is just a memory."[25] *Just* a memory, Jack Blades and Tommy Shaw? If it's never over, how can yesterday be just a memory, anyway?

My Double Life (Reprise)

After teaching, writing, serving on college committees, answering emails, and doing my administrative work, every weekend I now somehow find myself in an '80s hard rock and heavy metal tribute band, wearing a wig that isn't even as outrageous as my real hair was in 1989, changing my clothes in a trailer, or just as often, a bathroom or kitchen, so I can rock out on my guitar for crowds in bars, clubs, casinos, and, sure, wineries, to fans mainly in their 40s, 50s, and 60s. Together, we all imagine that it's 1989, a time machine of memory and sound where the technology we need isn't a *Back to the Future*-esque DeLorean. It's not on a phone, computer, or server, either. It's drums, guitars, and amplifiers whose basic constructions haven't changed much in over half a century. Smoke machines. Bright lights on stage, dim lights in the house. It works best if no one can see too clearly. This is true of all nostalgia. Luckily, our vision isn't what it used to be.

We play to younger crowds, too—all-ages shows at county fairs, homecomings, and, sure, apple orchards. There I can see the novelty, and maybe beauty, of what we're doing. Twenty-somethings and teens love us. Maybe it's that phantom nostalgia for a time they missed. Or maybe it's a stranger thing: *it's new to them*.

Kids love us, and so do actual toddlers, who know to dance. Why shouldn't they love us? We're jumping around, singing at the top of our lungs, playing as hard as we can. *We're playing.* There's that word again. We're doing what kids do, and we're giving them license to do the same. The music is loud. We're banging our heads and having a great time. In an era when shit like energy drinks and video games and clothes use "rock star" as their brand name, the '80s metal look—wild hair, and no one cares if it's a wig anymore, boots with skulls, and a loaded six-string in my hand—reflects the platonic ideal of what a rock star should look like. It's also a childhood wish. The streaming generation's only context for the music is *The '80s*, a genre, not a time period, instantly available now, untethered from the context of the artist or era-accurate listening and recording technology, the PMRC, the Cold War, or anything. Philosopher George W.S. Trow wrote an alarmist essay called "Within the Context of No Context" in 1980. He was concerned about what television was doing to our understanding of knowledge. That medium that now feels old-fashioned, even wholesome, an object of warm nostalgia itself, something families and friends used to watch together at the same time, and at the same time as everyone else was watching, and they were all watching the same things, unlike now.

And if not *The '80s* as a genre, then, our bands—Van Halen, Bon Jovi, Mötley Crüe, Joan Jett and the rest—are just "rock" to them. No subgenre, no subcategory. Not even hard rock, not even heavy metal. And, if not rock, it's something I can't believe: Classic Rock. In 2004, Bowling for Soup released the song "1985," with the knowingly horrific line "When did Mötley Crüe become classic rock?"[26] In 2023, we were as far away from 2004's "1985" as "1985" was from 1985. When did Bowling for Soup become classic rock? When will Mötley Crüe become Golden Oldies?

And yet, for all I've written here, it does not register to my band's audience that the music is part of a cultural or literary lineage, or any lineage at all. It doesn't register to me, either. The literary tradition of heavy metal melts away. People ask me what I'm thinking when I perform on stage. I think all the time. And yet, the answer is: *nothing.* Gloriously, nothing. Nothing—but a good time. We exist simply as a live rock band, who look like real rock stars, here, after the end of history. Which rock stars we look like, exactly, does not matter. We're playing rock-star music, with nothing prerecorded, that most of the kids and even 20-somethings have never heard live—and, in some cases, have never heard at all. So many kids and teens have told me at our Missouri and Illinois fairs that we, Top Gunz: The '80s Party Rock Experience, were their first concert. My fleeting thought is that we are not really a concert. But we are, for them.

For four hours, minus two quick breaks to refresh the eyeliner I sweated off and use the bathroom, because I am in my 50s, we play the supernova hits. Every song is a sing-along, an anthem, a banger, as we did not say back then. "Don't Stop Believin'." "Rock You Like a Hurricane." "Panama." "Sweet Child O' Mine." "Metal Health." "Pour Some Sugar on Me." And, of course, "Livin' on a Prayer." They get it. *They get it.*

People, so many people, ask to take pictures with us. I, a person who spent much of my life avoiding cameras, alone, reading books, am on thousands of strangers' social media feeds, festooned with guitar and party emojis. They ask for our autographs. I sign "Dr. NoiZe," and no one thinks it's strange. They think it's awesome. We pose for pictures with children, instructing them to stick out their tongues and throw the horns with their pointer and pinky fingers, as their parents egg them on. By request, I signed a baby. Parents tell me how their kids are enrolled in after-school rock classes, learning some of the songs we're playing—'80s heavy metal and the pedagogical tradition. The music that the PMRC worried would harm children has, forty years on, become a character-building extracurricular. The Filthy Fifteen list has practically become kids' music itself.

The thing is this: *it always has been kids' music.* This is not its weakness. This is its strength. The child is father to the man.

In 1985, songs by Twisted Sister, AC/DC, and Judas Priest comprised three of the PMRC's Filthy Fifteen. Twenty years later, a version of Twisted Sister's "I Wanna Rock" concluded *The SpongeBob SquarePants Movie* (2004). After that, AC/DC's "Highway to Hell" was featured in *Megamind* (2010). In 2023, Judas Priest's "Breaking the Law" was in *Nimona*. It's not a surprise or coincidence that all of these movies were about outcasts: a girl accused of being a monster. An alien villain who would be a hero. An anthropomorphic sponge who longed to be a restaurant manager. '80s heavy metal has so far overshot the mainstream that it landed squarely in the realm of children's entertainment. In 2020, Dee Snider rewrote "We're Not Gonna Take It" as an illustrated children's book about toddlers defying their parents during meal-, bed-, and bath times. At this rate, I'm hoping to see a WASP song make it into a kids' film. Maybe something about animals.

What made metal go from the Senate to SpongeBob?

It was always, proudly, kids' music, but there is more. The kids turned out all right. Not today's kids. It's too soon to know. Here's hoping. I mean *us*, if you're one of us, the '80s metal kids, now long grown. Raising kids as parents ourselves and, in some cases, grandparents. Taking care of their own parents, and worrying about what *they're* listening to now. Holding down jobs. Taking out the trash. The kids the PMRC claimed to be so worried about. It turns out, we're fine. Better than fine. The summary of a 2015 article in the peer-reviewed journal *Self and Identity*, titled "Three Decades Later: The Life Experiences and Mid-Life Functioning of 1980s Heavy Metal Groupies, Musicians, and Fans," reports that

> research in the 1980s suggested that young "metalheads" were at risk for poor developmental outcomes. No other study has assessed this group as adults; thus, we examined 1980s heavy metal groupies, musicians, and fans at middle age . . . Results revealed that metal enthusiasts did often experience traumatic and risky "sex, drugs, and rock-n-roll" lives. However, the "metalhead" identity also served as a protective factor against negative outcomes. They were significantly happier in their youth and better adjusted currently than either middle-aged or current college-age youth comparison groups. Thus, participation in fringe style cultures may enhance identity development in troubled youth.[27]

School didn't enhance identity development. Heavy metal did. The hair, derided as superficial, strengthened and declared the identity. The metalhead identity then served as a protective factor. But we already knew that. Bon Jovi told us, in 1986: *We've got each other. And that's a lot.*

Not only were the PMRC wrong. They were exactly, precisely, spectacularly wrong. In the best, most important sense of the literary tradition, for all of its representations of violence, drugs, sex, and the occult—no, *because of them*— heavy metal made life better. It had been good.

It always was.

It still is.

Notes

Throughout this book, I relied on my own lyrical transcriptions, together with https://www.azlyrics.com/. Since most of the lyrics on this website are unpunctuated, I took the liberty of adding what sounded to me like appropriate punctuation marks throughout to aid in reading. I have also opted for electronic editions of many books so that readers may access them more easily.

Preface

1 Sigmund Freud, *The Uncanny*, 1919, https://web.mit.edu/allanmc/www/freud1.pdf.
2 Megadeth, "Sweating Bullets," *Countdown to Extinction*, Capitol Records, 1992.
3 Metallica, "Master of Puppets," *Master of Puppets*, Elektra Records, 1986.
4 Metallica. "The way The Duffer Brothers have incorporated music into Stranger Things has always been next level, so we were beyond psyched for them to include 'Master of Puppets' in such a pivotal scene. We were all stoked to see the final result and when we did, we were totally blown away . . . it's so extremely well done, so much so, that some folks were able to guess the song just by seeing a few seconds of Joseph Quinn's hands in the trailer! How crazy cool is that? It's an incredible honor to be such a big part of Eddie's journey and to once again be keeping company with all of the other amazing artists featured in the show." Instagram, July 5, 2022, https://www.instagram.com/tv/Cfom8d8twqG/.
5 There is disagreement about the very first rock & roll song, but in addition to "Rock Around the Clock," earlier contenders lay down their own archetypes as well. "Rocket 88" (1951), a song of sexual double entendre, is about a car that's like a woman, or maybe vice versa. Or maybe a car that's like a man, or vice versa. Another first-rock-song contender is "60 Minute Man" (1951), a single-entendre song worthy of AC/DC, about the male speaker's sexual prowess.
6 Chuck Berry, "School Days," *After School Session*, Chess Records, 1957.
7 Ibid.
8 Sam Cooke, "Wonderful World," *The Wonderful World of Sam Cooke*, Keen Records, 2002.
9 Alice Cooper, "School's Out," *School's Out*, Warner Bros. Records, 1972.
10 WASP, "School Daze," *W.A.S.P.*, Capitol Records, 1984.
11 Van Halen, "And the Cradle Will Rock . . .," *Women and Children First*, Warner Bros. Records, 1980.

12 Pink Floyd, "Another Brick in the Wall, Part 2," *The Wall*, Columbia Records, 1979.

13 Extreme, "Mutha (Don't Wanna Go to School Today)," *Extreme*, A&M Records, 1989.

14 Brittany Wong, "The Next Lesson in High School English Class? Taylor Swift and the Drake-Kendrick Beef," *HuffPost*, May 14, 2024, https://www.huffpost.com/entry/taylor-swift-kendrick-lamar-english-classes_l_664272b7e4b0409df02998b7.

15 Megadeth, "Sweating Bullets."

Introduction

1 "Sir Salman Rushdie Visits Campus For The Newhouse Center for the Humanities' Newly Launched Distinguished Thinkers Program," *Wellesley College News*, November 12, 2015, https://www.wellesley.edu/news/2015/november/node/76076#:~:text=%22Literature%20is%20where%20I%20go,The%20Observer%2C%20London%20in%201989.

2 Tipper Gore, *Raising PG Kids in an X-Rated Society* (New York: Random House, 1987).

3 Jon Wiederhorn and Katherine Turman, *Louder Than Hell: The Definitive Oral History of Metal* (New York: It Books, 2014), 3. Many other writers and musicians have pondered the question, "What is heavy metal?" For the purposes of this book, I'm using the eminently recognizable term "heavy metal" for the bands under discussion, even though some of my examples will not fit every reader's definition. Just as "rock & roll" came to embody the music of the 1950s and early '60s as a historical category, I'm using "heavy metal" to encompass much of the heavy rock from 1978, beginning with *Van Halen I*, through 1991, with the release of *Nevermind*. This is not by any means meant to suggest that heavy metal ended in 1991, or that this book can possibly be comprehensive. Readers may also notice an emphasis on American bands as well as those European bands that broke through in the US. This reflects my own experience as an American and is similarly not meant to diminish the contributions of the global metal groups that did not happen to become American household names during this period.

4 *Griffin v. California*, 378 US 184 (1964), https://supreme.justia.com/cases/federal/us/378/184/.

5 William Shakespeare, "Venus and Adonis," 1593, https://www.poetryfoundation.org/poems/56962/venus-and-adonis-56d239f8f109c.

6 "Life of Lord Byron," Newstead Abbey Byron Society, http://www.newsteadabbeybyronsociety.org/life.htm.

7   Lord Byron, "She Walks in Beauty," 1815, https://www.poetryfoundation.org/poems/43844/she-walks-in-beauty.
8   Samuel Taylor Coleridge, "Kubla Khan," 1816, https://www.poetryfoundation.org/poems/43991/kubla-khan.
9   John Donne, "The Flea," 1623, https://www.poetryfoundation.org/poems/46467/the-flea.
10 Andrew Marvell, "To His Coy Mistress," 1681, https://www.poetryfoundation.org/poems/44688/to-his-coy-mistress.
11 "On Charles Baudelaire's *Les Fleurs du mal*," PEN America, https://pen.org/on-charles-baudelaires-les-fleurs-del-mal/#:~:text=In%20August%20of%201857%2C%20less,that%20these%20pieces%20would%20%E2%80%9Cnecessarily.
12 Ibid.
13 Oscar Wilde, *The Picture of Dorian Gray* (London: Ward, Lock & Co., 1890).
14 Allen Ginsberg, *Howl*, https://www.poetryfoundation.org/poems/49303/howl.
15 "The 'Howl' Heard Round the World," *Encyclopaedia Britannica*, https://www.britannica.com/story/the-howl-heard-round-the-world.
16 Quoted from Trent Hill, "The Enemy Within," in *Present Tense*, ed. Anthony DeCurtis (Durham: Duke University Press, 1992), 60.
17 Ibid., 61.
18 Quoted from John Brackett, "The ASCAP-BMI Feud, Status Panic, and the Struggle for Cold War Consensus," *Journal of the Society for American Music* 15, no. 2 (May 4, 2021): 171–191.
19 Ibid.
20 Ibid.
21 Quoted in Hill, "Enemy Within," 61.
22 Because all of those artists have songs called "Out for Blood."
23 Kory Grow, "PMRC's 'Filthy 15': Where Are They Now?" *Rolling Stone*, September 15, 2017, 2025, https://www.rollingstone.com/music/music-lists/pmrcs-filthy-15-where-are-they-now-60601/.
24 Gore, *Raising PG Kids in an X-Rated Society*, 11.
25 Ibid., 12.
26 Geoff Shelton, "Former Second Lady Tipper Gore Banging the Drum for a Better World," *TomTom Magazine*, February 2019, https://tomtommag.com/2019/02/former-second-lady-tipper-gore-banging-the-drum-for-a-better-world/.
27 Gore, *Raising PG Kids*, 17.
28 Prince, "Little Red Corvette," *1999*, Warner Bros. Records, 1982.
29 Gore, *Raising PG Kids*, 17.
30 Ibid., 32.
31 Ibid.

32. PMRC. Video. Rising to the Challenge, produced by Torn Vision, Inc., 1989. Cited by Reebee Garofalo, *Rockin' Out: Popular Music in the USA*, 5th ed. (Upper Saddle River: Prentice Hall, 2011), 357.
33. *Dee Snider's PMRC Senate Hearing Speech (Full)*, YouTube video, 30:28, posted by Douglas Stewart, May 4, 2012, https://www.youtube.com/watch?v=S0Vyr1TylTE.
34. Dee Snider, *Shut Up and Pass the Mic* (New York: Gallery Books, 2013), 336.
35. Gore, *Raising PG Kids*, 33.
36. Snider, *Shut Up*, 345.
37. Garofalo, *Rockin' Out*, 356.
38. Robert Walser, *Running with the Devil: Power, Gender, and Madness in Heavy Metal Music* (Middletown: Wesleyan University Press, 1993), 139.

Chapter 1

1. Margaret Thatcher, "Speech at Soviet Official Banquet," Margaret Thatcher Foundation, March 30, 1987, https://www.margaretthatcher.org/document/106776.
2. Ozzy Osbourne, "Killer of Giants," *The Ultimate Sin*, Epic Records, 1986.
3. In the 1980s, many people only had access to three television networks, plus a public broadcasting station, and possibly a few more local affiliates. Then, in addition, there were the tiny independent UHF stations. The reception was inconsistent at best. They may be best remembered now for the Weird Al movie. But at the time, UHF stations provided the possibility of watching something outside of the mainstream. As it happened, both of my originals bands appeared on different UHF programs in the late '80s and early '90s, to no fame or fanfare whatsoever.
4. In *I Want My MTV*, Tom Petty said that the "You Got Lucky" video borrowed from *Mad Max* (106); metal manager Doc McGhee similarly said, "In the '80s, every video had to look like *Escape From New York*" (163). Quoted in Rob Tannenbaum and Craig Marks, *I Want My MTV: The Uncensored Story of the Music Video* (New York: Plume, 2011).
5. Ibid., 152.
6. Ibid., 118.
7. William S. Burroughs, *The Soft Machine*, 1961, [PDF file], https://avalonlibrary.net/ebooks/William%20Burroughs%20-%20The%20Soft%20Machine.pdf.
8. Ibid.
9. Robert Christgau, review of *1984* by Van Halen, https://www.robertchristgau.com/get_album.php?id=8062.

10 I actually looked this up. See "The Loudest Known Sound Ever," American Academy of Audiology, https://www.audiology.org/the-loudest-known-sound-ever/.
11 Van Halen, "Ain't Talkin' 'Bout Love," *Van Halen*, Warner Bros. Records, 1978.
12 Bee Gees, "Stayin' Alive," *Saturday Night Fever: The Original Movie Soundtrack*, RSO Records, 1977.
13 *Saturday Night Fever*, directed by John Badham (Paramount Pictures, 1977).
14 Sex Pistols, "God Save the Queen," *Never Mind the Bollocks, Here's the Sex Pistols*, Virgin Records, 1977.
15 The Clash, "London Calling," *London Calling*, CBS Records 36328, 1979.
16 Van Halen, "Atomic Punk," *Van Halen*, Warner Bros. Records, 1978.
17 Van Halen, "Runnin' with the Devil," *Van Halen*, Warner Bros. Records, 1978.
18 Van Halen, "DOA," *Van Halen II*, Warner Bros. Records, 1979.
19 Neil Young, "Rockin' in the Free World," *Freedom*, Reprise Records, 1989.
20 "The 500 Greatest Songs of All Time," *Rolling Stone*, February 16, 2924, https://www.rollingstone.com/music/music-lists/best-songs-of-all-time-1224767/.
21 Prince, "Let's Go Crazy," *Purple Rain*, Warner Bros. Records, 1984. Prince is the most metal non-metal artist of the '80s. The man wore a wicked mullet, eye shadow, heels, and a poet shirt with a Victorian coat that would make Britany Fox jealous. His voice could hit the stratosphere, and his guitar solos were legendary. It was his song, after all, that got Tipper Gore's goat in the first place.
22 Kimmy Yam, "Eddie Van Halen Endured 'Horrifying' Racist Environment Before Becoming Rock Legend," *NBC News*, October 9, 2020, https://www.nbcnews.com/news/asian-america/eddie-van-halen-endured-horrifying-racist-environment-becoming-rock-legend-n1242663.
23 David Segal, "David Lee Roth Hoping to Take Classic Rock to Promised Land," *The Washington Post*, May 29, 2003, https://www.washingtonpost.com/archive/lifestyle/2003/05/29/david-lee-roth-hoping-to-take-classic-rock-to-promised-land/cf41edf8-1535-4ae8-bb66-002b76824dc4/.
24 Wiederhorn and Turman, *Louder Than Hell*, 90.
25 Ibid.
26 Judas Priest, "Breaking the Law," *British Steel*, Columbia Records, 1980.
27 Ibid.
28 Judas Priest, "Living After Midnight," *British Steel*, Columbia Records, 1980.
29 Djuna Barnes, *Nightwood* (New York: New Directions, 1936), 87.
30 Van Halen, "I'll Wait," *1984*, Warner Bros. Records, 1984.
31 Yes, the name of Courtney Love (née Harrison) appears to be a literary pun.
32 Van Halen, "Panama," *1984*, Warner Bros. Records, 1984.

33 Van Halen, "Hot for Teacher (Official Video)," YouTube video, 5:35, posted by Van Halen, March 4, 2015, https://www.youtube.com/watch?v=6M4_Ommfvv0.
34 Gore, *Raising PG Kids*, 18.
35 George Orwell, *1984*, 1949, https://gutenberg.net.au/ebooks01/0100021.txt.
36 Tom Beaujour and Richard Bienstock, *Nöthin' But a Good Time: The Uncensored History of the '80s Hard Rock Explosion* (New York: St. Martin's Press, 2021).
37 Ibid., 117.
38 Ibid., 115.
39 Ibid., 303–304.
40 Ibid., 281.
41 Ibid., 236.
42 Mötley Crüe, "Too Young to Fall in Love," *Shout at the Devil*, Elektra, 1983.
43 Mötley Crüe with Neil Strauss, *The Dirt: Confessions of the World's Most Notorious Rock Band* (New York: HarperCollins, 2001), 2.
44 Ibid., 5.
45 Ibid., 32 and *passim*.
46 Ibid., 150.
47 Ibid., 67.
48 Ibid., 146–147.
49 Ibid., 163.
50 Ibid., 193.
51 Beaujour and Bienstock, *Nöthin' But a Good Time*, 143.
52 Ibid.
53 Ibid., 163.
54 Ibid., 327.
55 Ibid., 441.
56 Poison, "Nothin' But a Good Time," *Open Up and Say . . . Ahh!*, Enigma Records, 1988.
57 Prince, "1999," *1999*, Warner Bros. Records, 1982.
58 Jean-Paul Sartre, *No Exit and Three Other Plays* (original French title: *Huis Clos*), translated from the French by Stuart Gilbert (New York: Vintage International, 1989), 44.
59 Ozzy Osbourne, "I Don't Know," *Blizzard of Ozz*, Jet Records, 1980.
60 William Shakespeare, *As You Like It*, Act 2, Scene 7. 1623, https://www.poetryfoundation.org/poems/45470/as-you-like-it-ii-vii-all-the-worlds-a-stage.
61 Ozzy Osbourne, "Crazy Train," *Blizzard of Ozz*, Jet Records, 1980.
62 The PCP acronym is coincidental to the other use of "PCP" but seems fitting.
63 Joseph Heller, *Catch-22* (New York: Simon & Schuster, 1961), 47–48.
64 Ozzy Osbourne, "Revelation (Mother Earth)," *Blizzard of Ozz*, Jet Records, 1980.

65 That is, a new section follows each previous section without repetition; other through-composed rock songs include "Bohemian Rhapsody" and "Paranoid Android."
66 Robert Frost, "Fire and Ice," *The Poetry Foundation*, https://www.poetryfoundation.org/poems/45580/fire-and-ice.
67 Osbourne, "Killer of Giants."
68 Patrick Goldstein, "Jimmy Swaggart Blasts Porn Rock," *Los Angeles Times*, August 3, 1986, https://www.latimes.com/archives/la-xpm-1986-08-03-ca-1235-story.html.
69 *Holy Bible: New International Version* (International Bible Society, 1984).
70 Ozzy Osbourne, "I Don't Want to Change the World," *No More Tears*, Epic Records, 1991.
71 Ozzy Osbourne (@ozzyosbourne), "KANYEWEST ASKED PERMISSION TO SAMPLE A SECTION OF A 1983 LIVE PERFORMANCE OF "IRON MAN" FROM THE US FESTIVAL WITHOUT VOCALS & WAS REFUSED PERMISSION BECAUSE HE IS AN ANTISEMITE AND HAS CAUSED UNTOLD HEARTACHE TO MANY. HE WENT AHEAD AND USED THE SAMPLE ANYWAY AT HIS ALBUM LISTENING PARTY LAST NIGHT. I WANT NO ASSOCIATION WITH THIS MAN!" Instagram, February 9, 2024, https://www.instagram.com/ozzyosbourne/p/C3JTmo9PY1A/?hl=en.
72 Tesla, "Modern Day Cowboy," *Mechanical Resonance*, Geffen Records, 1986.
73 Before the 1980s, Moody Blues, Fleetwood Mac, Cher, Deep Purple, Black Sabbath, and Uriah Heep all used Gypsy imagery for song titles; during the 80s, so did Dio, Saxon, Loudness, and Cinderella. I'm using that word here as an indication of the time and because all of the songs use it. The preferred term in the United States today is Romani.
74 Bon Jovi, "Wanted Dead or Alive," *Slippery When Wet*, Mercury Records, 1986.
75 Bon Jovi, "Livin' on a Prayer," *Slippery When Wet*, Mercury Records, 1986.
76 Journey, "Don't Stop Believin'," *Escape*, Columbia Records, 1981.
77 Aristotle, *Physics*, VI:9, 239b10.
78 *8 Mile*, directed by Curtis Hanson (Universal Pictures, 2002).
79 There is also a racial subtext to both *Rocky* and *8 Mile*: that, when it comes to toughness and authenticity, class beats race. Rocky and Rabbit's lower- and working-class status give them more grit and gravitas than privileged Apollo or Papa Doc, who are both Black, but, following the films" logic, have grown soft in their middle- and upper-class comforts. It's a striking sociological stance.
80 Bon Jovi, *It's My Life*, *Crush*, Island Records, 2000.
81 John Keats, *Ode on a Grecian Urn*, 1819, https://www.poetryfoundation.org/poems/44477/ode-on-a-grecian-urn.

82 Noel Monk, with Joe Layden, *Runnin' with the Devil: A Backstage Pass to the Wild Times, Loud Rock, and the Down and Dirty Truth Behind the Making of Van Halen* (New York: Dey Street Books, 2017), 265.

83 Saul Austerlitz, "How Glam Metal Helped End the Cold War: The Moscow Music Peace Festival," *Rolling Stone*, September 27, 2017, https://www.rollingstone.com/feature/moscow-music-peace-festival-how-glam-metal-helped-end-the-cold-war-201218/.

84 Scorpions, "Wind of Change," *Crazy World*, Mercury Records, 1990.

85 Patrick Radden Keefe, *Wind of Change*, podcast series, Crooked Media, 2020, https://crooked.com/podcast-series/wind-of-change/.

86 Alex Hopper, "Remember When Metallica Played to a Crowd of 1.6 Million in Moscow?" *American Songwriter*, October 13, 2023, https://americansongwriter.com/remember-when-metallica-played-to-a-crowd-of-1-6-million-in-moscow/.

Chapter 2

1 William Shakespeare, *Macbeth*, Act 2, Scene 1, 1623, Folger Shakespeare Library, https://www.folger.edu/explore/shakespeares-works/macbeth/read/.

2 Twisted Sister, "Under the Blade," *Under the Blade*, Atlantic Records, 1982.

3 Tipper Gore, "The Smut and Sadism of Rock," *Newsday* (Suffolk Edition), Melville, New York, August 28, 1985, 59, https://www.newspapers.com/article/newsday-suffolk-edition/119414909/.

4 *Dee Snider's PMRC Senate Hearing Speech (Full)*. See the Introduction for a longer version of this same quotation.

5 Edgar Allan Poe, "The Tell-Tale Heart," 1843, https://www.gutenberg.org/files/2148/2148-h/2148-h.htm#chap2.20.

6 Terry Eagleton, *How to Read Literature* (New York: Yale University Press, 2013), 85, uses this fairy tale as a thought exercise in misinterpretation as well.

7 Edgar Allan Poe, "The Raven," 1845, https://www.poetryfoundation.org/poems/48860/the-raven.

8 Robert O'Harrow Jr., "2 Fairfax Mothers Want 8th-Grade Text Banned," *The Washington Post*, August 19, 1994, https://www.washingtonpost.com/archive/local/1994/08/20/2-fairfax-mothers-want-8th-grade-text-banned/ff6248aa-41df-476c-957f-1182430c928f/.

9 Sociologists, in keeping with Erving Goffman, might say we all play versions of ourselves, but certainly rock stars do it in a bigger, or at least more public, manner.

10 "Sir Salman Rushdie Visits Campus For The Newhouse Center for the Humanities' Newly Launched Distinguished Thinkers Program."

11 Twisted Sister, "Under the Blade."
12. Adam Vitcavage, "Two Kinds of Aboutness: The Millions Interviews Michael Chabon," *The Millions*, November 22, 2016, https://themillions.com/2016/11/two-kinds-aboutness-millions-interviews-michael-chabon.html.
13 *Back to School*, directed by Alan Metter (Orion Pictures, 1986).
14 Roland Barthes, "The Death of the Author," in *Image, Music, Text*, trans. Stephen Heath (New York: Hill and Wang, 1996), 143.
15 Ibid.
16 Ibid., 146.
17 Queen, "We Will Rock You," *News of the World*, EMI Records, 1977.
18 Ozzy Osbourne, "You Can't Kill Rock and Roll," *Diary of a Madman*, Jet Records, 1981.
19 Kiss, "Crazy Nights," *Crazy Nights*, Mercury Records, 1987.
20 Loudness, "Crazy Nights," *Thunder in the East*, Atco Records, 1985. In fairness to Loudness, theirs came first, in 1985, versus Kiss's 1987 release.
21 Judas Priest, "Parental Guidance," *Turbo*, Columbia Records, 1986.
22 Scorpions, "Rock You Like a Hurricane," *Love at First Sting*, Mercury Records, 1984. Scorpions, who are German, and Led Zeppelin, who are English, use "inches" for their phallic imagery when both Germany and England use the metric system. (England adopted it in 1965, four years before "Whole Lotta Love.") Maybe "centimeter" has too many syllables, doesn't scan well, or just sounds smaller. It's hard to take "give her centimeters" seriously. "Rock You Like a Hurricane" also has enough fantastic mixed metaphors of different animals combined with different weather phenomena to deserve its own chapter. Maybe next time.
23 Stone Temple Pilots, "Sex Type Thing," *Core*, Atlantic Records, 1992.
24 Twisted Sister, "Under the Blade."
25 Judas Priest, "The Ripper," *Sad Wings of Destiny*, Gull Records, 1976.
26 Judas Priest, "Eat Me Alive," *Defenders of the Faith*, Columbia Records, 1984.
27 Mötley Crüe, "Bastard," *Shout at the Devil*, Elektra Records, 1983.
28 "MOTLEY CRUE's Nikki Sixx explains the meaning behind the song 'Bastard' from Shout at the Devil," interview from 1984, YouTube, uploaded by The Rogue Trip, June 20, 2022, https://www.youtube.com/watch?v=MaINW4cASNs.
29 William Shakespeare, *Romeo and Juliet*, Act I, Scene 1, 1597, Folger Shakespeare Library, https://www.folger.edu/explore/shakespeares-works/romeo-and-juliet/read/.
30 *This Is Spinal Tap*, directed by Rob Reiner (United States: Embassy Pictures, 1984).
31 René Magritte, "The Treachery of Images" (French: "La Trahison des images")," painting, 1929.
32 Metal Church, "Of Unsound Mind," *Of Unsound Mind*, Elektra Records, 1986.

33 Tipper Gore also made time to attack *Dungeons & Dragons*, too. See Justin Moyer, "The Tangled Cultural Roots of *Dungeons & Dragons*," *The New Yorker*, October 27, 2022, https://www.newyorker.com/books/page-turner/the-tangled-cultural-roots-of-dungeons-dragons.

34 Twisted Sister, "We're Not Gonna Take It," *Stay Hungry*, Atlantic Records, 1984.

35 Rachel Martin and Phil Harrell, "Don't Get It Twisted: 'We're Not Gonna Take It' Can Be Anyone's Protest Song," *NPR*, August 27, 2018, https://www.npr.org/2018/08/27/641562734/dont-get-it-twisted-we-re-not-gonna-take-it-can-be-anyone-s-protest-song.

36 Larisha Paul, "Dee Snider Endorses Ukrainians' Use of 'We're Not Gonna Take It,'" *Rolling Stone*, February 28, 2022, https://www.rollingstone.com/music/music-news/dee-snider-endorses-ukrainians-use-of-were-not-gonna-take-it-1313512/.

37 *Dee Snider's PMRC Senate Hearing Speech.*

38 Shakespeare, *Macbeth.*

39 Twisted Sister, "Horror Teria: Captain Howdy/Street Justice," *Stay Hungry*, Atlantic Records, 1984. Snider would later revisit this song's theme for his horror movie, *Strangeland* (1998).

40 Ibid.

41 Metallica, "One," *. . .And Justice for All*, Elektra Records, 1988.

42 Metallica Fanpage (@metallica___fanpage), "Metallica Fact #49," Instagram, April 6, 2021, https://www.instagram.com/metallica___fanpage/p/CPfzQjAgteR/.

43 White Lion, "When the Children Cry," *Pride*, Atlantic Records, 1987.

44 White Lion, "Little Fighter," *Big Game*, Atlantic Records, 1989.

45 Kevin Wuench, "Thursday Lost and Found: The Story of White Lion's 'Little Fighter,'" *Tampa Bay Times*, July 23, 2014, https://www.tampabay.com/thursday-lost-and-found-the-story-of-white-lions-little-fighter/2189694/.

46 White Lion, "Cry for Freedom," *Pride*, Atlantic Records, 1987.

47 Beaujour and Bienstock, *Nöthin'" But a Good Time*, 354.

48 Living Colour, "Cult of Personality," *Vivid*, Epic Records, 1988.

49 Megadeth, "Peace Sells," *Peace Sells. . . but Who's Buying?*, Capitol Records, 1986.

50 As I write, in 2024, pronouns are political in relation to gender identity. But, as this chapter suggests, pronouns have been the most political part of speech for a long time.

51 Megadeth, "Peace Sells," YouTube, 4:01, posted by Megadeth, November 16, 2010, https://www.youtube.com/watch?v=rdEupVsL07E.

52 Tannenbaum and Marks, *I Want My MTV*, 543.

53 Ibid., 149.

Chapter 3

1. Don DeLillo, *Great Jones Street* (Boston: Houghton Mifflin, 1973), 1.
2. Bon Jovi, "In and Out of Love," *7800° Fahrenheit*, Mercury Records, 1985.
3. Metallica, "Master of Puppets."
4. Black Sabbath, "Trashed," *Born Again*, Vertigo Records, 1983.
5. Def Leppard, "High 'n' Dry (Saturday Night)," *High 'n' Dry*, Mercury Records, 1981.
6. Talking Heads, "Psycho Killer," *Talking Heads: 77*, Sire Records, 1977.
7. Quiet Riot, "Metal Health," *Metal Health*, Pasha Records, 1983.
8. Plato, *Phaedrus*, trans. Harold N. Fowler, Perseus Digital Library (Tufts University, 2025), https://www.perseus.tufts.edu/hopper/text?doc=Perseus%3Atext%3A1999.01.0174%3Atext%3DPhaedrus%3Apage%3D265.
9. Ibid.
10. If you're reading this note, now you know it wasn't Bruce Dickinson. It's Emily Dickinson, "I Felt a Funeral in My Brain," 1896, *Poetry Foundation*, https://www.poetryfoundation.org/poems/47657/i-felt-a-funeral-in-my-brain.
11. Ibid.
12. Iron Maiden, "Powerslave," *Powerslave*, EMI Records, 1984.
13. Iron Maiden, "Can I Play with Madness," *Seventh Son of a Seventh Son*, EMI Records, 1988.
14. Emily Dickinson, "I Died for Beauty," 1890, *Poetry Foundation*, https://www.poetryfoundation.org/poems/47486/i-died-for-beauty.
15. Emily Dickinson, "Pain has an Element of Blank," 1890. *Poetry Foundation*, https://www.poetryfoundation.org/poems/47535/pain-has-an-element-of-blank.
16. Anthrax, "Madhouse," *Spreading the Disease*, Island Records, 1985.
17. Armored Saint, "Mad House," *March of the Saint*, Chrysalis Records, 1984.
18. Suicidal Tendencies, "Institutionalized," *Suicidal Tendencies*, Frontier Records, 1983.
19. Ozzy Osbourne, "Diary of a Madman," *Diary of a Madman*, Jet Records, 1981. Once again, as with "Crazy Train," it is possible that bassist Bob Daisley wrote the lyrics. I'm going to ascribe them to Ozzy here, since they have become intrinsic to his popular persona, and let Ozzy, Daisley, and the courts determine ownership.
20. Lewis Carroll, *Alice's Adventures in Wonderland*, ed. Henry L. S. Dyer, 1865 (Project Gutenberg, 1998), 75, https://www.gutenberg.org/ebooks/11.
21. Metallica, "Welcome Home (Sanitarium)," *Master of Puppets*, Elektra, 1986.
22. "Metallica's 'One' was Inspired by One Flew Over the Cuckoo's Nest," *Far Out Magazine*, October 27, 2020, https://faroutmagazine.co.uk/metallica-song-one-flew-over-the-cuckoos-nest/.
23. Ken Kesey, *One Flew Over the Cuckoo's Nest* (New York: Viking Press, 1962), 23.

24 Albert Camus, *The Myth of Sisyphus*, trans. Justin O'Brien (New York: Alfred A. Knopf, 1955), https://archive.org/details/AlbertCamusTheMythOfSisyphus.
25 There is much more to say about "Suicide Solution"; Walser's and Weinstein's books both feature excellent analyses.
26 Metallica, *Ride the Lightning* (Los Angeles: Elektra Records, 1984).
27 Joe DiVita, "Why Do Metallica Hate the 'Ride the Lightning' Song 'Escape'?" *Loudwire*, September 6, 2023, https://loudwire.com/why-do-metallica-hate-ride-the-lightning-song-escape/.
28 Metallica, "The Thing That Should Not Be," *Master of Puppets*, Elektra, 1986.
29 Neil Young, "Hey Hey, My My," *Rust Never Sleeps*, Reprise, 1979.
30 Metallica, "Fade to Black," *Ride the Lightning*, Elektra, 1984.
31 Camus, *Myth of Sisyphus*.
32 Wallace Stevens, "The Emperor of Ice Cream," 1923, *The Collected Poems of Wallace Stevens*, https://archive.org/details/collected-poems-wallace-stevens.
33 Black Sabbath, "Paranoid," *Paranoid*, Vertigo, 1970.
34 Metallica, "Nothing Else Matters," *Metallica*, Elektra, 1991.
35 Camus, *Myth of Sisyphus*.
36 Don DeLillo, *White Noise* (New York: Penguin, 1985), 72.
37 DeLillo, *Great Jones Street*, 24.
38 Ibid., 86.
39 Ian Winwood, *Bodies: Life and Death in Music* (London: Faber & Faber, 2022), 7.
40 Megadeth, *In My Darkest Hour*, on *So Far, So Good . . . So What!*, Capitol Records, 1988.
41 Then again, the military suicide rate is 1.5 times higher than the civilian rate, so maybe nothing would be done.
42 Elvis Presley, *Heartbreak Hotel*, RCA Victor, 1956.
43 Winwood, *Bodies*, 34.
44 Ibid., 14.
45 Ibid., 172.
46 Ibid., 154.

Chapter 4

1 Skid Row, "I Remember You," *Skid Row*, Atlantic Records, 1989.
2 D. H. Lawrence, *Lady Chatterley's Lover* (Project Gutenberg, 1928), https://www.gutenberg.org/cache/epub/73144/pg73144-images.html.
3 *This Is Spinal Tap*.

4 AC/DC, "Let Me Put My Love Into You," *Back in Black*, Atlantic Records, 1980; KISS, "Burn Bitch Burn," *Animalize*, Mercury Records, 1984.
5 "Theatre of Cruelty," *Encyclopaedia Britannica*, last modified September 11, 2019, https://www.britannica.com/topic/Theatre-of-Cruelty.
6 Mötley Crüe, *The Dirt*, 140.
7 W.A.S.P., *Animal (F**k Like a Beast)* (12-inch single; Music For Nations, 1984).
8 Zach Schonfeld, "Parental Advisory Forever: An Oral History of the PMRC's War on Dirty Lyrics," *Newsweek*, September 19, 2015, https://www.newsweek.com/2015/10/09/oral-history-tipper-gores-war-explicit-rock-lyrics-dee-snider-373103.html.
9 Def Leppard, "Animal," *Hysteria*, Mercury, 1987.
10 Nine Inch Nails, "Closer," *The Downward Spiral*, Interscope, 1994.
11 "VH1 Classics' Greatest Videos of All Time," *Pulse Music Board*, https://pulsemusic.proboards.com/thread/72321/vh1-classics-greatest-videos-time.
12 *This Is Spinal Tap*.
13 Nickelback, "Animal," *All the Right Reasons*, Roadrunner Records, 2005.
14 Maroon 5, "Animal," *V*, Interscope Records, 2014.
15 Guns N' Roses, "Patience," *G N' R Lies*, Geffen Records, 1988.
16 Guns N' Roses, "Used to Love Her," *G N' R Lies*, Geffen Records, 1988.
17 Buckcherry, "I'm Sorry," *15*, Eleven Seven Music, 2006.
18 Sigmund Freud, "The Most Prevalent Form of Degradation in Erotic Life" (1912), *Psychoanalytic Electronic Publishing*, https://pepweb.org/browse/document/se.011.0177a?page=P0177.
19 Sigmund Freud, *The Question of Lay Analysis* (London: Imago Publishing Co. Ltd., 1947), 35, https://archive.org/details/dli.ernet.12168/mode/2up?q=d.
20 The Clovers, "Devil or Angel," Atlantic Records, 1956.
21 Alice Cooper, "Poison," *Trash*, Epic Records, 1989.
22 Alice Cooper, "I'm Eighteen," *Love It to Death*, Warner Bros. Records, 1971.
23 Mötley Crüe, "Looks That Kill," *Shout at the Devil*, Elektra Records, 1983.
24 Mötley Crüe, *The Dirt*, 115.
25 Damn Yankees, "High Enough," *Damn Yankees*, Atlantic Records, 1990.
26 Journey, "Separate Ways (Worlds Apart)," *Frontiers*, Columbia Records, 1983.
27 Black Sabbath, "Evil Woman," *Black Sabbath*, Vertigo Records, 1970.
28 The Eagles, "Witchy Woman," *Eagles*, Asylum Records, 1972.
29 Electric Light Orchestra, "Evil Woman," *Face the Music*, Jet Records, 1975.
30 Cliff Richard, "Devil Woman," *Devil Woman*, EMI, 1976.
31 Black Sabbath, "Lady Evil," *Heaven and Hell*, Vertigo Records, 1980.
32 The Cult, "Fire Woman," *Sonic Temple*, Beggars Banquet Records, 1989.
33 Type O Negative, "Black No. 1 (Little Miss Scare-All)," *Bloody Kisses*, Roadrunner Records, 1993.

34 Flight of the Conchords, "Demon Woman," *Flight of the Conchords*, Sub Pop Records, 2008.
35 Aerosmith, "Angel," *Permanent Vacation*, Geffen Records, 1987.
36 Poison, "Fallen Angel," *Open Up and Say. . . Ahh!*, Enigma Records, 1988.
37 The Black Crowes, "She Talks to Angels," *Shake Your Money Maker*, Def American Recordings, 1990.
38 Tannenbaum and Marks, *I Want My MTV*, 149.
39 Whitesnake, "Here I Go Again," *Whitesnake*, Geffen Records, 1987.
40 Def Leppard, "Women," *Hysteria*, Mercury Records, 1987.
41 Genesis 2:18–24, *The Holy Bible: New King James Version* (Nashville: Thomas Nelson, 1987), 2:18–24.
42 Producer Mutt Lange and Joe Elliott later were having some tea, and Elliott asked if Lange wanted one lump or two. Lange responded, "I don't care, just pour some sugar on me," and a song was born.
See Jeff Cornell, "10 Best Def Leppard Songs," *Loudwire*, August 4, 2015, https://loudwire.com/best-def-leppard-songs/?utm_source=tsmclip&utm_medium=referral.
43 "Women (Def Leppard Song)," *Wikipedia*, last modified December 30, 2024, https://en.wikipedia.org/wiki/Women_(Def_Leppard_song).
44 Genesis 3:6–7, *The Holy Bible: New King James Version* (Nashville: Thomas Nelson, 1987), 3:6–7.
45 John Milton, *Paradise Lost*, Book XII, lines 586–587, 1667 (Project Gutenberg, 2008), https://www.gutenberg.org/cache/epub/26/pg26-images.html.
46 Milton, *Paradise Lost*, Book XII, lines 646–647.
47 Guns N' Roses, "It's So Easy," *Appetite for Destruction*, Geffen Records, 1987.
48 Ibid.
49 Nickelback, "Rock Star," *All the Right Reasons*, Roadrunner Records, 2005.
50 Elvis Presley, "Fame and Fortune," *G.I. Blues*, RCA Victor, 1960, LP.
51 C. G. Jung, *The Collected Works of C.G. Jung, Volume 9 (Part 1): Archetypes and the Collective Unconscious*, ed. Gerhard Adler and R. F. C. Hull, 2nd ed. (Princeton: Princeton University Press, 1969), 161.
52 Guns N' Roses, "Sweet Child O' Mine," *Appetite for Destruction*, Geffen Records, 1987.
53 Jung, *Collected Works*, 161.
54 Mötley Crüe, "Stick To Your Guns / Toast Of The Town," Leathür Records, 1981.
55 Mötley Crüe, "Take Me to the Top," *Too Fast for Love*, Elektra, 1981.
56 George Carlin, "Baseball vs. Football," YouTube, uploaded by rlcook75, August 23, 2008, https://www.youtube.com/watch?v=aIkqNiBASfI.
57 Mötley Crüe, "Home Sweet Home," *Theatre of Pain*, Elektra, 1985.

58 Poison, "Every Rose Has Its Thorn," *Open Up and Say... Ahh!*, Enigma, 1988.
59 William Shakespeare, "Sonnet 35," in *The Sonnets of William Shakespeare*, ed. George Wyndham (Project Gutenberg, 2008), https://www.gutenberg.org/ebooks/1041.
60 David Marchese, "Eddie Vedder on the Power of Music, the Pain of Loss, and the Art of Reinvention," *The New York Times Magazine*, January 30, 2022, https://www.nytimes.com/interactive/2022/01/31/magazine/eddie-vedder-interview.html.
61 Mötley Crüe, "Piece of Your Action," *Too Fast for Love*, Elektra, 1981; Gore, "Smut."
62 Wiederhorn and Turman, *Louder Than Hell*, 92.
63 Hill, "Enemy Within," 55.
64 Mötley Crüe, "Girls, Girls, Girls," *Girls, Girls, Girls*, Elektra, 1987.
65 Harold Bloom, *The Western Canon: The Books and School of the Ages* (New York: Harcourt Brace, 1994).
66 Lita Ford, "Kiss Me Deadly," *Lita*, RCA Records, 1988.
67 Monk, *Runnin' with the Devil*, 195.
68 "Lita Ford: 'I Had Affairs with a Lot of Guitar Players and Lead Singers in the Music Industry,'" *Blabbermouth*, January 29, 2018, https://blabbermouth.net/news/lita-ford-i-had-affairs-with-a-lot-of-guitar-players-and-a-lot-of-lead-singers-in-the-music-industry.
69 Joan Jett and the Blackhearts, "I Love Rock 'n Roll," *I Love Rock n Roll*, Boardwalk Records, 1981.
70 I first explored the idea of Jett's gender reversal of the original Arrows song in a 2012 blog post. Amazingly, Alan Merrill, the singer/songwriter from The Arrows, read it. He sent me a direct message telling me I was ugly, among other insults. I wrote back, truthfully, that I was amazed and flattered to hear from him. He didn't write back again.
71 The Donnas, "Take It Off," *Spend the Night*, Atlantic Records, 2002.
72 Greg Kennelty, "Lzzy Hale on Joining Skid Row for Live Shows: 'There Will Be Blood Left on the Stage,'" *Metal Injection*, March 21, 2024, https://metalinjection.net/news/lzzy-hale-on-joining-skid-row-for-live-shows-there-will-be-blood-left-on-the-stage.

Chapter 5

1 Dante Alighieri, *The Inferno*, trans. John Ciardi (New York: Signet Classics, 2009), 18.
2 Venom, "Welcome to Hell," *Welcome to Hell*, Neat Records, 1981.

3 Susan Baker, statement at the PMRC (Parents Music Resource Center) Senate Hearing, *American Rhetoric*, https://www.americanrhetoric.com/speeches/susanbakerpmrchearingstatement.htm.
4 Wiederhorn and Turman, *Louder Than Hell*, 269.
5 Ryan Bray, "Danzig's 1988 Debut Album Exposed a Flawed Attempt at Censorship," *Consequence*, August 30, 2018, https://consequence.net/2018/08/danzig-1988-debut-album-exposed-flawed-attempt-censorship/.
6 Danzig, "Mother," *Danzig*, 1988.
7 Mercyful Fate, "Into the Coven," *Melissa*, Roadrunner Records, 1983.
8 Venom, "Possessed," *Possessed*, Neat Records, 1985.
9 Grow, "PMRC's 'Filthy 15': Where Are They Now?"
10 Ozzy Osbourne, *I Am Ozzy* (New York: Grand Central Publishing, 2010), 118.
11 Alaa Elassar, "Black Sabbath Is Selling Black Lives Matter Shirts and Donating All the Proceeds to the Movement," *CNN*, June 21, 2020, https://www.cnn.com/2020/06/21/entertainment/black-sabbath-black-lives-matter-trnd/index.html.
12 Black Sabbath, "Black Sabbath," *Black Sabbath*, Vertigo, 1970. The trifecta!
13 Jon Wiederhorn, "The Devil's Chord: The Eerie History of Diabolus in Musica," *Fender*, https://www.fender.com/articles/chords/the-devils-chord-the-eerie-history-of-diabolus-in-musica.
14 "Stairway to Heaven Chords 'Centuries Old,' Court Hears," *The Irish Times*, June 18, 2016, https://www.irishtimes.com/culture/music/stairway-to-heaven-chords-centuries-old-court-hears-1.2690598.
15 I was able to find only one controversy, when Colorado teacher in 2006 showed a 33-year-old tape of Charles Gounod's *Faust* to first, second, and third graders, who were frightened. See Vivien Schweitzer, "Teacher Draws Criticism for Screening *Faust* Excerpt," *Playbill*, February 3, 2006, https://playbill.com/article/teacher-draws-criticism-for-screening-faust-excerpt.
16 Robert Johnson, "Me and the Devil Blues," *King of the Delta Blues Singers*, Columbia, 1937.
17 Black Sabbath, "N.I.B.," *Black Sabbath*, Vertigo, 1970.
18 Johnson, "Me and the Devil Blues."
19 Robert Johnson, "Cross Road Blues," *King of the Delta Blues Singers*, Columbia, 1936.
20 Dan Wilcock, "The Devil Didn't Make Him: Debunking the Robert Johnson Myth," *American Blues Scene*, August 16, 2022, https://www.americanbluesscene.com/2022/08/devil-didnt-make-him-debunking-robert-johnson-myth-3dw/.
21 Quoted in Patricia R. Schroeder, *Robert Johnson, Mythmaking, and Contemporary America* (Urbana: University of Illinois Press, 2004), 156.
22 "ReMastered: Devil at the Crossroads," directed by Brian Oakes (Netflix, 2019).

23 Eugene wins by resorting to his original training in classical guitar, which in some ways defeats the point of the film itself. The implicit message is, in the end, that a white person should stick with stereotypically white music if he wants to succeed.
24 Johnson, "Cross Road Blues."
25 Langston Hughes, "Mother to Son," 1922, *Poetry Foundation*, https://www.poetryfoundation.org/poems/47559/mother-to-son.
26 AC/DC, "Highway to Hell," *Highway to Hell*, Atlantic Records, 1979.
27 "The Devil Worshippers," *20/20*, ABC, aired May 16, 1985.
28 Mötley Crüe, "Shout at the Devil," *Shout at the Devil*, Elektra, 1983.
29 Mötley Crüe, *The Dirt*, 88.
30 Milton, *Paradise Lost*, Book 1, lines 250–259.
31 Paradise Lost, "Paradise Lost," on *Lost Paradise*, Century Media, 1990.
32 Milton, *Paradise Lost*, Book 1, line 19; Eminem, "The Real Slim Shady," on *The Marshall Mathers LP*, Aftermath Entertainment/Interscope Records, 2000; AC/DC, "T.N.T.," on *T.N.T.*, Albert Productions, 1975.
33 There is also a political allegory that could be the subject of a whole other book, and it is: *Milton and Religious Controversy: Satire and Polemic in Paradise Lost* by John N. King (Cambridge UP, 2000).
34 Milton, *Paradise Lost*, Book 2, lines 799–802.
35 Slayer, "Hell Awaits," on *Hell Awaits*, Metal Blade Records, 1985.
36 Milton, *Paradise Lost*, Book 1, line 263.
37 *The Wild One*, directed by Laslo Benedek (Columbia Pictures, 1953).
38 Milton, *Paradise Lost*, Book IV, lines 73–78.
39 Ozzy Osbourne, "Bark at the Moon," *Bark at the Moon*, Jet Records, 1983.
40 Iron Maiden, "The Number of the Beast," *The Number of the Beast*, EMI, 1982.
41 Iron Maiden, "Powerslave."
42 William Blake, *The Marriage of Heaven and Hell* (1790–1793), "The Voice of the Devil."
43 Percy Bysshe Shelley, "On the Devil, and Devils," *The Anarchist Library*, 1880, https://theanarchistlibrary.org/library/percy-bysshe-shelley-on-the-devil-and-devils.
44 See Stanley Fish, *Surprised by Sin: The Reader in Paradise Lost* (London: Macmillan, 1967).
45 Alighieri, *The Inferno*, 8.
46 Steel Panther, "Death to All But Metal," *Feel the Steel*, Universal Republic Records, 2009.
47 Alighieri, *The Inferno*, 101.
48 Nine Inch Nails, "Hurt," *The Downward Spiral*, Interscope Records, 1994.
49 Papa Roach, "Scars," *Getting Away with Murder*, DreamWorks Records, 2004.

50 Guns N' Roses, "Get in the Ring," *Use Your Illusion II*, Geffen Records, 1991.
51 Megadeth, "Hook in Mouth," *So Far, So Good. . . So What!*, Capitol Records, 1988.
52 Ozzy Osbourne, "Suicide Solution," *Blizzard of Ozz*, Jet Records, 1980.
53 Slayer, "Hell Awaits."
54 This catchphrase comes from Dana Carvey's Church Lady on *Saturday Night Live*, beginning in 1986, already spoofing the absurdity of the Satanic Panic.
55 Slayer, "On Crypts of Eternity," *Hell Awaits*, Metal Blade Records, 1985.
56 Slayer, "Praise of Death," *Hell Awaits*, Metal Blade Records, 1985.
57 Pat Benatar, "Hell Is for Children," *Crimes of Passion*, Chrysalis Records, 1980.
58 Gloria Naylor, *Linden Hills* (New York: Viking Penguin, 1985), no page number.
59 Sartre, *No Exit*, 45.
60 Van Halen, "Runnin' With the Devil."
61 I can't tell if the line in "Heaven and Hell" is "The ending is just the beginnin'" or "The ending is just a beginner." Lyric websites are divided. The first makes more sense but doesn't rhyme with the previous line's "sinner"; the second rhymes but is not grammatically parallel. It's always a mystery.
62 Black Sabbath, "Neon Knights," *Heaven and Hell*, Warner Bros., 1980.
63 Black Sabbath, "Sabbath Bloody Sabbath," *Sabbath Bloody Sabbath*, Warner Bros., 1973.
64 Dio, "The Last in Line," *The Last in Line*, Warner Bros., 1984.
65 Blake, *Marriage of Heaven and Hell*, "Proverbs of Hell."
66 Black Sabbath, "Heaven and Hell," *Heaven and Hell*, Warner Bros., 1980.
67 Ibid.
68 Ibid.
69 Blake, *Marriage of Heaven and Hell*, "Proverbs of Hell."
70 Black Sabbath, "Heaven and Hell."
71 Dio, "Hungry for Heaven," *The Last in Line*, Warner Bros., 1984.
72 Blake, *Marriage of Heaven and Hell*, "Proverbs of Hell."
73 Dio, "Holy Diver," *Holy Diver*, Warner Bros., 1983.
74 William Blake, "The Tyger," *Poetry Foundation*, published 1794, https://www.poetryfoundation.org/poems/43687/the-tyger.
75 Dio, "Mystery," *The Last in Line*, 1984.
76 John McHugh, "Mystery," in *The Catholic Encyclopedia*, vol. 10 (New York: Robert Appleton Company, 1911), http://www.newadvent.org/cathen/10662a.htm.
77 Dio, "Shame on the Night," *The Last in Line*, Vertigo, 1984.
78 Dio, "Sacred Heart," *Sacred Heart*, Warner Bros., 1985.
79 Credit to this Reddit thread for helping me aggregate all these "rainbow" songs: u/serkophis. "When Tony Iommi Told Dio to Stop Putting Rainbows in His Lyrics,"

Reddit, *r/dio*, August 21, 2021, https://www.reddit.com/r/dio/comments/p72stn/when_tony_iommi_told_dio_to_stop_putting_rainbows/.

80 "Ronnie James Dio Handwritten & Signed Thoughts on Rainbow Themes in His Various Songs and Albums," Heritage Auctions, https://entertainment.ha.com/itm/movie-tv-memorabilia/ronnie-james-dio-handwritten-signed-thoughts-on-rainbow-themes-in-his-various-songs-and-albums/a/997012-1146.s.

81 Genesis 9:14. *The Holy Bible: New King James Version*, 1987.

82 This is also the reason for the LGBTQIA+ community's adoption of the rainbow as a symbol.

83 William Wordsworth, "My Heart Leaps Up," 1807, *Poets.org*, Academy of American Poets, https://poets.org/poem/my-heart-leaps.

84 William Shakespeare, *Hamlet*, Act 3, Scene 1. 1623, in *The Folger Shakespeare*, ed. Barbara A. Mowat and Paul Werstine (Washington, DC: Folger Shakespeare Library, 2011), https://www.folger.edu/explore/shakespeares-works/hamlet/read/.

85 Tannenbaum and Marks, *I Want My MTV*, 449.

86 Metallica, "Enter Sandman," *Metallica*, Elektra, 1991.

87 Ibid.

88 Ibid.

89 Rich Hobson, "The Story Behind the Song: Enter Sandman," *Metal Hammer*, September 20, 2022, https://www.loudersound.com/features/enter-sandman-metallica-story-behind-song.

90 Freud, *The Uncanny*, 2.

91 E. T. A. Hoffman, "The Sandman," trans. John Oxenford, 1816, 1, https://www.ux1.eiu.edu/~rlbeebe/sandman.pdf.

92 Ibid., 2.

93 Futurist Masahiro Mori built upon this idea and Freud's essay in his own conception of the Uncanny Valley, or people's discomfort with inhuman but human-like images.

94 The Chordettes, "Mr. Sandman," *The Chordettes' Greatest Hits*, Cadence Records, 1954.

95 Metallica, "Enter Sandman."

96 Black Sabbath, "The Wizard," *Black Sabbath*, Vertigo Records, 1970.

97 See Mara Leveritt, *Devil's Knot: The True Story of the West Memphis Three* (New York: Simon & Schuster, 2003).

98 Patrick Doyle, "How Rockers Helped Free the West Memphis Three," *Rolling Stone*, September 1, 2011, https://www.rollingstone.com/music/music-news/how-rockers-helped-free-the-west-memphis-three-174460/.

99 "Addiction Doc Who Swapped Drugs for Sex, Had Baby with Patient Gets Long Prison Sentence," *WTAE Pittsburgh*, June 2, 2016, https://www.wtae.com/article

/addiction-doc-who-swapped-drugs-for-sex-had-baby-with-patient-gets-long-prison-sentence/7480392.
100 Hear "N Aid, "Stars," *Stars: Hear N Aid*, Shrapnel Records, 1986.
101 Melissa FitzGerald, *Band Aid: The Song That Rocked the World* (TV movie), 2004, YouTube video, 58:13, uploaded by Peter Campbell, December 13, 2023, https://www.youtube.com/watch?.
102 Al Newstead, "The Greatest Night In Pop: We Are The World Documentary Review," *ABC News*, January 31, 2024, https://www.abc.net.au/news/2024-02-01/we-are-the-world-documentary-the-greatest-night-in-pop-review/103414458.
103 Supporters insist this line is meant to be sarcastic. Whatever.
104 Michael Jackson and Lionel Richie, "We Are the World," *We Are the World* album, USA for Africa, CBS Records, 1985.
105 "Reissue of Eighties Metal All-Star Project HEAR 'N AID Will Arrive 'Sometime Soon', Says Wendy Dio," September 25, 2023, https://blabbermouth.net/news/reissue-of-eighties-metal-all-star-project-hear-n-aid-will-arrive-sometime-soon-says-wendy-dio.
106 "The Greatest Night in Pop," directed by Bao Nguyen (Netflix, 2024).
107 "Rare!! Dio 'Stars'—Behind the Scenes—Making Metal History HQ Best Quality," YouTube, uploaded by M. RileyJunior, June 1, 2016, https://www.youtube.com/watch?v=zM89fYqvvWw&t=901s.
108 "Tipper Gore Widens War on Rock," *The New York Times*, January 4, 1988, https://www.nytimes.com/1988/01/04/arts/tipper-gore-widens-war-on-rock.html.

An Ode to Guitar Solos

1 Miloš Forman, dir., *Amadeus*, Warner Bros., 1984.
2 Immanuel Kant, *Critique of Judgment*. 1790, ed. Nicholas Walker, trans. James Creed Meredith (Oxford University Press, 2009).

Conclusion

1 Walt Whitman, "Song of Myself" (1892 version), in *Poetry Foundation*, https://www.poetryfoundation.org/poems/45477/song-of-myself-1892-version.
2 Faith No More, "Epic," *The Real Thing*, Slash Records, 1989.
3 Tannenbaum and Marks, *I Want My MTV*, 530.
4 Ibid., 532.

5 Ibid.
6 Ibid., 533.
7 Ibid.
8 Michael Azerrad, *Come As You Are: The Story of Nirvana* (New York: Crown, 1993), 179–80.
9 Rage Against the Machine, "Killing in the Name," *Rage Against the Machine*, Epic Records, 1992.
10 Kurt Andersen, "The Best Decade Ever? The 1990s, Obviously," *New York Times*, February 6, 2015, https://www.nytimes.com/2015/02/08/opinion/sunday/the-best-decade-ever-the-1990s-obviously.html.
11 Soundgarden, "Rusty Cage," *Badmotorfinger*, A&M Records, 1991.
12 Alice in Chains, "Man in the Box," *Facelift*, Columbia Records, 1990.
13 Pearl Jam, "Release," *Ten*, Epic Records, 1991.
14 Smashing Pumpkins, "Bullet with Butterfly Wings," *Mellon Collie and the Infinite Sadness*, Virgin Records, 1995.
15 The Faces, "Ooh La La," *Ooh La La*, Warner Bros., 1973.
16 Bob Seger, "Against the Wind," *Against the Wind*, Capitol Records, 1980.
17 Poison, "Something to Believe In," *Flesh & Blood*, Capitol Records, 1990.
18 Poison, "Cry Tough," *Look What the Cat Dragged In*, Enigma Records, 1986.
19 Berry, "School Days."
20 DeLillo, *White Noise*, 258.
21 Led Zeppelin, "Rock and Roll," *Led Zeppelin IV*, Atlantic Records, 1971.
22 Van Halen, "Right Now," *For Unlawful Carnal Knowledge*, Van Halen Music, 1991.
23 Autograph, "Turn Up the Radio," *Sign In Please*, RCA, 1984.
24 Taylor Swift, "Is It Over Now? (Taylor's Version)," *1989 (Taylor's Version)*, Republic Records, 2024.
25 Damn Yankees, "High Enough," *Damn Yankees*, Warner Bros. Records, 1990.
26 Bowling for Soup, "1985," *A Hangover You Don't Deserve*, Jive Records, 2004.
27 Tasha R. Howe, Christopher L. Aberson, Howard S. Friedman, Sarah E. Murphy, Esperanza Alcazar, Edwin J. Vazquez, and Rebekah Becker, "Three Decades Later: The Life Experiences and Mid-Life Functioning of 1980s Heavy Metal Groupies, Musicians, and Fans," *Self and Identity* (2015), https://doi.org/10.1080/15298868.2015.1036918.

Selected Bibliography

This list provides some of the major works cited and possibilities for further reading. For a comprehensive list of citations, please see each chapter's endnotes.

Alighieri, Dante. *The Inferno*. Translated by John Ciardi. Signet Classics, 2009.
Barnes, Djuna. *Nightwood*. New Directions, 1936.
Barthes, Roland. "The Death of the Author." In *Image, Music, Text*, translated by Stephen Heath, 143. Hill and Wang, 1996.
Beaujour, Tom, and Richard Bienstock. *Nöthin' But a Good Time: The Uncensored History of the '80s Hard Rock Explosion*. St. Martin's Press, 2021.
Blake, William. *Collection*. Annotated Classics, 2015.
Bloom, Harold. *The Western Canon: The Books and School of the Ages*. Harcourt Brace, 1994.
Burroughs, William S. *The Soft Machine*. 1961. Grove Press, 1992.
Camus, Albert. *The Myth of Sisyphus*. Translated by Justin O'Brien. Alfred A. Knopf, 1955.
Carroll, Lewis. *Alice's Adventures in Wonderland*. 1865. Sky, 2024.
Christie, Ian. *Sound of the Beast: The Complete Headbanging History of Heavy Metal*. HarperCollins, 2003.
Coleridge, Samuel Taylor. *Major Works*. Oxford UP, 2009.
DeLillo, Don. *Great Jones Street*. Houghton Mifflin, 1973.
DeLillo, Don. *White Noise*. Viking Penguin, 1985.
Dickinson, Emily. *Selected Poems*. Oxford, 2008.
Foucault, Michel. *Madness and Civilization: A History of Insanity in the Age of Reason*. Vintage, 1988.
Freud, Sigmund. *Collected Works*. CreateSpace, 2010.
Ginsberg, Allen. *Howl and Other Poems*. City Lights, 1959.
von Goethe, J. W. *Faust*. Oxford Classic, 2008.
Heller, Joseph. *Catch-22*. Simon & Schuster, 1961.
Hoffman, E. T. A. "The Sandman." Translated by John Oxenford, 1816.
Hughes, Langston. *Collected Poems*. Vintage Classics, 1995.
Jung, C. G. *The Collected Works of C.G. Jung, Volume 9 (Part 1): Archetypes and the Collective Unconscious*. Edited by Gerhard Adler and R. F. C. Hull, 2nd ed. Princeton UP, 1969.
Kesey, Ken. *One Flew Over the Cuckoo's Nest*. Viking Press, 1962.
Milton, John. *Paradise Lost*. 1667. Penguin Classics, 2003.

Monk, Noel, with Joe Layden. *Runnin' with the Devil: A Backstage Pass to the Wild Times, Loud Rock, and the Down and Dirty Truth Behind the Making of Van Halen*. Dey Street Books, 2017.

Mötley Crüe, with Neil Strauss. *The Dirt: Confessions of the World's Most Notorious Rock Band*. HarperCollins, 2001.

Naylor, Gloria. *Linden Hills*. Penguin, 1986.

Orwell, George. *1984*. Signet, 1949.

O'Neill, Andrew. *A History of Heavy Metal*. Headline, 2018.

Shakespeare, William. *Complete Works*. Modern Library, 2022.

Tannenbaum, Rob, and Craig Marks. *I Want My MTV: The Uncensored Story of the Music Video*. Plume, 2011.

Walser, Robert. *Running with the Devil: Power, Gender, and Madness in Heavy Metal Music*. Wesleyan University Press, 1993.

Weinstein, Deena. *Heavy Metal: The Music and Its Culture*. Da Capo, 1991.

Wilde, Oscar. *The Picture of Dorian Gray*. Ward, Lock & Co., 1890.

Winwood, Ian. *Bodies: Life and Death in Music*. Faber & Faber, 2022.

Discography

This list provides the names of the major albums referenced throughout this book.

AC/DC, *Back in Black*, Atlantic, 1980.
AC/DC, *Highway to Hell*, Atlantic, 1979.
Aerosmith, *Permanent Vacation*, Geffen, 1987.
Anthrax, *Spreading the Disease*, Island, 1985.
Armored Saint, *March of the Saint*, Chrysalis, 1984.
Autograph, *Sign In Please*, RCA, 1984.
The Black Crowes, *Shake Your Money Maker*, Def American Recordings, 1990.
Black Sabbath, *Black Sabbath*, Vertigo, 1970.
Black Sabbath, *Born Again*, Vertigo, 1983.
Black Sabbath, *Heaven and Hell*, Vertigo, 1980.
Black Sabbath, *Paranoid*, Vertigo, 1970.
Bon Jovi, *7800° Fahrenheit*, Mercury, 1985.
Bon Jovi, *Crush*, Island Records, 2000.
Bon Jovi, *New Jersey*, Mercury, 1988.
Bon Jovi, *Slippery When Wet*, Mercury, 1986.
Cooper, Alice, *Love It to Death*, Warner Bros., 1971.
Cooper, Alice, *School's Out*, Warner Bros., 1972.
Cooper, Alice, *Trash*, Epic, 1989.
The Cult, *Sonic Temple*, Beggars Banquet, 1989.
Damn Yankees, *Damn Yankees*, Atlantic, 1990.
Danzig, *Danzig*, 1988.
Def Leppard, *High 'n' Dry*, Mercury, 1981.
Def Leppard, *Hysteria*, Mercury, 1987.
Def Leppard, *Pyromania*, Mercury, 1983.
Dio, *Holy Diver*, Warner Bros., 1983.
Dio, *The Last in Line*, Vertigo, 1984.
Dio, *Sacred Heart*, Warner Bros., 1985.
Extreme, *Extreme*, A&M, 1989.
Faith No More, *The Real Thing*, Slash, 1989.
Ford, Lita, *Lita*, RCA, 1988.
Guns N' Roses, *Appetite for Destruction*, Geffen, 1987.
Guns N' Roses, *G N' R Lies*, Geffen, 1988.
Iron Maiden, *The Number of the Beast*, EMI, 1982.

Iron Maiden, *Powerslave*, EMI, 1984.
Iron Maiden, *Seventh Son of a Seventh Son*, EMI, 1988.
Joan Jett and the Blackhearts, *I Love Rock 'n Roll*, Boardwalk, 1981.
Johnson, Robert, *Complete Recordings*, Columbia, 1990.
Journey, *Escape*, Columbia, 1981.
Journey, *Frontiers*, Columbia, 1983.
Judas Priest, *British Steel*, Columbia, 1980.
Judas Priest, *Defenders of the Faith*, Columbia, 1984.
Judas Priest, *Sad Wings of Destiny*, Gull, 1976.
Judas Priest, *Turbo*, Columbia, 1986.
Kiss, *Crazy Nights*, Mercury, 1987.
Kiss, *Lick It Up*, Mercury, 1983.
Led Zeppelin, *Led Zeppelin IV*, Atlantic, 1971.
Living Colour, *Vivid*, Epic, 1988.
Loudness, *Thunder in the East*, Atco, 1985.
Megadeth, *Countdown to Extinction*, Capitol, 1992.
Megadeth, *Peace Sells... but Who's Buying?*, Capitol, 1986.
Megadeth, *So Far, So Good... So What!*, Capitol, 1988.
Mercyful Fate, *Melissa, Roadrunner*, 1983.
Metallica, *...And Justice for All*, Elektra, 1988.
Metallica, *Master of Puppets*, Elektra, 1986.
Metallica, *Metallica*, Elektra, 1991.
Metallica, *Ride the Lightning*, Elektra, 1984.
Mötley Crüe, *Girls, Girls, Girls*, Elektra, 1987.
Mötley Crüe, *Shout at the Devil*, Elektra, 1983.
Mötley Crüe, *Theatre of Pain*, Elektra, 1985.
Mötley Crüe, *Too Fast for Love*, Elektra, 1981.
Ozzy Osbourne, *Bark at the Moon*, Jet, 1983.
Ozzy Osbourne, *Blizzard of Ozz*, Jet, 1980.
Ozzy Osbourne, *Diary of a Madman*, Jet, 1981.
Ozzy Osbourne, *No More Tears*, Epic, 1991.
Ozzy Osbourne, *The Ultimate Sin*, Epic, 1986.
Poison, *Flesh & Blood*, Capitol, 1990.
Poison, *Look What the Cat Dragged In*, Enigma, 1986.
Poison, *Open Up and Say... Ahh!*, Enigma, 1988.
Prince, *1999*, Warner Bros., 1982.
Prince, *Purple Rain*, Warner Bros., 1984.
Quiet Riot, *Metal Health*, Pasha, 1983.
Ratt, *Out of the Cellar*, Atlantic, 1984.
Scorpions, *Crazy World*, Mercury, 1990.
Scorpions, *Love at First Sting*, Mercury, 1984.

Skid Row, *Skid Row*, Atlantic, 1989.
Slayer, *Hell Awaits*, Metal Blade, 1985.
Tesla, *Mechanical Resonance*, Geffen, 1986.
Twisted Sister, *Stay Hungry*, Atlantic, 1984.
Twisted Sister, *Under the Blade*, Atlantic, 1982.
Type O Negative, *Bloody Kisses*, Roadrunner, 1993.
Van Halen, *1984*, Warner Bros., 1984.
Van Halen, *For Unlawful Carnal Knowledge*, Van Halen Music, 1991.
Van Halen, *Van Halen*, Warner Bros., 1978.
Van Halen, *Van Halen II*, Warner Bros., 1979.
Venom, *Possessed*, Neat Records, 1985.
Venom, *Welcome to Hell*, Neat Records, 1981.
W.A.S.P., *W.A.S.P.*, Capitol, 1984.
White Lion, *Big Game*, Atlantic, 1989.
White Lion, *Pride*, Atlantic, 1987.
Whitesnake, *Whitesnake*, Geffen, 1987.

Index

Note: Page numbers followed by "n" refer to notes.

8 Mile 68, 225 n.79
20/20 170, 235 n.27
27 Club 165
60 Minutes 197

AC/DC 10, 12, 210
    Back in Black (1980) 126, 127
    "Dirty Deeds Done Dirt Cheap" 88
    "Highway to Hell" 169, 216
    Johnson, Brian 123
    "Let Me Put My Love Into You" 27, 126
    Scott, Bon 123, 169
    "T.N.T" 171
    "You Shook Me All Night Long" 48, 82
Aerosmith
    "Angel" 139–40
    "Back in the Saddle" 63
    Tyler, Steven 139
Alan Parsons Project 76
Alice In Chains 208, 209
    Dirt 121, 122
    "Down in a Hole" 121
    "Godsmack" 121
    "Junkhead" 121
    "Rain When I Die" 121
    "Sickman" 121
    Staley, Layne 121, 122, 209
Aliens (1986) 2
Amadeus (1984) 202
American Graffiti (1973) 51
American Society of Composers, Authors and Publishers (ASCAP) 23, 24
Anderson, Pamela 150
"Angel of the Morning" 139
Angel Witch
    "Angel Witch" 139
Animal House (1978) 90
Anthrax 10, 33, 111, 112, 182
    Belladonna, Joey 207
    "Madhouse" 108–10

anti-Semitism 62
apocalypse 16, 30, 37, 38, 40–1, 45, 46, 57, 59, 63, 134
Appleseed, Johnny 78
Armored Saint
    "Mad House" 173
Arrows, The 156, 233 n.70
ASCAP, *see* American Society of Composers, Authors and Publishers (ASCAP)
Autograph
    "Turn Up the Radio" 203, 213
Avenged Sevenfold
    "Almost Easy" 111

Back to School (1986) 80, 81
Badlands 208
    Gillan, Ray 208
Baez, Joan 195
Baker, James 25
Baker, Susan 25, 27, 160, 169
Bakker, Jim 62
Band Aid
    "Do They Know It's Christmas?" 197
Barnes, Djuna
    Nightwood 48
Barry, James
    "Satan and His Legions Hurling Defiance toward the Vault of Heaven" 176
Barrie, J. M.
    Peter Pan 192
Barthes, Roland 86
    "Death of the Author, The" 80
    jouissance 86
Bashō, Matsuo 213
Baudelaire, Charles 103
    "Vampire's Metamorphoses, The" 22
Baum, L. Frank 59
Beach Boys 211
Beatles, The 111, 146

"Day Tripper" 103
"Doctor Robert" 103
"Everybody's Got Something to Hide Except Me and My Monkey" 103
"Help" 146
Lennon, John 42, 60, 123, 210
"Twist and Shout" 170
"With A Little Help from My Friends" 103
Beaujour, Tom and Bienstock, Richard
Nöthin' But a Good Time: The Uncensored History of the '80s Hard Rock Explosion 52, 55, 58, 78
Bee Gees
"Stayin' Alive" 45
Behind the Music 100, 123
Belafonte, Harry 197
Benatar, Pat
"Hell is for Children" 183–4
"You Better Run" 83
Berry, Chuck 210, 211
"Maybellene" 51
"School Days" 12, 13
Biffy Clyro 123
Big Bopper, The 210
Bill Haley & His Comets
"Rock Around the Clock" 12, 213, 219 n.5
Black Crows, The 95
"She Talks to Angels" 140
Black Death 95
Black Flag 95
Black Label Society 95
Black Lives Matter 162
Black Oak Arkansas 95
Black Rebel Motorcycle Club 76
Black Sabbath 42, 58, 95, 137, 162, 163, 175
Butler, Geezer 163
"Heaven and Hell" 186, 188, 191
Iommi, Tony 135, 156, 163
"Iron Man" 106
"Killing Yourself to Live" 88
"Lady Evil" 138
"Neon Knights" 185, 187
"NIB" 165, 176
"Sign of the Southern Cross, The" 190

"Trashed" 27, 102, 103, 114
"Turn Up the Night" 187
"Wishing Well" 190
Black Veil Brides 95
Blackboard Jungle (1955) 12–13
Blade Runner (1982) 49, 50
Blake, William 9, 33, 61, 186, 191, 211
Marriage of Heaven and Hell 176, 186–8
Songs of Innocence and of Experience 188
"Tyger, The" 188–9
Bloom, Allan
Closing of the American Mind, The 172
Bloom, Harold
Western Canon, The 155
Blue Öyster Cult 198
"Burnin' For You" 82, 84
BMI, see Broadcast Music, Inc. (BMI)
Bon Jovi 32, 36, 37, 64, 202, 206, 210, 215
Blaze of Glory 66
"It's My Life" 69
Keep the Faith 66
"Livin' on a Prayer" 38, 66–9, 149
"In and Out of Love" 100
"Runaway" 41
Slippery When Wet 69–70
"Wanted Dead or Alive" 65, 66, 169
"You Give Love a Bad Name" 82, 84
Bonham
"Wait for You" 133
Book of Mormon, The 168
Bosch, Hieronymus 181, 196
Bowie, David 10, 77
Bowling for Soup 215
Brackett, John 24
Brando, Marlon 12, 173
Broadcast Music, Inc. (BMI) 23
Brothers Grimm 75
Brown, James 148
Buckcherry
"Crazy Bitch" 131, 132, 137, 139, 147
"I'm Sorry" 131, 132, 147
Bunyan, Paul 78
Burroughs, William
Soft Machine, The 32, 40, 41, 44, 80

Index

Bush, George 68, 98, 209
Butler, Judith 154
Byron, Lord
   Byronic hero 122
   "Childe Harold's Pilgrimage" 21

Calvino, Italo
   If on a Winter's Night a Traveler 82
Camus, Albert
   Myth of Sisyphus, The 115, 117, 118
Carlin, George
   "Baseball *vs.* Football" 149
   "Seven Words You Can't Say on Television" 95
Carroll, Lewis
   Alice's Adventures in Wonderland 82, 111
Carver, Raymond 75
Cash, Johnny
   "Hurt" 180
Chabon, Michael 79–80
Charles, Ray 197
Chaucer, Geoffrey
   Canterbury Tales 42
Cheap Trick
   "I Want You to Want Me" 83, 84
Child's Play 10
Chordettes, The
   "Mr. Sandman" 195
Christgau, Robert 43
Christie, Ian
   Sound of the Beast: The Complete Headbanging History of Heavy Metal 32
Ciardi, John 178
Cinderella
   Kieffer, Tom 207
Clapton, Eric 166, 202
Clash, The 45, 70
Clink, Mike 148
Clinton, Bill 28, 97, 98, 209
Clovers, The
   "Devil or Angel" 132–3
Cochran, Wayne
   "Last Kiss" 140
cold war 2, 16, 23, 24, 30, 33, 36, 38, 40–2, 46, 51, 58–64, 70, 72, 74, 101, 110, 183, 211, 215

Coleridge, Samuel Taylor 32, 103
   "Kubla Khan" 21
   "Rime of the Ancient Mariner, The" 9, 21
Collins, Phil 197
Collins, Wilkie
   Woman in White, The 78
Cooke, Sam
   "Wonderful World" 13
Cooper, Alice 13, 21–2, 133–4, 153
   "I'm Eighteen" 134
   "Poison" 133, 137
   "School's Out" 13, 32, 145
Corrosion of Conformity 10
cowboys 63–6
Crocket, Davy 78
Crossroads (1986) 168, 234 n.22
Crow
   "Evil Woman" 137
Crow, The 92
Cult, The
   Astbury, Ian 138
   Duffy, Billy 138
   "Fire Woman" 138
Cutting Crew
   "(I Just) Died in Your Arms" 120
Cycle Sluts from Hell 10
Cypress Hill
   "Insane in the Membrane" 111
   "(Rock) Superstar" 146

Daisley, Bob (Ozzy Osbourne) 59
"Dallas" 63
Damn Yankees 214
   "High Enough" 135
   Shaw, Tommy 214
Danger Danger 10
Dangerfield, Rodney 80
Dangerous Toys 10
Daniels, Charlie
   "Devil Went Down to Georgia, The" 168
Dante Alighieri 180, 183, 193
   Divine Comedy, The 42, 163, 177
   Inferno 33, 44, 160, 163, 167, 176–9, 181, 183, 184
   Purgatory 177
   symbolic retribution 179–81

Danzig, Glen   138, 160
　"Am I a Demon"   160
　"Devil on Hwy 9"   160
　"Devil's Angels"   160
　"Devil's Plaything"   160
　"Heart of the Devil"   160
　"Mother"   161
Davis, Miles   65
Day After, The (1983)   38
Dean, James   12
Death Wish (1974)   92
Decline of Western Civilization Part II: The Metal Years, The (1988)   53
Deep Purple   42, 190
　Gillan, Ian   102, 164
　"Highway Star"   164
Def Leppard   16, 129, 132, 136, 156, 208, 210
　"Bringin' On the Heartbreak"   39
　Clark, Steve   208
　Elliot, Joe   143, 232 n.42
　"Foolin'"   209
　"High 'n' Dry (Saturday Night)"   27, 102, 103
　Hysteria   129
　"Me and My Wine"   102, 103
　"Photograph"   38-9, 50
　"Pour Some Sugar on Me"   143, 216
　Pyromania   90, 142
　"Wasted"   103
　"Women"   142-4, 147
DeLillo, Don   120-3
　Great Jones Street   99-100, 119-20
　White Noise   119, 212
Denver, John   27
Diamond Head
　"Am I Evil?"   163
Dickens, Charles   42, 78
Dickinson, Emily   33, 105, 166
　"I Felt a Funeral, in my Brain"   107
　"I Died for Beauty"   107
　"Pain has an Element of Blank"   107
Dio   7
　"All the Fools Sailed Away"   189, 191
　Bain, Jimmy   198
　"Breathless"   187, 190
　Campbell, Vivian   198
　"Die Young"   115

"Dream Evil"   190
"Evil Eyes"   187, 190
"Holy Diver"   188
"Hungry for Heaven"   188
"I Speed at Night"   187
"Last in Line, The"   37, 185
"Mystery"   189, 191
"Otherworld"   190
"Rainbow in the Dark"   187, 190, 202
Ronnie James   7, 31, 33, 38, 61, 138, 185-91, 198, 199
"Sacred Heart"   7, 187, 189-90
"Shame on the Night"   187, 189
Dirty Harry (1970)   92
Disney   192
Dixon, Willie   163-4
　"You Need Love"   164
Dokken   10, 39, 52, 198
　"Dream Warriors"   174
　"In My Dreams"   44
　Lynch, George   44, 52, 53, 199
Donnas, The
　"Take It Off"   157
Donne, John   21-2
　"Flea, The"   21
Doré, Gustave   9, 159, 175
Dostoyevsky, Fyodor   15, 106
Dr. Strangelove (1964)   63
Dungeons & Dragons (*D&D*)   2-11, 15, 53, 89, 196, 206
　Fiend Folio, The   7
　Monster Manual   3
　Player's Handbook   9
Dunn, Sam
　"Metal Evolution"   36
Duran Duran   197
　Rhodes, Nick   40
Dylan, Bob   16, 59, 77, 120, 197, 198
　"Blowin' In the Wind"   64

Eagles, The   137-8
　"Desperado"   63
　"Witchy Woman"   137
Easton, Sheena
　"Sugar Walls"   27
Egan, Jennifer
　Visit From the Goon Squad, A   82
Electric Ladyland Studios   10

Electric Light Orchestra
   "Evil Woman" 138
"Electronic Curtain" 24
Eliot, T. S. 16
Elvis (2022) 121, 123, 124
Enuff Z'Nuff 10
Escape From New York (1981) 37, 38, 41, 92
escape/escapism 4, 13, 36, 40, 57, 110, 111, 116, 119, 120, 126, 135, 167, 196
ET (1982) 2
"Evening (The Fall of Day)" 7
Extreme 206
   Bettencourt, Nuno 202
   "Get the Funk Out" 202–3
"Eye of the Beholder" 93

Faith No More 91, 206, 210
Faulkner, William 103
female gaze 155–8
"Final Fantasy" 4
Firestarter (1984) 2
Fish, Stanley 176
Fitzgerald, F. Scott 103
Flaubert, Gustave
   Madame Bovary 25
Flight of the Conchords
   "Demon Woman" 139
Flynn, Gillian
   Gone Girl 26
Foo Fighters 122, 123
   Hawkins, Taylor 123
Ford, Lita 25, 156, 202
   "Close My Eyes Forever" 115, 203
   "Kiss Me Deadly" 155, 156
Foucault, Michel 107, 112–14
   Madness and Civilization 108–9
Four Aces, The
   "Mr. Sandman" 195
Freed, Alan 24
French Revolution 42
Freud, Sigmund 1, 15, 32, 100, 135, 138, 147, 194
   Beyond the Pleasure Principle 39
   castration 134–6
   Interpretation of Dreams, The 38
   "Most Prevalent Form of Degradation in Erotic Life, The" 131–2

Self and Identity 217
   separation anxiety 134–6, 141
"Friday Night Videos" 36
Fukuyama, Francis
   "End of History?, The" 211

Garden of Eden 143, 171
Geefs, Guillaume
   "The Lucifer of Liège" 175
Ghost 168
   Forge, Tobias 78
Ginsberg, Allen 22–3, 25
   "Howl" 22, 23
Geldof, Bob 197, 198
Goethe, Johann Wolfgang von
   Faust 164–6, 168
   Faust Part Two 168
Goffman, Erving 226 n.9
Goonies (1985) 2
Gore, Al, Jr. 25, 27, 28, 89, 97–8, 209
Gore, Albert, Sr. 24–6
Gore, Tipper 27–9, 39, 51, 62, 70, 74–5, 78, 79, 85, 86, 89, 91, 98, 101, 103, 104, 121, 124, 128, 130, 153, 154, 161, 179, 197, 199
   Raising PG Kids in an X-Rated Society 25, 26
   "Smut and Sadism of Rock, The" 74
Grand Guignol, The 127
Grease (1978) 45
Great White
   "Angel Song, The" 140
Greatest Night in Pop, The (2024) 198
Green Day 122
   "Basket Case" 111
Guns N' Roses 32–3, 52, 132, 140, 206, 207, 210
   Appetite for Destruction 130, 145, 148
   "Get in the Ring" 181
   Lies 130
   "Nightrain" 148
   "Out Ta Get Me" 148
   "Paradise City" 148
   "Patience" 130–2
   "Rocket Queen" 148
   Rose, W. Axl 130–1, 145, 147, 148, 150

Slash   202
"Sweet Child O' Mine"   145, 147–8, 181, 202, 216
"Used to Love Her"   88, 130–2, 144
"Welcome to the Jungle"   148
"You Could Be Mine"   83, 84
"You're Crazy"   148
Gypsies (Romani)   65, 225 n.73

"Hair Nation"   56
Hale, Lzzy   157
Hammer, Mike   155
Hanks, Tom   121
Headbangers Ball (1987–2012)   208
Hear N' Aid   31
   "Stars"   197–9
Heller, Joseph
   Catch-22   60, 109, 113
Hellfire Club   5
Hemingway, Ernest   32, 103
   Farewell to Arms, A   9
   "For Whom the Bell Tolls"   9, 116
Hendrix, Jimi   10, 119, 165, 202
   "Manic Depression"   111
   "Star-Spangled Banner, The"   43, 44
Henry, John   78
"High in High School"   13
High Noon (1952)   63
Hill, Trent   153
Hobbes, Thomas
   Leviathan   3
Hoffmann, E. T. A.
   "Sandman, The" ("Der Sandmann")   194, 196
Holly, Buddy   210
   "It's So Easy"   145
Holst, Gustav
   "Mars, The Bringer of War"   163
Homer
   Odyssey, The   137
Hot Tub Time Machine (2010)   150
How to Make a Monster (1958)   175
HuffPost   16
Hughes, Langston
   "Mother to Son"   169
Hunt, Brad   55
Hunt for Red October, The (1990)   38

Ice Cube
   "No Vaseline"   180
International Society for Metal Music Studies   32
Iron Curtain   24, 70–2
Iron Maiden   7, 21, 32, 33, 105, 196, 202, 207
   "Can I Play With Madness?"   106
   Dickinson, Bruce   33, 105–7, 207
   "Duellists, The"   91
   "Flash of the Blade"   91
   Harris, Steve   105
   "Killers"   86
   "Number of the Beast, The"   175
   "Powerslave"   9, 106

Jack the Ripper   86, 87, 92, 93, 96
Jackson, Michael   197
   Thriller   49, 51
Jane's Addiction   210
Jefferson Airplane
   "White Rabbit"   111
Jett, Joan   156, 215
   "I Hate Myself for Loving You"   82
   "I Love Rock 'n' Roll"   156
Joel, Billy   197, 201
   "Big Shot"   83
   "Pressure"   83
   "We Didn't Start the Fire"   209
   "You May Be Right"   83
   "You're Only Human"   83
Johnson, Robert   165–9
   "Cross Road Blues"   165, 166, 176, 184
   "Hellhound on My Trail"   165, 166
   "Me and the Devil Blues"   165
Jones, Quincy   197
Joplin, Janis   119, 122, 165
Journey
   "Don't Stop Believin'"   67, 216
   "Separate Ways"   136
Joyce, James   42
   Ulysses   25
Judas Priest   70, 119, 154, 198, 202, 207
   "Breaking the Law"   48, 216
   British Steel   47
   Downing, K. K.   47
   "Eat Me Alive"   27, 86, 87, 126, 130

Halford, Rob 198, 207
"Living After Midnight" 48
"Parental Guidance" 84
"Ripper, The" 86, 87
Jung, Carl 33
"Psychology of the Child Archetype, The" 147

Kafka, Franz 42
Kant, Immanuel
 Critique of Judgement 202
Karate Kid, The (1984) 168
Keats, John 137
 "Ode on a Grecian Urn" 69
Kerslake, Kevin 206
Kesey, Ken 113, 114
 One Flew Over the Cuckoo's Nest 32
Kierkegaard, Søren 50
King, Rodney 209
King, Stephen 41
 Carrie 2
 Maximum Overdrive 174–5
Kinison, Sam
 "Wild Thing" 62
Kinks, The
 "You Really Got Me" 44, 82
Kiss 10, 12, 161
 "Burn Bitch Burn" 127
 Carr, Eric 208
 "Crazy Nights" 84
 "Let's Put the X in Sex" 22
 "Lick It Up" 37
 "Rock and Roll All Nite" 12, 48, 146
 Simmons, Gene 161
 Stanley, Paul 84, 161
Kitaen, Tawny 140–1, 157
Kix
 "Don't Close Your Eyes" 115
Korn
 "Coming Undone" 111
 "Insane" 111
Krokus 13, 38
 "Screaming in the Night" 37
 Storace, Marc 37, 39

Lady Gaga 77–8
Lamar, Kendrick 16
Lange, Mutt 232 n.42

Lauper, Cyndi
 "She Bop" 27
LaVey, Anton 161
Lawrence, D. H.
 Lady Chatterley's Lover 25, 126
Lawrence, Jack 24
Led Zeppelin 42, 43, 169, 212, 213
 "Battle of Evermore, The" 7
 "Crunge, The" 148
 "Heartbreaker" 163
 "Misty Mountain Hop" 7
 "In My Time of Dying" 120
 Page, Jimmy 202
 Plant, Robert 7, 148
 "Ramble On" 7
 "Rock and Roll" 212–13
 "Stairway to Heaven" 164
 "Whole Lotta Love" 164, 227 n.22
Lee, Jake E. (Ozzy Osbourne) 53, 59, 61
Life of Agony 10
Liszt, Franz 163
Little Nicky (2000) 169
Living Colour
 "Cult of Personality" 96, 203
 Reid, Vernon 202
Lollapalooza 210
Lovecraft, H. P. 116
Loverboy
 "Working for the Weekend" 57

madness 22, 29–31, 60, 100, 104–14, 116, 120, 167, 175, 196
Macchio, Ralph 168
McCarthy, Joseph 23–5, 70
 McCarthyite moralism 90
McCarthyism 23, 70
McCartney, Paul 123
McGhee, Doc 71, 78
McInerney, Jay
 Bright Lights, Big City 82
McLachlan, Sarah
 "Angel" 139
McLuhan, Marshall 210
Mad Max (1979) 38
Madonna
 "Dress You Up" 27
Magritte, René
 "Treachery of Images, The" 87

male gaze   31, 137, 153, 155–7
Mallet, David   38–9
Malmsteen, Yngwie   164
Mann, Thomas   164
Mannequin (1987)   144
Marilyn Manson   153
Marlowe, Christopher   164
Maroon 5
  Levine, Adam   130
Marvel Cinematic Universe   178
Marvell, Andrew
  "To His Coy Mistress"   22
Mary Jane Girls
  "In My House"   27
Megadeth   1, 16, 22, 36, 57–8, 98, 202
  Friedman, Marty   182
  "In My Darkest Hour"   120
  Killing Is My Business. . . And Business Is Good (1985)   96
  "Killing Is My Business. . .and Business Is Good!"   88
  Mustaine, Dave   16, 96, 97, 172
  "Peace Sells"   96–7
  Peace Sells. . . But Who's Buying? (1986)   96
  "Skin O' My Teeth"   115
  So Far, So Good. . . So What! (1988)   96
  "Sweating Bullets"   1, 16–17
  "Tout Le Monde, A"   115
Megamind (2010)   216
Mengele, Josef   88
Mercyful Fate
  "Into the Coven"   27, 161, 182
  King Diamond   161
Metal Church
  "Of Unsound Mind"   76, 88
Metal Studies   31, 119
Metallica   7–10, 32, 36, 72, 98, 101, 114, 116, 182, 191–5, 206, 210, 219 n.4
  And Justice for All   93, 94
  Black Album, The   192
  Burton, Cliff   93, 118
  "Call of Ktulu, The"   116
  "Creeping Death"   88, 116
  "Dyers Eve"   93
  "Enter Sandman"   192–5
  "Escape"   116
  "Fade to Black"   116–18, 124
  "Fight Fire with Fire"   93, 116
  "Frayed Ends of Sanity, The"   94
  "Leper Messiah"   62
  Hammett, Kirk   192
  Hetfield, James   101, 102, 117, 122, 124, 192, 193, 195
  Master of Puppets   7–8, 94–5, 102, 103, 112, 116
  "Memory Remains, The"   117, 118
  Metal Up Your Ass   93
  "Nothing Else Matters"   118
  Ride the Lightning   9, 93, 116, 118
  "Shortest Straw, The"   93
  "Trapped Under Ice"   116
  Ulrich, Lars   113, 197
  "Welcome Home (Sanitarium)"   94, 112–14
Metcalf, Mark   90
Michael, George   197
Midnight in Paris (2011)   213
Milton, John   9, 183, 187
  Paradise Lost   142, 167, 168, 170–3, 175, 176, 196
Misfits, The
  "Die, Die My Darling"   88
Molly Hatchet   7
Monk, Noel   51, 70–1, 156
Morahan, Andy   207
Morrison, Jim   119, 122, 165
Moscow Music Peace Festival   71, 207
Mothra vs. Godzilla (1964)   175
Mötley Crüe   36, 52–5, 58, 70, 71, 89, 98, 101, 122, 127, 146, 154, 207, 208, 215
  "Bastard"   27, 86, 87, 150
  Corabi, John   150
  Decade of Decadence   22
  Dirt, The   54, 55, 78, 80, 134, 156, 170
  "Girls, Girls, Girls"   153–5, 157
  "Home Sweet Home"   113, 145, 148–50, 166
  Lee, Tommy   150
  "Looks That Kill"   54, 134, 137
  Mars, Mick   198
  "Merry Go Round"   54
  Mötley Crüe   150
  Neil, Vince   53, 149, 150, 198, 207

"Piece of Your Action" 153
"Shout at the Devil" 6, 31, 54, 148, 170, 173
"Smokin' in the Boys Room" 110
Sixx, Nikki 53, 54, 87, 136, 149, 156
"Take Me to the Top" 149
Theatre of Pain 127, 148–9
"Toast of the Town" 149
Too Fast for Love 54, 148
"Too Young to Fall in Love" 54
"Without You" 82
"You're All I Need" 88
Mozart, Wolfgang Amadeus 164, 202
Mr. Big
   "To Be With You" 83
MTV 30, 36, 65, 97, 98, 209, 210
   "Choose or Lose" 97
   Real World, The 10, 208
Munsters, The 5
Muse
   "Madness" 111
"Mustang Sally" 50

Nabokov, Vladimir
   Lolita 25
Naylor, Gloria
   Linden Hills 184, 196
Neil, Simon 123
Nelson
   "After the Rain" 110
Nickelback
   "Animals" 130
   "Rockstar" 146
Nicks, Stevie 76
Night Ranger 202
   Blades, Jack 214
   Gillis, Brad 199
   "(You Can Still) Rock in America" 83
Nightmare Before Christmas, The (1993) 163
Nightmare on Elm Street, A (1984) 2
Nightmare on Elm Street 3 (1987) 174
Nimona (2023) 216
Nine Inch Nails 180
   Downward Spiral, The 129
Nirvana 121, 210
   Cobain, Kurt 117, 165, 210
   "I Hate Myself and Want to Die" 120
   Nevermind 47, 206–8, 220 n.3
   "Rape Me" 87
   "Smells Like Teen Spirit" 206
Nosferatu (1922) 175
Nuclear Assault
   "Hang the Pope" 179
NWA
   Straight Outta Compton (2015) 180

O'Barr, James 92
"O Come, All Ye Faithful" 90
O'Neill, Andrew
   History of Heavy Metal, A 32
One Million Years B.C. (1940) 175
Orpheus 17, 205
Orwell, George 211
   1984 48, 51
Osbourne, Sharon 53
Osbourne, Ozzy 36, 52, 58–62, 71, 72, 77, 101, 119, 162, 163, 173–4, 196, 197
   "Bark at the Moon" 173–5
   Blizzard of Ozz 59
   "Close My Eyes Forever" 115
   "Crazy Train" 60, 61, 64, 110, 111
   "Demon Alcohol" 174
   "Diary of a Madman" 110–11
   "I Don't Know" 61, 62
   "Killer of Giants" 35, 61
   "Mr. Crowley" 202
   No More Tears 62, 206
   No Rest for the Wicked 62
   "Revelation (Mother Earth)" 61, 93
   "Shot in the Dark" 133
   "Suicide Solution" 115–16, 174, 181
   "Thank God for the Bomb" 61
   Ultimate Sin, The 61, 63, 133
   "You Can't Kill Rock and Roll" 83
Osbournes, The 208
Overkill 10

Packard, Vance 23
Palahniuk, Chuck 15
   Fight Club 26
Pantera 25, 63
Papa Roach
   "Scars" 180
Paradise Lost (1996) 196

Paradise Lost (band)
  Lost Paradise 171
Parents Music Resource Center
  (PMRC) 25, 26, 28–30, 39, 51,
  70, 74, 77, 86–92, 97, 100, 101, 103,
  109, 114, 120, 126, 128, 129, 150,
  152–3, 158, 160, 161, 169, 175, 176,
  181, 187, 196, 197, 199, 208, 215–17
Parker, Dorothy 103
Payola hearings 23, 24, 70
Peacemaker 150
Pearl Jam 140, 152, 208
  "Animal" 129
  Vedder, Eddie 153, 197
Penny Dreadfuls 9
*Percy Jackson and the Olympians: The
  Lightning Thief* (2010) 169
Perot, Ross 97
Pink Floyd
  "Another Brick in the Wall Part 2" 13
  "Wish You Were Here" 111
Plato
  Phaedrus 104, 105
PMRC, *see* Parents Music Resource Center
  (PMRC)
Poe, Edgar Allan 15, 82
  "Raven, The" 76, 77
  "Tell-Tale Heart, The" 75, 77, 78, 88
Poison 52, 56–8, 206, 209, 212
  "Cry Tough" 69, 211
  DeVille, C. C. 140, 207
  "Every Rose Has Its Thorn" 145,
    150–2
  "Fallen Angel" 140
  Michaels, Bret 33, 55, 57, 150–2, 207,
    211
  "Nothin' But a Good Time" 57, 110
  "Something to Believe In" 62, 211
  "Talk Dirty to Me" 211–12
Presley, Elvis 122, 153–4
  "Fame and Fortune" 146–7
Primus 210
Prince 223 n.21
  "1999" 57–8
  "Darling Nikki" 26, 27, 103, 128
  "Let's Go Crazy" 57
  "Little Red Corvette" 26
  Purple Rain 26

Prometheus 35, 40
Proust, Marcel 42

Queen
  Mercury, Freddie 47, 208
  "We Will Rock You" 82, 83
Queensrÿche 38, 58, 198, 206
  "Queen of the Reich" 37
  Tate, Geoff 198
Queer Theory 154
Quiet Riot 39, 70, 112, 198
  DuBrow, Kevin 39, 198
  "Cum On Feel the Noise" 109
  "Metal Health" 104, 109, 110, 173,
    209, 216
Quinn, Joseph 1, 2, 219 n.4
Quirk, Justin
  *Nothin' But A Good Time: The
    Spectacular Rise and Fall of Hair
    Metal* 52

Rachtman, Riki 56
Rage Against the Machine 209
  "Killing in the Name Of" 172,
    208
  Morello, Tom 209
Rainbow
  "Catch the Rainbow" 190
  "Kill the King" 190
  "Rainbow Eyes" 190
  "Stargazer" 190
Ramones, The 13
  "I Wanna Be Sedated" 111
  "Rock and Roll High School" 13
Ratt 52, 53, 64, 208
  Crosby, Robbin 53, 208
  Croucier, Juan 52
  "Round and Round" 6, 203
  "Wanted Man" 65
Ready Player One (2018) 49, 90
Reagan, Ronald 30, 42, 65, 101
reality TV 208
Rebel Without a Cause 12
Red Dawn (1984) 38
Red Hot Chili Peppers 210
Reigndance 10
REM 38
  "Try Not to Breathe" 120

"ReMastered: Devil at the
    Crossroads" 167
Rhoads, Randy (Ozzy Osbourne) 93, 202
Richard, Cliff
    "Devil Woman" 138
Richardson, Samuel
    Clarissa 78
    Pamela 78
Richie, Lionel 197, 202
Rimmer, William 7
    "Evening (The Fall of Day)"
Road Warrior, The (1981) 37, 38, 41, 63, 92, 134
Rock of Ages (2012) 90
rock star (concept) 11, 20–3, 30, 43, 46, 52, 62, 65, 66, 78, 93, 100, 101, 111–23, 145, 146, 155, 156, 167, 177, 215
"Rocket 88" 219 n.5
Rocky 68, 225 n.79
Rolling Stone 46, 71
Rolling Stones, The 210
    Jones, Brian 119, 123, 165
    Richards, Keith 146, 166
Rollins, Henry 197
Ross, Diana 197
Roth, Philip 15
Rough Cutt 198
"Run to You" 84
Runaways, The 13, 156
Rushdie, Salman 20, 79

Sabbat
    "Cautionary Tale, A" 168
sadomasochism 27, 74, 79, 80, 104, 154, 160
Saigon Kick 10
Saint-Saëns, Camille
    "Danse macabre, Op. 40" 163
Salinger, J. D.
    Catcher in the Rye, The 26, 127
Sambora, Richie 156
    Stranger in This Town 66
Sartre, Jean-Paul 118
    Being and Nothingness? 58
    No Exit 58, 184, 196
Satanism 3, 160–2, 196, 209

Saturday Night Fever (1977) 45, 57
Scarface (1932) 63
Scarlet Letter, The 88
Schumann, Robert 106
Scorpions, The 6, 10, 70, 212
    Meine, Klaus 71, 72
    "Rock You Like a Hurricane" 6, 37, 82, 83, 109, 166, 203, 209, 216, 227 n.22
    Schenker, Rudolf 71
    "Still Loving You" 82
    "Wind of Change" 71
Screaming Trees
    Lanegan, Mark 123
Segal, David 47
Seger, Bob 43
    "Against the Wind" 211
Sex Pistols, The 45, 48, 57
Shakespeare, William 33, 151, 152
    As You Like It 59
    Hamlet 81, 91, 92, 115, 192
    Henry IV 91
    Macbeth 73, 91, 92
    Romeo and Juliet 87, 91, 92
    "Venus and Adonis" 20–1
Shelly, Mary
    Frankenstein 138, 162
Shelly, Percy 176
Simpsons, The 26
Sir Gawain and the Green Knight 42
Skid Row 157, 206
    Grönwall, Erik 157
    "I Remember You" 126
    "Youth Gone Wild" 157
Slade
    "Mama Weer All Crazee Now" 109
Slaughter
    "Fly to the Angels" 140
Slayer 10, 33, 114, 154, 196
    "Angel of Death" 88
    Araya, Tom 182
    Hanneman, Jeff 182
    Hell Awaits 182–4
    King, Kerry 153, 182
    "Praise of Death" 183
Slipknot
    "Duality" 111
Smashing Pumpkins 122, 209
    Corgan, Billy 209

256 Index

Smith, Patti   197
Snider, Dee   11, 27, 74, 75, 77, 79, 80, 82, 85–7, 89–91, 98, 197
   Shut Up and Pass the Mic   28
Socrates   104, 106, 110
Sophocles
   Oedipus Rex   134–5
Sopranos, The   68
Soundgarden   208
   Cornell, Chris   121, 209
South Park   26
Spektor, Regina   195
Spheeris, Penelope   53
Spirit
   "Taurus"   164
SpongeBob SquarePants Movie, The (2004)   216
Springsteen, Bruce   16, 197, 198
   "Born in the USA"   57
Star Wars (1977)   67
Steel Panther   43
   "Death to All but Metal"   179
   "Party Like Tomorrow is the End of the World"   40
Stepford Wives (1975)   144
Steppenwolf
   "Born to Be Wild"   40
Stevens, Wallace
   "Emperor of Ice-Cream, The"   118
Stevenson, Robert Louis   15
   Strange Case of Dr. Jekyll and Mr. Hyde   173, 174
Stewart, Potter   20
Stoker, Bram
   Dracula   42
Stone Temple Pilots
   "Sex Type Thing"   85, 87
   Weiland, Scott   85
Stormtroopers of Death   10
Stranger Things   2–7, 15, 16, 38, 101, 170, 213–14
   Montgomery, Dacre   7
   Munson, Eddie (fictional character)   1–3
Stratocaster   203
Strauss, Neil   78
Stryper
   To Hell with the Devil   176

Styx   43
   "Come Sail Away"   182
Suicidal Tendencies
   "Institutionalized"   109, 173
suicide   5, 9, 50, 93, 100, 112–19, 174, 180, 181, 209
Swaggart, Jimmy   62
Sweeney Todd (1979)   127
Swift, Taylor   16
   1989   214

Talking Heads, The
   "Psycho Killer"   104
Templeman, Ted   49
Tenacious D in the Pick of Destiny, The (2006)   168
Tesla
   "Modern Day Cowboy"   63–6
Tesla, Nikola   64
"That Metal Show"   36
Thatcher, Margaret   35
Theatre of Cruelty   127
Thicke, Robin
   "Blurred Lines"   85
Thin Lizzy
   "Cowboy Song"   63
This Is Spinal Tap (1984)   87, 95, 126, 129
   McKean, Michael   199
   Shearer, Harry   199
Tolkien, J. R. R.   7
   Lord of the Rings, The   7, 196
Travolta, John   45
Trick or Treat (1986)   5, 174
Triumph   70
Trow, George W. S.
   "Within the Context of No Context"   215
Trumbo, Dalton
   Johnny Got His Gun   94
Turner, Tina   197
Twisted Sister   32, 86, 89, 98, 104, 154, 198, 202, 216
   "Horror Teria: Captain Howdy"   92, 93
   "I Wanna Rock"   12, 216
   Ojeda, Eddie   198, 202
   "Street Justice"   92

"Under the Blade"   27, 39, 73–5, 79–82, 85–7, 91–3, 104, 108, 153, 197
"We're Not Gonna Take It"   27, 51
Tyketto   10
Type O Negative   10
  "Black No. 1"   138–9
  Silver, Josh   10
  Steele, Peter   138

U2   197, 198
Uncanny X-Men, The   6
Ure, Midge   197
USA for Africa   198, 199
  "We Are the World"   197–9, 202
US Festival   70–1

Vai, Steve   55, 168
Valens, Ritchie   210
Van Gogh, Vincent   106
Van Halen   10, 32, 36, 37, 48–52, 58, 59, 70, 114, 127, 156, 206, 212, 213, 215
  1984   49, 51, 211
  "Ain't Talkin' bout Love"   45
  "And the Cradle Will Rock . . ."   13
  Anthony, Michael   47, 65
  Diver Down   49
  "Eruption"   43, 44, 49, 55, 202
  Fair Warning   49
  "Feel Your Love"   45
  For Unlawful Carnal Knowledge   47, 207
  Hagar, Sammy   47, 207, 213
  "Hot for Teacher"   13, 51, 90, 133
  "House of Pain"   50
  "I'll Wait"   50
  "Jump"   49, 50, 203
  "Panama"   37, 50, 216
  "Pretty Woman"   65
  Roth, David Lee   13, 43, 47, 49, 65, 70, 77, 79, 168
  "Runnin' With the Devil"   48, 169
  Van Halen I   43, 47
  Van Halen II   46
  Van Halen, Alex   46, 49
  Van Halen, Eddie   5, 43, 45, 46, 49, 51, 55, 58, 59, 65, 156, 202, 207
  "You Really Got Me"   44, 82

Vanity
  "Strap On 'Robbie Baby'"   27
Varney the Vampire   9
Vatican Council of the Catholic Church   189
Venom   162
  Chronos   161
  "Possessed"   27, 161
  "Welcome to Hell"   160
VH1   36
Virgil   177–9
  Aeneid   107
Vonnegut, Kurt   80–1
  Cat's Cradle   80, 81
  Slaughterhouse-Five   80, 127
"Voyagers" (TV series)   37

Wall, The (1982)   13
Wall Street (1987)   55, 56
Walser, Robert   29
  Running with the Devil: Power, Gender, and Madness in Heavy Metal Music   31
Walsh, Joe
  "Life's Been Good"   146
WarGames (1983)   38
Warrant   208
  Lane, Jani   53, 208
WASP   10, 13, 22, 33, 126–30, 152
  "Animal (F**k Life a Beast)"   25, 27, 90, 126–30
  Holmes, Chris   53
  "I Want to Be Somebody"   127
  Lawless, Blackie   25, 198
  "School Daze"   13
Waters, Muddy   164
Weinstein, Deena
  Heavy Metal: The Music and Its Culture   31
Weird Science (1985)   144
Werman, Tom   52
West, Leslie (Mountain)   20, 25
West Memphis Three   196
Westworld (1973)   65, 144
Whalley, Tom   55
White Lion
  Big Game (1989)   95
  Bratta, Vito   96, 202

"Cry for Freedom" 96
"Little Fighter" 95–6
Pride 95
Tramp, Mike 96
"Wait" 203
"When the Children Cry" 95
Whitesnake
   Coverdale, David 141, 157
   "Here I Go Again" 141
   Saints & Sinners 141
   "Still of the Night" 141
White Trash 10
Whitman, Walt
   "Song of Myself" 205
Who, The
   Tommy (1969) 90
Widowmaker 11
Wiederhorn, Jon and Turman, Katherine
   Louder Than Hell: The Definitive Oral History of Metal 78
Wild One, The (1953) 12, 173
Wilde, Oscar 25
   Picture of Dorian Gray, The 22, 146
Williams, Tennessee 138

Williams, Wendy O.
   W.O.W. 90
Winehouse, Amy 165
Winger, Kip 206
Winwood, Ian 121
   Bodies: Life and Death in Music 120, 122–3
Wonder, Stevie 197
Woolf, Virginia 42
Wordsworth, William 211
   "Rainbow, The" 191
Wozniak, Steve 70
Wurtzel, Elizabeth 103
Wylde, Zakk (Ozzy Osbourne) 59

Young, Neil 46, 117
   "Hey Hey, My My" 117
   "Rockin' in the Free World" 46, 57
Young Guns II (1990) 66

Zappa, Frank 27, 168
Zeno
   Dichotomy Paradox 68
Zutaut, Tom 78, 170